D1120074

◆ ©ASSASSI PRODUCTIONS

G R E A T E R
DES MOINES

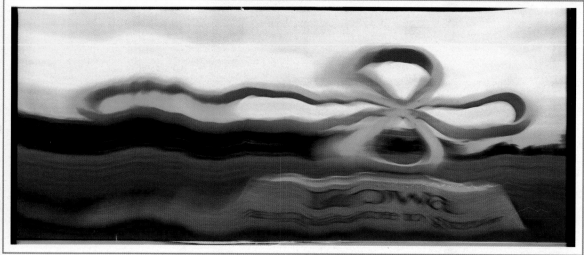

Iowa's Commercial Center

URBAN
TAPESTRY
SERIES
TOWERY
PUBLISHING, INC.

CLOCKWISE FROM TOP LEFT: (1&2) © JONATHAN POSTAL / TOWERY PUBLISHING, INC. (3) © GREG SCHEIDEMAN / [N]HAUS FOTO (4) © SCOTT CAVANAH / STUDIO AU

Contents

© SCOTT CAVANAH / STUDIO AU

LIBRARY OF CONGRESS CATALOGING-IN-PUBLICATION DATA

Greater Des Moines : Iowa's commercial center / introduction by Judy McCoy Davis ; art direction by Geoffrey Ellis.
     p. cm. — (Urban tapestry series)
    "Sponsored by the Greater Des Moines Chamber of Commerce Federation."
    Includes index.
    ISBN 1-881096-65-3 (alk. paper)
    1. Des Moines (Iowa)—Civilization.   2. Des Moines (Iowa)--Pictorial works.   3. Des Moines (Iowa)—Economic conditions. 4. Business enterprises—Iowa—Des Moines.   I. Davis, Judy McCoy, 1949- . II. Greater Des Moines Chamber of Commerce Federation. III. Series.
F629.D4G74 1999
977.7'58—dc21   98-52518

Printed in Canada

Copyright © 1999 by Towery Publishing, Inc.

All rights reserved. No part of this work may be reproduced or copied in any form or by any means, except for brief excerpts in conjunction with book reviews, without prior written permission of the publisher.

Towery Publishing, Inc., The Towery Building, 1835 Union Avenue, Memphis, TN 38104

Publisher: *J. Robert Towery*
Executive Publisher: *Jenny McDowell*
Associate Publisher: *Michael C. James*
National Sales Manager: *Stephen Hung*
Marketing Director: *Carol Culpepper*
Project Directors: *Dawn Park-Donegan, Lori Park-Wagner*
Executive Editor: *David B. Dawson*
Managing Editor: *Lynn Conlee*
Senior Editor: *Carlisle Hacker*
Editors/Profile Managers: *Susan Hesson, Brian Johnston*
Editors: *Mary Jane Adams, Jana Files, John Floyd, Heather Ramsey*
Assistant Editor: *Rebecca Green*
Editorial Assistant: *Sunni Thompson*
Caption Writer: *Jill Van Wyke*

Editorial Contributors: *Anne Marie Cox, Jennifer L. Irsfeld*
Creative Director: *Brian Groppe*
Photography Editor: *Jonathan Postal*
Photographic Consultant: *Mark Bassett*
Profile Designers: *Laurie Beck, Melissa Ellis, Kelley Pratt, Ann Ward*
Digital Color Supervisor: *Darin Ipema*
Digital Color Technicians: *John Brantley, Eric Friedl, Brent Salazar*
Production Resources Manager: *Dave Dunlap Jr.*
Production Coordinator: *Brenda Pattat*
Photographic Coordinator: *Robin McGehee*
Production Assistant: *Loretta Drew*
Print Coordinator: *Tonda Thomas*

© JONATHAN POSTAL TOWERY PUBLISHING, INC.

◆ © ASSASSI PRODUCTIONS

BY JUDY McCOY DAVIS

I IT MAY SEEM STRANGE TO SOME THAT I WAS CHOSEN TO WRITE ABOUT THE joys of living in Des Moines. I wasn't born here. I haven't lived here most of my life. In fact, I've only lived here eight years. ■ And yet, an argument could easily be made that that is exactly why I'm most qualified to write this essay. In today's mobile society, I have lived in

Des Moines longer than many stay in one city. I can relate to being a stranger in town. Being something of a newcomer, I have had to learn what Des Moines really is. My vision is not clouded by memories of past glory or the romanticization of my youth. And, since I've lived in several other cities, I have a good basis for comparison.

While all of this is true, I know I was chosen to write about Des Moines because I was fortunate enough to share in someone else's vision of this city. I'm speaking of Arthur Davis, my husband.

Some of you may have known Arthur—or may have known of him—as the highly successful, nationally respected senior partner in Iowa's largest law firm. Or, perhaps you knew him as an adviser to presidents and the éminence grise of the

© JAMES BLANK

Iowa Democratic Party. Or, more likely, you knew him as the mayor of Des Moines. On a sunny June day in 1995, with Claes Oldenburg's *Crusoe Umbrella* providing just a touch of shade in Nollen Plaza, Arthur Davis announced that he was running for mayor of Des Moines. His decision was a surprise to many. They had always ex-

THE *CRUSOE UMBRELLA* BY CLAES OLDENBURG (ABOVE) STANDS IN DOWNTOWN DES MOINES' NOLLEN PLAZA. THE SHIMMERING HEADQUARTERS OF EMC INSURANCE GROUP (OPPOSITE), COMPLETED IN 1997, IS ONE OF FOUR MAJOR DOWNTOWN OFFICE BUILDINGS ERECTED IN RECENT YEARS.

© EWING GALLOWAY, INC.

THE STATE CAPITOL, COMPLETED IN
1886, RISES MAJESTICALLY FROM A
HILLTOP IN THE MIDDLE OF THE CITY.
PICTURED HERE IN THE 1950S, THE
CAPITOL, WHICH FEATURES A 23-KARAT
GOLD DOME, IS NEARING COMPLETION
OF A 14-YEAR, $41 MILLION EXTERIOR
RENOVATION.

◆ © JIM DAY / TWODAYS PHOTOGRAPHY

pected him to run for governor or senator, and could not understand why he would run for the relatively thankless job of mayor. But Arthur saw becoming mayor not as an opportunity to receive thanks, but to give it.

Arthur wanted to say thank-you to the people of Des Moines for the 40 years of wonderful living he enjoyed here. A native of Sioux City, he came to Des Moines in 1955, after leaving the army. Back then, he had a job waiting for him at a Chicago law firm. But he stopped there only briefly, to say that he had decided Chicago was not the city where he wanted to establish roots and raise a family. Having no idea where he would go, Arthur was grateful when a Chicago attorney suggested Des Moines and graciously set up an interview here. While Arthur had always enjoyed seeing Iowa's capital city when visiting in his youth, this tall, skinny, Jewish attorney arrived in Des Moines in 1955 with all his possessions in his car, and knowing only a handful of folks.

© LYNDA RICHARDS

THE CAPITOL dome towers over gardens, sculptures, and memorials on its landscaped grounds.

Forty years later, as mayor of Des Moines, he often smiled, thinking back. Des Moines had indeed been good to him. Its location in the heartland had attracted many agriculture-related industries. Being the state capital, Des Moines is home to a plethora of statewide trade associations and governmental organizations. Over the years, Des Moines had also grown to be one of the insurance capitals of the nation. All these were factors in the growth of Arthur's law practice, as were the quality and the work ethic of the young attorneys who worked with him, and who were similarly attracted to Des Moines. ☛

▲ © SCOTT CAVANAH / STUDIO AU

From here, one can affect state legislation as well as have input in national laws. Iowa's first-in-the-nation presidential caucuses, which bring so many candidates and campaign workers to Iowa for extended periods, create an unbelievable network of contacts. Almost every office in Washington, D.C., has someone with warm memories of months spent in Iowa, and of the Iowans, such as Arthur, who befriended them.

Des Moines provided Arthur not only with a good place to work, but also with a great place to live. Home was only minutes away from his office. Quiet, yet friendly, neighborhoods provided the ideal setting for raising a family. Des Moines is a community that encourages participation, and Arthur easily found outlets for his boundless energy and his desire to contribute.

Long before he was mayor, Arthur loved showing Des Moines to visitors. First-time visitors were his favorites, for he knew how many surprises were in store for them. Des Moines is not the low-lying, slow-paced city out in the cornfields that these visitors were likely expecting. Far from being flat and featureless, Des Moines is a city of rolling hills covered with glorious trees and lush flowers—just what you would expect from the home of America's favorite horticultural magazine, *Better Homes and Gardens*. Des Moines has a vibrant downtown with a multitude of tall, architecturally significant buildings linked together by a skywalk system that allows you to move throughout the downtown area in perfect comfort no matter what the weather—snow, rain, or blistering sun. ☛

DES MOINES' OFFICE BUILDINGS, MEETING FACILITIES, HOTELS, RESTAURANTS, SHOPS, PARKING GARAGES, AND CULTURAL ATTRACTIONS ARE CONNECTED BY NEARLY THREE MILES OF CLIMATE-CONTROLLED SKYWALKS.

© PAUL GATES BPC
© MARK BASSETT

Arthur's office at the top of the Financial Center provided a panoramic view of the city—so very green in summer, so colorful in autumn—with ribbons of blue water meandering in from the north and the west. You could watch new buildings rising from the ground, reaching for the sky; or, you could look down on the Court Avenue entertainment district, with its old-fashioned streetlights giving a warm glow to outdoor dining. On Saturday mornings, from spring to fall, Court Avenue's lively farmer's market is a mecca for all, with its produce, baked goods, art, and entertainment.

Arthur especially enjoyed taking visitors to baseball games in Sec Taylor Stadium. Who couldn't enjoy America's favorite pastime in this newly restored, pristine park strategically set at the convergence of the Des Moines and Raccoon rivers? It is always a thrill to hear "The Star-Spangled Banner" played as the flag waves against the magnificent backdrop of the Iowa Capitol, its dome gleaming, standing stately on the hill just beyond the outfield fence. It's a sight you only expect to see in the

THE FINANCIAL CENTER (OPPOSITE) IS JUST ONE SYMBOL OF DES MOINES' STRONG WORK ETHIC—BALANCED BY SOME FUN AND PLAY AT SEC TAYLOR STADIUM, WHERE THE CAPITOL STANDS SENTRY BEYOND THE OUTFIELD FENCE.

◆ © STEVE O'BRIEN

IA 6660 FF

IA 5435 CC

JUST NORTHWEST OF DES MOINES, THE
6,000-ACRE SAYLORVILLE LAKE PRO-
VIDES NUMEROUS OPPORTUNITIES FOR
YEAR-ROUND OUTDOOR RECREATION.

▲ © RON LEVINE

movies, but it's just one of a myriad of breathtaking sights you find in Des Moines.

Those who knew Arthur might laugh at the thought of his serving as a tour guide, for they know he had no sense of direction whatsoever. But you see, when Arthur was giving a tour, that didn't really make any difference. If he found himself on the south side, he might drive through Ewing Park to enjoy the lilac arboretum, or he'd take visitors to a wonderful old family-owned Italian market where complete strangers are treated like old friends. If he ended up on Des Moines' north side, he might drive his visitors through the curving streets of Beaverdale, lined with its signature brick homes; show them the restoration going on in the River Bend neigh-

GREATER DES MOINES

borhood; or drive beyond the city limits to Saylorville Reservoir to watch sailboats crisscross the waves.

On the east side, Arthur's favorite spot to explore was the Iowa State Fairgrounds. Not only are the grounds beautiful, but with three or four different activities in progress at most times, there is always something for everyone's interest. Today, Arthur might keep on driving east, taking his visitors to the Walnut Creek National Wildlife Refuge and Neal Smith Prairie Learning Center, where they could see not only buffalo, but also what the prairie was like in the days when these majestic creatures roamed. ☛

THE IOWA STATE FAIR IS AN ANNUAL CELEBRATION OF THE STATE'S RICH AGRICULTURAL HERITAGE, DRAWING MORE THAN 800,000 PEOPLE DURING ITS SUMMERTIME RUN AT THE DES MOINES FAIRGROUNDS.

© STEVE BAKER / HIGHLIGHT PHOTOGRAPHY

© JONATHAN POSTAL / TOWERY PUBLISHING, INC.

On the west side, Arthur could count on rave reviews after a visit to the Science Center at Greenwood Park. When we rounded the curve on Tonawanda Drive, even visitors from England were taken aback by the beauty and majesty of Salisbury House, a treasure rightfully included on an A&E Network broadcast of *America's Castles*. And while Arthur wasn't much of a shopper, he knew both shoppers and non-shoppers alike enjoyed stopping in Valley Junction, a historic district in West Des Moines full of funky boutiques, art galleries, and antique stores.

But Des Moines is much more than the things that Arthur could show off during a drive around town. It is more than tall buildings, flowing rivers, beautiful parks, and the state capitol. It's people. It's attitude. It's a way of both looking at the world and participating in that world.

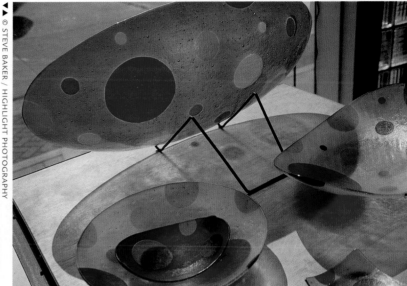

© STEVE BAKER / HIGHLIGHT PHOTOGRAPHY

Like Arthur, there are many people living in Des Moines who could live anywhere in the world. Some are retired, some turned down other job opportunities to take a position in a Des Moines company, and still others work all over the country, but call Des Moines home and return here on the weekends. Why?

The answer might be summed up in the hackneyed, overused expression "quality of life." But this sounds trite, the explanations too full of platitudes. I know it's more than safe streets and a sense of being secure in your home and in your neighborhood. It's more than education. It's more than being considered the best place in the country to raise children, an accolade bestowed on Iowa in 1998 by the Washington, D.C.-based Children's Rights Council. I think it's about community. Des Moines is not a city where you'll always be considered an outsider if you weren't

GALLERIES SPECIALIZING IN UNIQUE AND EXQUISITE ART MIX WITH ANTIQUE STORES, CLOTHING BOUTIQUES, RESTAURANTS, AND OTHER ONE-OF-A-KIND SHOPS IN HISTORIC VALLEY JUNCTION.

▲ © MIKE WHYE

GREATER DES MOINES

SALISBURY HOUSE, A 42-ROOM REPLICA OF KING'S HOUSE IN SALISBURY, ENGLAND, FEATURES AN IMPRESSIVE COLLECTION OF ART AND TREASURES FROM AROUND THE WORLD.

© JOHN F. SCHULTZ

CENTRAL IOWA BOASTS A VIBRANT THE-
ATER SCENE, WITH TOURING BROADWAY
SHOWS, DES MOINES METRO OPERA,
UNIVERSITY PERFORMANCES, AND COM-
MUNITY PLAYHOUSES. RECENT PRODUC-
TIONS HAVE INCLUDED *DON GIOVANNI,*
ALBERT HERRING, AND *MISS SAIGON.*

born here. Nor is it a city so impersonal that you never get to know your neighbors, much less interact with them. Des Moines is a community that brings people together—for fun, for work, and for problem solving.

The citizens of Des Moines aren't waiting to see what the future may bring; they are trying to shape that future. A city-appointed strategic planning committee made up of people from all walks of life, from all parts of town, gathered input and forged a multifaceted plan that enumerated their hopes and dreams for the city. The city wide strategic plan covers growth, finances, economic development, infrastructure, public safety, neighborhood revitalization, housing, education, parks, recreation, culture, the downtown area, transportation, and governance—all issues essential to a community's growth and vitality. With this road map in hand, business leaders, neighborhood activists, and average citizens work together on a daily basis to bring the city's plan to fruition.

Before moving to Des Moines in 1990, I operated a retail shop in a smaller city,

© COURTESY DES MOINES PLAYHOUSE

© JOHN F. SCHULTZ

© JOAN MARCUS

Dubuque, which often required doing business in much larger cities, such as New York and Chicago. I found Des Moines to be the best of both worlds. It has the friendliness you associate with small-town living. It also has the activities and amenities associated with large metropolises, but without the accompanying hassles. If you love music, you will enjoy the weekly summertime concerts on the State Capitol grounds and in the Simon Estes Riverfront Amphitheater on the Des Moines River. You'll want to attend the Metro Opera or partake in Jazz in July. If you love theater, you'll have plenty of performances to choose from—at the community theater, the Drama Workshop, a dinner theater, or local colleges and universities, and Des Moines' state-of-the-art civic center, which has demonstrated its capabilities by hosting touring Broadway productions of *The Phantom of the Opera* and *Miss Saigon*. If you want to do more than watch, the 80-year-old Des Moines Playhouse—one of the oldest continuously operating community theaters in the country—provides ample opportunity for would-be thespians, including educa-

THE DES MOINES PLAYHOUSE, ONE OF THE OLDEST COMMUNITY THEATERS IN THE NATION, FEATURES LOCAL DRAMATIC TALENT VOLUNTEERING IN PRODUCTIONS SUCH AS (BELOW, FROM OPPOSITE LEFT) *THE SOUND OF MUSIC*, *AIN'T MISBEHAVIN'*, *THE WIZ*, AND *LAUGHTER ON THE 23RD FLOOR*.

© COURTESY DES MOINES PLAYHOUSE

◆ © JONATHAN POSTAL / TOWERY PUBLISHING, INC.

tional programs, workshops, and classes for all ages. Youngsters can try out their newfound skills in the Kate Goldman Children's Theatre.

If you gotta have your sports, the Cubs (baseball), the Barnstormers (football), and the Buccaneers (ice hockey) are just a few of the teams awaiting you. If you prefer something more unusual, perhaps rugby or rowing, you'll find it here. You can play the ponies at Prairie Meadows Racetrack and Casino, or you can ride your ponies at Polo on the Green. If you are a runner or a biker, you'll have difficulty finding more beautiful paths than those extending along Des Moines' rivers and creeks. It's the perfect place to train for RAGBRAI (the *Register's* Annual Great Bike Ride Across Iowa) or for the annual Dam to Dam 20K race. If you prefer to watch others test their times, the nationally re- nowned Drake Relays at- tracts top athletes from across the country. The Des Moines Country Club, host of the 1999

© MIKE WHYE

U.S. Senior Open, is just one of the fine golf facilities in the area. Even in winter your golfing skills won't get rusty with Des Moines' indoor ranges and the annual Skywalk Open Golf Tournament. Admittedly, the latter is more about fun than fitness, but it does allow young and old to test their putting skills through three challenging courses set up in the downtown skywalks.

You won't run out of things to do in Des Moines. Blank Park Zoo, White Water University, and Adventureland Park provide entertainment for people of all ages. You might want to visit the past at the State of Iowa Historical Buildings, or expe- rience it firsthand at Living History Farms. You might want to take in the 15,000

A FOOT-STOMPING GOOD TIME CAN BE HAD AT ADVENTURELAND PARK, WITH ITS 100-PLUS AMUSEMENT RIDES, SHOWS, AND ATTRACTIONS (OPPOSITE). EXERCISE ENTHUSIASTS FIND FITNESS AND CAMARA- DERIE IN ROWING ON THE DES MOINES RIVER (ABOVE).

◆ © BARBARA KNIGHT

plants under the dome of the Des Moines Botanical Center, or gaze at a dome full of stars at the planetarium in the Science Center at Greenwood Park. From the Pella Tulip Festival to the Renaissance-style entertainment at the Salisbury House May Festival, special events fill the weekends throughout the year.

Des Moines does not lament its location, it revels in it. It is at the crossroads of our nation, figuratively and literally. This is where Interstate 35 crosses Interstate 80, not only providing for the nation's transportation needs, but ensuring a con-

© JONATHAN POSTAL / TOWERY PUBLISHING, INC.

stant interaction between Iowans and people from across the nation and around the world.

Des Moines is where rural and urban meet. You may not be able to see farm fields from the heart of the city, but Des Moines does not allow you to forget your ties to the land. *Successful Farming* and the Iowa State Fair; Pioneer Hi-Bred International and the

World Food Prize; farmers' markets and Iowa State University, one of the nation's premier agronomy schools, only 35 miles away—they're all reminders that farming is business, big business, vital business, not just to our state or to our country, but to the world.

Often called the heartland, this is where you can really get the pulse of the nation. It is no accident that presidential hopefuls must first test their political timber in Iowa. Nor is it a surprise that more producers do their test marketing in Des Moines than anywhere else in the country. ☛

CENTRAL IOWA IS A BLEND OF RURAL AND URBAN, COEXISTING IN CAREFUL BALANCE AT PLACES LIKE THE DES MOINES BOTANICAL CENTER (ABOVE).

© PLUMMER-JOHNSON, INC.

WHETHER IT'S AN ART FESTIVAL ON THE CITY'S RIVER BRIDGES OR A GATHERING AT NOLLEN PLAZA, DES MOINES IS BIG ENOUGH TO OFFER INNUMERABLE OPPORTUNITIES—BUT SMALL ENOUGH FOR INDIVIDUALS TO MAKE THEIR MARK.

Arthur saw his abiding faith in the people of Des Moines fully justified when cancer forced his resignation just 15 months after he took office. Not only did the people shower him with words of encouragement, but also they didn't hesitate to take up the causes and concerns he was fostering. One of Arthur's goals was to see the city make better use of its rivers; how pleased he would be to see the success of the art festival now taking place on three bridges spanning the river in downtown Des Moines. He'd smile at the development of Gray's Lake, for he wanted it to entice visitors as they traveled from the airport to downtown and the State Capitol.

It's appropriate that Arthur's penultimate day was Thanksgiving Day, for giving through your actions and not through your words is the legacy he left us. Since Arthur's death, many friends and acquaintances have asked me if I'll stay in Des Moines or if I'll leave. I smile. One never knows what the future will bring or where it may take you, but I know that Des Moines—this wonderful city that has embraced me with open arms—will always be the city I call home. ■

◆ © SCOTT CAVANAH / STUDIO AU

© DAVID CANNONE

Nᴇᴡ ᴏꜰꜰɪᴄᴇ ʙᴜɪʟᴅɪɴɢꜱ ʀᴇᴀᴄʜ for the skies, reflecting Des Moines' ambitions and optimism. Although Iowa is an agricultural state, the city's workforce is overwhelmingly white-collar, as insurance, finance, health care, education, government, publishing, and other industries drive business activity.

© STEVE BAKER / HIGHLIGHT PHOTOGRAPHY

© STEVE BAKER / HIGHLIGHT PHOTOGRAPHY

ALTHOUGH DES MOINES IS enjoying growth and progress, reminders of its past remain in architectural treasures.

▼ © MARK BASSETT   ▲ © KAY PRALL

C OME RAIN OR SHINE, RESI-
dents enjoy two longtime
landmarks: the illuminated
Travelers Insurance sign and the
Claes Oldenburg *Crusoe Umbrella*
at Nollen Plaza.

© STEPHEN ELLWANGER   © TOM AND CAROLYN TENNEY

THE DES MOINES ART CENTER, nestled in a hilly park amid towering oaks, houses an impressive collection of 19th- and 20th- century works. The quadrangle with a reflecting pool is one of the museum's distinctive architectural features.

© PAUL GATES BPC

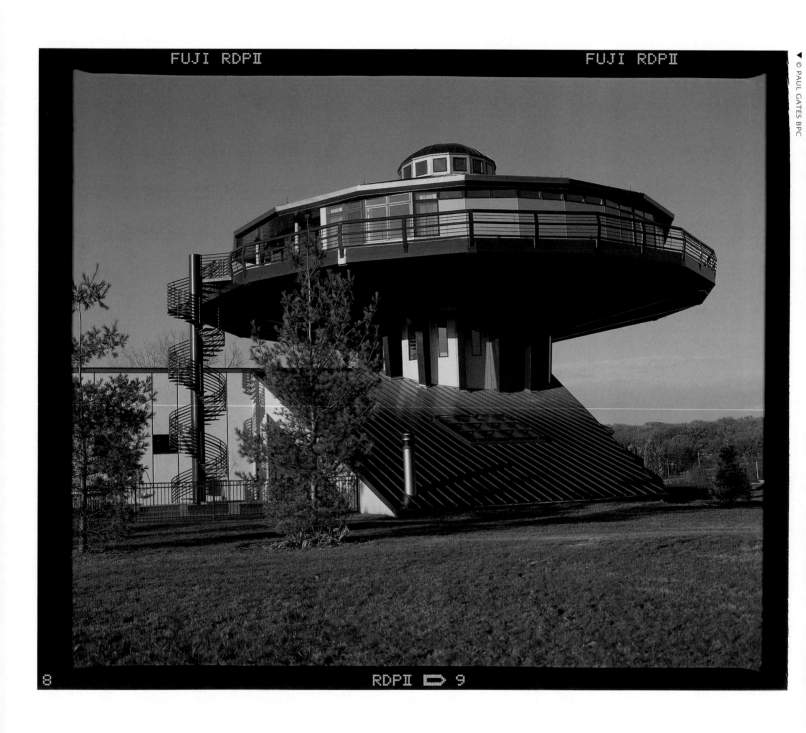

© PAUL GATES BPC

MILLIONAIRE LeMAR KOETHE enjoys the high life in his space-age house in nearby Dallas County. The futuristic home features a huge party room, a 20-car garage, a balcony that surrounds the second floor, an eclectic art collection, security-guard mannequins, and a third-floor cupola with a telescope for stargazing.

© RICHARD CUMMINS / PHOTOPHILE

SALISBURY HOUSE WAS BUILT BY cosmetics tycoon Carl Weeks in the 1920s. He and his wife filled the 42-room Tudor man- sion with art, furniture, stained glass, tapestries, and furnishings collected on their world travels. Since 1954, the building has housed the Iowa State Educa- tion Association.

© RICHARD CUMMINS / PHOTOPHILE

© STEVE BAKER / HIGHLIGHT PHOTOGRAPHY

The detailed archways of buildings in Des Moines' historic downtown district are echoed in the ornate halls of the 70-year-old Salisbury House (OPPOSITE).

© DAMON G. BULLOCK / DIAMOND STAR PHOTOGRAPHY

D RAKE UNIVERSITY, FOUNDED
in 1881, blends a liberal arts
education with strong professional training. The university
enrolls about 3,100 full-time
undergraduate students.

© DAMON G. BULLOCK / DIAMOND STAR PHOTOGRAPHY

GREATER DES MOINES

© PAUL GATES BPC

S CHOOLS AND LIBRARIES HAVE
long enjoyed support in
Iowa, among the most literate
states in the nation. Iowa's students routinely test at or near
the top in college entrance exams.

▼ © JONATHAN POSTAL / TOWERY PUBLISHING, INC.

▼ © JONATHAN POSTAL / TOWERY PUBLISHING, INC.

GREATER DES MOINES

© JONATHAN POSTAL / TOWERY PUBLISHING, INC.

© JONATHAN POSTAL / TOWERY PUBLISHING, INC.

RECOGNIZING THE CHARM AND historic value of turn-of-the-century homes, preservationists are restoring them to their original splendor in several neighborhoods, including Sherman Hill, River Bend, and the Drake area.

▼ © PAUL GATES BPC

GREATER DES MOINES

© PAUL GATES BPC

PLEASANT HILL, A BURGEONING suburb east of Des Moines, attracts families with its good schools, low crime rate, and reasonably priced homes.

◆ © DAMON G. BULLOCK / DIAMOND STAR PHOTOGRAPHY

DEDICATED IN 1906, THE POLK County Courthouse sits on the edge of downtown—a true architectural treasure anchoring one end of historic Court Avenue.

© JONATHAN POSTAL / TOWERY PUBLISHING, INC.

© TY C. SMEDES

© TY C. SMEDES

© TY C. SMEDES

© TY C. SMEDES

© JONATHAN POSTAL / TOWERY PUBLISHING, INC.

© TY C. SMEDES
© TY C. SMEDES
© TY C. SMEDES
© TY C. SMEDES
© JONATHAN POSTAL / TOWERY PUBLISHING, INC.
© TY C. SMEDES

Dozens of grotesques—
some whimsical, others
more sinister—ornament the
doors, windows, and facade of
the courthouse.

▲ © JONATHAN POSTAL / TOWERY PUBLISHING, INC.

▲ © PAUL GATES BPC

GREATER DES MOINES

▲ © JONATHAN POSTAL / TOWERY PUBLISHING, INC.

THE STATEHOUSE IS ACCENTED with statues and monuments that commemorate Iowa's history, including its pioneers and war veterans. Iowa celebrated its sesquicentennial in 1996.

© JONATHAN POSTAL / TOWERY PUBLISHING, INC.

© MIKE WHYE

DES MOINES IS A HUB FOR STATE,
county, and municipal pol-
itics. In 1997, the city elected its
first African-American mayor,
Preston Daniels, a neighborhood
advocate.

I N AN AMBITIOUS RENOVATION, the statehouse law library was refurbished to its original splendor (RIGHT AND OPPOSITE). Five tiers of books, accessed by a spiral staircase, soar above the library's reading room.

© PAUL GATES BPL

IMPOSING VICTORIAN ARCHITEC-
ture reflects the opulence of
the 19th century. The Davis
County Courthouse (PAGE 68)
stands regally at the center of
nearby Bloomfield, Iowa. Terrace
Hill (PAGE 69) was built by Iowa's
first millionaire in 1869, and since
1972, has been the residence of
the governor.

© DAMON G. BULLOCK / DIAMOND STAR PHOTOGRAPHY

© DAMON G. BULLOCK / DIAMOND STAR PHOTOGRAPHY

◆ © DAMON G. BULLOCK / DIAMOND STAR PHOTOGRAPHY

CAPITAL SQUARE IN DOWNTOWN Des Moines opened in 1983 and is one of the largest office complexes in Polk County. It opens onto Nollen Plaza, a favorite lunchtime gathering spot in warm weather.

© SCOTT CAVANAH / STUDIO AU   ▲   © RICHARD CUMMINS / PHOTOPHILE

THE SOOTHING WATERFALL, fountains, and pool at Nollen Plaza beckon locals to relax amid the bustle of downtown.

© SCOTT LAVANAH / STUDIO AU

GREATER DES MOINES

© SCOTT CAVANAH / STUDIO AU

Residents of The Plaza condominiums downtown (OPPOSITE) enjoy urban living with a view of Nollen Plaza. Others find the fountains there to be practical as well as pleasurable.

© SCOTT CAVANAH / STUDIO AU

GREATER DES MOINES

© SCOTT CAVANAH / STUDIO AU

S OMETHING OLD, SOMETHING new, something borrowed, and something . . . VROOM? Waterworks Park—with its colorful gardens, arboretum, and sce- nic fountain—is a popular place for picnics as well as weddings. One bridal party opted to forgo the traditional limousine, choosing motorcycles instead.

© RON LEVINE

© RON LEVINE

THE IOWA STATE FAIR UNITES Iowans from all walks of life in a grand celebration each August that features everything from top-notch country music to cooking-with-lard contests. While some fairgoers make use of golf carts to navigate the sprawling fairgrounds, daredevil Robbie Knievel (ABOVE) relied on his motorcycle. In a 1998 appearance, Robbie—son of Evel Knievel—hurdled 15 semitrailer trucks, breaking the record of 13 held by his father.

© TOM AND CAROLYN TENNEY

THE STATE FAIR HAS ALWAYS provided plenty of "novelty acts," be it a female auto mechanic in 1949, the Altoona Kitchen Band, or an accordion-playing contest.

© TOM AND CAROLYN TENNEY

▲ © RON LEVINE

▶▶ © RON LEVINE

▶▶ © RON LEVINE

Nothing compares to the dizzying rides and festive lights of the Iowa State Fair's midway at night.

©JONATHAN POSTAL / TOWERY PUBLISHING, INC.

© JONATHAN POSTAL / TOWERY PUBLISHING, INC.

WHETHER IT'S COWBOY ATTIRE on a young Blank Park Zoo visitor or The Outlaw thrill ride at Adventureland, Iowans enjoy a touch of the Old West.

© JONATHAN POSTAL / TOWERY PUBLISHING, INC.

© JONATHAN POSTAL / TOWERY PUBLISHING, INC.

© LYNDA RICHARDS

THE CARNIVAL ATTRACTIONS at Adventureland Park lure those eager to conquer a game of chance and take home the big prize.

© JOHNATHAN POSTAL / TOWERY PUBLISHING, INC.

© JOHNATHAN POSTAL / TOWERY PUBLISHING, INC.

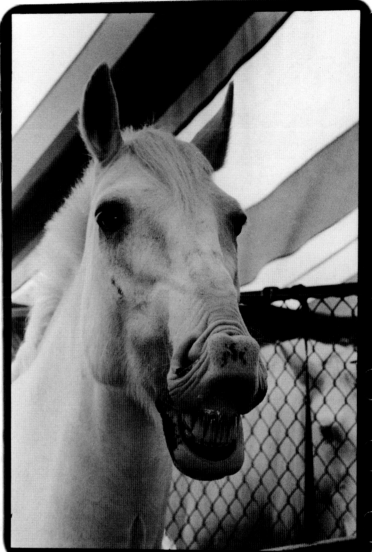

S OMETIMES IT'S NOT CLEAR exactly who's in charge among the trainers and animals of the Royal Hanneford Circus at Adventureland Park, where a good Charlie Chaplin impersonation elicits even an equine smile.

▲ © PAUL GATES BPC

▲ © PAUL GATES BPC

W HEN THE CIRCUS COMES TO Des Moines, it's a traffic-stopping event through downtown as the animals parade from the rail yard to the circus arena.

▼ © JONATHAN POSTAL / TOWERY PUBLISHING, INC.

© PAUL GATES BPC

DES MOINES POLICE OFFICERS are a visible presence on the city's streets and work hand in hand with residents to keep neighborhoods safe.

© JONATHAN POSTAL / TOWERY PUBLISHING, INC.

▼ © JONATHAN POSTAL / TOWERY PUBLISHING, INC.

WHETHER IT'S FIGHTING crime or fighting fires, the city has its share of professional forces ready to respond.

© JOHN F. SCHULTZ

GREATER DES MOINES

© NANCY FERGUSON

FIRE SYMBOLIZES FEAR FOR some, faith for others. For youth parading in the March for Jesus, tongues of flame ignite religious devotion.

WORDS FROM ON HIGH BOLDLY proclaim their messages: The Door of Faith Mission offers a bed and meal for the homeless (OPPOSITE); a rooftop cross bears witness to the most basic tenet of the Christian faith.

© DAMON G. BULLOCK / DIAMOND STAR PHOTOGRAPHY

THE BASILICA OF ST. JOHN, with its soaring ceiling, towering arches, and stunning stained glass, has long been a center of worship in the community (LEFT AND PAGE 102). The church was designated a national historic landmark in 1987 and named a basilica in 1989 by Pope John Paul II.

Nearly 300 churches and synagogues represent some 80 denominations in the Des Moines area, among them St. Ambrose Cathedral (PAGES 103 AND 105), and St. John's Lutheran Church (PAGE 104).

© PAUL CRO'S DEL

© JONATHAN POSTAL / TOMKEY PUBLISHING, INC.

© BUD LEE / THE ARTISTS AND WRITERS GROUP

F OR MANY IN DES MOINES, A sense of community and sustenance come together in symbols of faith.

© STEVE BAKER / HIGHLIGHT PHOTOGRAPHY

© KAY PRALL

© JONATHAN POSTAL / TOMFRY PUBLISHING, INC.

WHETHER IT BE OLD GLORY or an old barber pole, Iowans are proud to display the red, white, and blue.

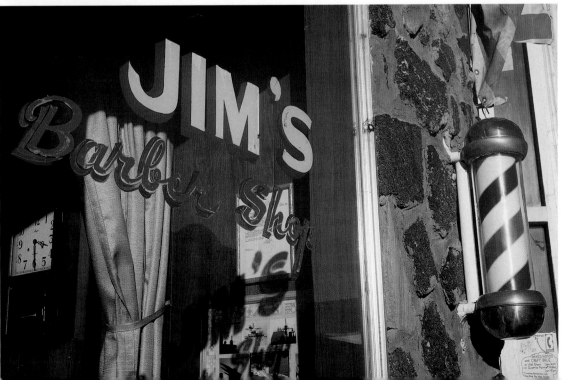

© BUD LEE / THE ARTISTS AND WRITERS GROUP

ONE OF IOWA'S MOST FAMOUS sons is Marion Morrison, better known as John Wayne, who was born in Winterset in 1907. The Duke's modest, four- room house has been restored to its 1907 appearance, and visitors can enjoy rare photos, memorabilia from Wayne's film career, and a collection of celebrity letters. Souvenir seekers will find plenty to choose from at the gift shop.

▲ ▲ © JONATHAN POSTAL / TOWERY PUBLISHING, INC.

© JONATHAN POSTAL / TOWERY PUBLISHING, INC.

CONFEDERATE AND UNION soldiers meet again in an annual Civil War reenactment in Boone, Iowa, a railroad town that celebrates its heritage each September during the Pufferbilly Days festival.

© JOHN F. SCHULTZ

GREATER DES MOINES

© JONATHAN POSTAL / TOWERY PUBLISHING, INC.

THE BOONE AND SCENIC VALLEY Railway owns one of the few newly built diesel locomotives in the world, taking passengers on scenic excursions through the Des Moines River Valley.

© COURTESY OF STATE HISTORICAL SOCIETY OF IOWA-DES MOINES

© PAUL GATES BPC

© COURTESY OF STATE HISTORICAL SOCIETY OF IOWA-DES MOINES

© PAUL GATES BPC

Aviation in Des Moines has come a long way from the day in 1914 when famed driver Eddie Rickenbacker raced pioneer flier Lincoln Beachey at the Iowa State Fair, winning by five seconds (OPPOSITE TOP). In 1946, the United Airlines Mainliner (TOP) arrived, and today, the Des Moines International Airport is served by 12 airlines, including American, Trans World, and United. More than 200 private and corporate aircraft are also based there.

▲ © MIKE WHYE

H OT-AIR BALLOONS LIFT PILOTS and passengers—not to mention spectators' imaginations—at the National Balloon Classic held south of Des Moines in nearby Indianola. One of the festival's biggest draws is the twice-daily mass ascension, when dozens of colorful craft take to the skies at once.

© T. C. SMEDES

© KEN SLAKPINO

GREATER DES MOINES

© TY SMEDES

© KEN SCARPINO

AIRPLANES TAKE FLIGHT AT local air shows, but sometimes even the most dazzling displays can't compete with the simple wonder of a soaring flock of Canada geese.

Not far from the fast-paced city, you'll find quiet marshes, ponds, and lakes that are home to wildlife such as the iridescent wood duck (PAGES 122 AND 123).

◆ © TY C. SMEDES

◆ © T.Y.C. SMEDES

FROM THE ORDINARY TO THE extraordinary: The crow of a rooster heralds the start of just another day on the farm. The growing population of bald eagles at Lake Red Rock, meanwhile, heralds the return of the magnificent bird from the brink of extinction.

▼ © CURTIS STAHR

GREATER DES MOINES

IT'S NOT AT ALL UNCOMMON TO spy wildlife in the area's many parks—or even in your own backyard.

© PAUL GATES BPC

© TY C. SMEDES

RESIDENTS IN THIS NEIGHBOR-hood are seeing spots. The "cow house," as it is known on Des Moines' east side, is painted in a Holstein pattern that reflects the owner's bovine mania. The real thing, bred for its delicious milk, might wonder about the fuss.

© JONATHAN POSTAL / TOWERY PUBLISHING, INC.

© BUD LEE / THE ARTISTS AND WRITERS GROUP

W<small>HO WOULD QUARREL WITH</small> this firearms policy, posted as it is under such an intimidating enforcer (OPPOSITE)? In Iowa, however, hunters and trappers are far more likely to nab deer, pheasant, and raccoon than a snarling bear.

◆ © PAUL GATES BPC

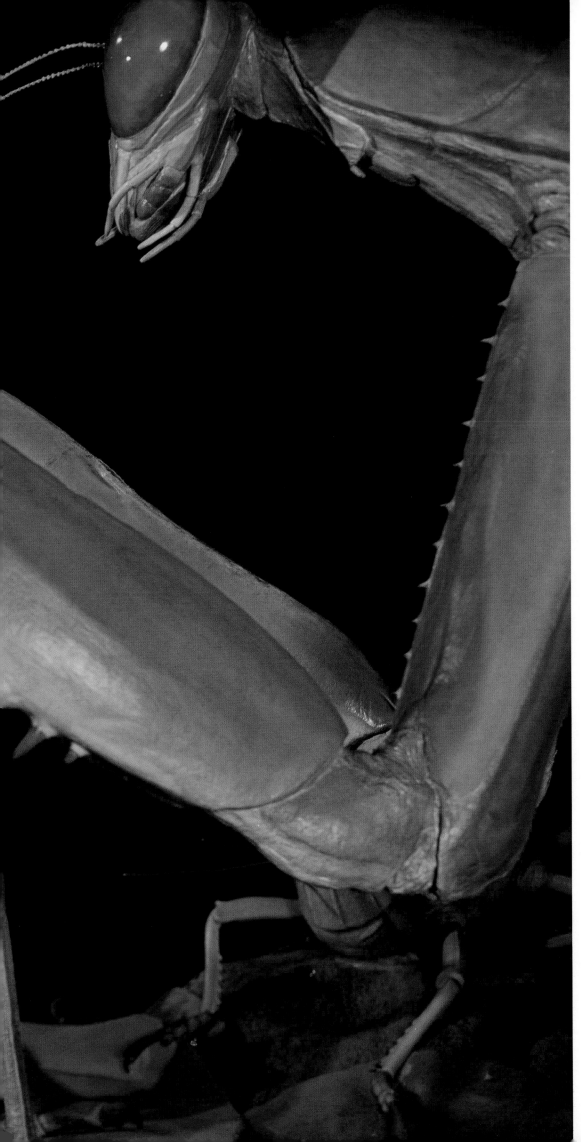

A BIGGER-THAN-LIFE PRAYING mantis in the Science Center of Iowa is one of many displays that help to open doors of discovery for children and adults.

THE DES MOINES BOTANICAL Center transports Iowans to a tropical paradise under one of the largest geodesic domes in the country (PAGES 134-137). Stunning displays of plants and flowers change throughout the year, and children delight in the free-flying birds and exotic fish in the ponds.

© MIKE WHYE

© SCOTT CAVANAH / STUDIO AU

▲ © DAMON G. BULLOCK / DIAMOND STAR PHOTOGRAPHY

▲ © TY C. SMEDES

GREATER DES MOINES

SOME 50 MILES SOUTHEAST OF the city, everyone is Dutch for a day when Pella hosts its annual tulip festival in early May. Townspeople honor their heritage by dressing in authentic costumes, performing Dutch dances and songs, baking rich pastries, and, of course, proudly showing off the stunning tulip gardens.

© DAVID G. BULLOCK / DIAMONDSTAR PHOTOGRAPHY

▼ © JONATHAN POSTAL / TOWERY PUBLISHING, INC.

▼ © JONATHAN POSTAL / TOWERY PUBLISHING, INC.

© PAUL GATES BPC

Living History Farms has been called the best agricultural museum in the world. The 600-acre open-air museum tells the story of how Iowa's prairies were transformed into some of the most productive farmland in the world.

▼ © PAUL GATES BPC

© JONATHAN POSTAL / TOWERY PUBLISHING, INC.

MUSEUM INTERPRETERS AT Living History Farms dress in period costume and re-create the daily routines of early Iowans, including those who lived on a farm in 1900.

▲ © MIKE WHYE

THE PIONEER TOWN OF WALNUT Hill at Living History Farms features an old-style General Store, stocked with reproductions of items from 1875.

Built in 1870, the Italianate Victorian mansion at the farm site (PAGES 148 AND 149) is listed on the National Register of Historic Places.

© JAMES BLANK

▼ © PAUL GATES BPC

© TY C. SMEDES

A GRICULTURE HAS COME A LONG way from the days of horse-drawn plows and two-cylinder tractors. Modern farmers rely on the latest in computer technology, but Iowans still harbor a nostalgia for simpler times.

© MARK BASSETT

GREATER DES MOINES

© RICHARD CUMMINS / PHOTOPHILE

LOCALS NEED NOT DRIVE FAR to be reminded of Iowa's agrarian roots. Weathered barns and sheds of long ago dot the rural landscape surrounding Des Moines.

◆ © STEVE O'BRIEN

E VEN THOSE IN THE CITY SENSE
when harvesttime arrives in
the countryside. Farmers trans-
port their crops to the local
grain elevator, where they are
loaded onto railcars for shipping.

© SCOTT CAVANAH / STUDIO AU

THE DOWNTOWN FARMERS' Market (PAGES 158-163) draws up to 5,000 shoppers on Saturday mornings from May to October. Market regulars can follow the rhythm of the summer: strawberries in June, sweet corn in July, and bell peppers in August. Vendors also sell everything from pepper sauce to Indian pastries, from honey to homegrown popcorn.

▲ © GREG SCHEIDEMAN / [N]HAUS FOTO

▼ © GREG SCHEIDEMAN / [N]HAUS FOTO

▲ © SCOTT CAVANAH / STUDIO AU

THE BIKE TRAIL THAT BEGINS downtown follows the Des Moines River north to Saylorville Lake and beyond. The scenic trail is one of many in central Iowa that invites bicyclists to view the countryside from a vantage point not possible by car.

© BOB NANDELL / DES MOINES REGISTER

GREATER DES MOINES

© DOUG WELLS / DES MOINES REGISTER

THOSE WITH A COMPETITIVE bent can pit their strength and endurance against other athletes in events such as the Big Creek Triathlon (OPPOSITE) and the Iowa bicycle racing championship (ABOVE).

PROFESSIONAL AND SEMIPRO-fessional sports thrive in Des Moines. The Menace soccer team, members of the Premier Developmental Soccer League, and the International Basketball Association's Dragons serve up fast-paced athletic excitement.

THE IOWA BARNSTORMERS provide hard-hitting excitement with arena football. Played indoors on a smaller field, the fast-paced game attracts avid fans.

© JONATHAN POSTAL / TOWERY PUBLISHING, INC.

NOTHING CAN COMPARE TO a sultry summer evening spent at the ballpark cheering on the Iowa Cubs, the Triple-A affiliate of the Chicago Cubs. Harboring dreams of making it to "the bigs," minor-leaguers play their hearts out in front of devoted fans. The club regularly ranks in the top 10 in division attendance.

KRAFT

Simple Answers

Good food for busy lives.

BiC

BiC

POWERADE

USWEST

life's better here

USA OLYMPICS
Proud Sponsor

Fairtron

PRAIRIE MEADOWS
RACETRACK AND CASINO

Coca-Cola

VICTORS
SPORTS CLUB
A SPORTS BAR AND GRILL
7500 - DOUGLAS

COMPETITIVE
edge
ADVERTISING SPECIALTY MFG. CO.
T-SHIRTS • AD SPECIALTIES

PLUMB
AND FITT
LOCAL

MIDLAND
HOMES
"The Best Value Anywhere!"
www.midland-homes.com

Tompkins
hose and fittings
2535 DELAWARE   DSM

YOU JUS
CAN'T
THE B

© STEVE BAKER, HIGHLIGHT PHOTOGRAPHY

UD LIGHT. BEER

KNOW WHEN TO SAY WHEN...
Budweiser
KING OF BEERS

MORTON SYSTEM SAVER Pellets

BALL STRIKE OUT

AT 1 2 3 4 5 6 7 8 9 10 R H E

SITORS

WA

6:10

UPS

kahler corporate identity & apparel
kahler & co. 334-0334
specialties

Intensive Carin
MER
Where The Experts

WELLMARK
Blue Cross and Blue Shield of Iowa

ACHESON *AUTO* **WORKS**

COST CUTTER
(FAMILY HAIR CARE)
We're your style

▼ © PAUL GATES BPC

© PAUL GATES BPC

Football fans love fall, when the Iowa State University Cyclones return to the field for another season in the Big 12 athletic conference. Halftime entertainment by the Cyclone marching band is always a highlight of a football Saturday in nearby Ames.

© JONATHAN POSTAL / TOWERY PUBLISHING, INC.

V INE STREET BALLET IN WEST
Des Moines is a training
ground for some of the area's
best dancers, including Julie
Grooters-Affrunti (OPPOSITE).
The young company prides
itself on the diversity of its
dancers' styles as well as its
performances.

© JONATHAN POSTAL / TOWERY PUBLISHING, INC.

P AINTER JACK WILKES (OPPOSITE) and musical composer and performer Linda Robbins Coleman (ABOVE) are two members of a small but vibrant community of artists who call Des Moines home.

© JONATHAN POSTAL / TOWERY PUBLISHING, INC.

INTERNATIONALLY RENOWNED opera tenor Simon Estes (OPPOSITE) hails from Centerville, Iowa, and returns regularly for performances in the area. The Des Moines Symphony, guided since 1988 by conductor and music director Joseph Giunta (LEFT), has reached a high level of performance excellence during its 60-year history.

▲▼ © JONATHAN POSTAL / TOWERY PUBLISHING, INC.

▲▲ © JONATHAN POSTAL / TOWERY PUBLISHING, INC.

W ITH DEEP CONCENTRATION and studied precision, members of the Des Moines Symphony transform notes on a page into the transcending language of music.

◄ © RAY F. HILLSTROM JR. / HILLSTROM STOCK PHOTO, INC.

Art imitates life—or is it the other way around? Passersby can almost hear the song of the musicians captured in bronze at the Fine Arts Center at Drake University (ABOVE). With fiddles and a banjo, street musicians entertain along Court Avenue (OPPOSITE).

© JONATHAN POSTAL / TOWERY PUBLISHING, INC.

JAZZ LOVERS CAN GET THEIR fix from performers like sax player Julius Brooks (PAGE 188) and trumpeter Jim Oatts (PAGE 189), both longtime fixtures on the city's music scene.

▲ © SCOTT CAVANAH / STUDIO AU

JAZZ, BLUES, COUNTRY, CLASSICAL, bluegrass, folk, or rock and roll: Guitarists playing any style of music can find the instrument of their dreams at Last Chance Guitars.

GUITARISTS ROB LUMBARD AND Frank Tribble have deep musical roots in Des Moines. Both are frequent performers at clubs, as well as at community events such as Jazz in July, a series of daily concerts at different sites throughout the city.

▲ © DAVID PETERSON / DES MOINES REGISTER

© DOUG WELLS / DES MOINES REGISTER

Central Iowa is a "must stop" on the tour circuit for big-name musicians and bands. The Artist (opposite) and Smashing Pumpkins (above) are just two of the numerous acts to have played before captive crowds at Hilton Coliseum in Ames, just north of Des Moines.

C OFFEE AFICIONADOS CAN GET their caffeine fix at any number of locations in Des Moines. Java Joes (OPPOSITE) in downtown's Court Avenue district and Zanzibar's (ABOVE) on Ingersoll Avenue are two favorites, serving up specialty drinks along with good conversation.

WHEN THE OCCASION CALLS for a special night out, Des Moines can serve up any number of fine restaurants. The Embassy Club (TOP), 801 Steak and Chop House (BOTTOM), and Raccoon River Brewing Co. (OPPOSITE) spotlight the region's traditional dishes, serving them with an updated flair.

© JONATHAN POSTAL / TOWERY PUBLISHING, INC.

© JONATHAN POSTAL / TOWERY PUBLISHING, INC.

For many Iowans, a day isn't complete without a stop at the local café. More than just a place to get heaping plates of pancakes or tuna salad sand-wiches, diners are the heart of many towns, the place where community news and happenings are exchanged—and debated—among patrons.

© JONATHAN POSTAL / TOWERY PUBLISHING, INC.

At Stella's Blue Sky Diner, a culinary adventure seekers can order a malt served in a rather unconventional way (OPPOSITE). Fifties-style eats are on the menu along with the usual burgers, fries, and patty melts.

LARUE MILLER

W HO SAYS SHOPPING CAN'T be fun? It's impossible to resist the treasures at A-Okay Antiques in Valley Junction (OPPOSITE) or the Booneville General Store (TOP). And who could pass up a storefront bearing this intriguing salutation (BOTTOM)?

© RAY F. HILLSTROM JR. / HILLSTROM STOCK PHOTO, INC.

© STEVE BAKER / HIGHLIGHT PHOTOGRAPHY

ZOMBIE
BELL RINGER
HOWARD STERN
CIGARETTE
LOADS
BANGERS
NOT INTENDED FOR SALE TO MINORS
GLO NECKLACE

ADVENTUROUS IOWANS CAN play make-believe anytime of the year thanks to the wares offered by area wig and mask shops.

▲▼ © JONATHAN POSTAL / TOWERY PUBLISHING, INC.

© JONATHAN POSTAL / TOWERY PUBLISHING, INC.

FROM FINE ART TO FOLK ART TO bigger-than-life art, Iowans create and collect it all.

© JONATHAN POSTAL / TOWERY PUBLISHING, INC.

A N OLD-FASHIONED SALON treats its regulars to more than just a shampoo and style. The weekly visit promises an hour of pampering, primping, and conversation, leaving customers ready to face the world anew.

© KEVIN WOLF / DES MOINES REGISTER

GREATER DES MOINES

© DAVID PETERSON / DES MOINES REGISTER

A SKATEBOARD AND AN OPEN stretch of concrete allow area teens to challenge each other with leaps, spins, and other up-in-the-air maneuvers.

▼ © PAUL GATES BPC

© PAUL GATES BPC

CALM WATERS AND SUNNY
skies beckon boaters to
Saylorville Lake for a relaxing
day outdoors.

© DAMON G. BULLOCK / DIAMOND STAR PHOTOGRAPHY

© RICHARD CUMMINS / PHOTOPHILE

Central Iowans treasured the area's covered bridges long before they were made famous in the 1992 Robert Waller novel *The Bridges of Madison County*. Of the original 19 bridges built in the late 1800s, today only six remain, all of which are listed on the National Register of Historic Places.

S OME OF MADISON COUNTY'S bridges, including the Holliwell (OPPOSITE BOTTOM) and the Hogback (BOTTOM), have been renovated. The Roseman Bridge, the most notable, is a popular place to post notes, remembrances, and graffiti (OPPOSITE TOP).

To make the movie version of *The Bridges of Madison County*, the film crew located an abandoned farmhouse and fully restored it to serve as Francesca's house.

© COURTESY OF STATE HISTORICAL SOCIETY OF IOWA-DES MOINES

© COURTESY OF STATE HISTORICAL SOCIETY OF IOWA–DES MOINES

THE DAYS OF STREETCARS, horse-drawn wagons, and gas lamps are long gone, but Walnut Street (OPPOSITE) and Locust Street (ABOVE) remain busy commercial thoroughfares in downtown Des Moines.

© COURTESY OF STATE HISTORICAL SOCIETY OF IOWA-DES MOINES

© KEN SCARPINO

GREATER DES MOINES HAS evolved from the days of covered wagons into a thriving commercial center offering fiber optics, digital communication, and other advanced technologies that form a solid link between the city and the rest of the world (PAGES 224-229).

◆ © RICHARD CUMMINS / PHOTOPHILE

◆ © TOM AND CAROLYN TENNEY

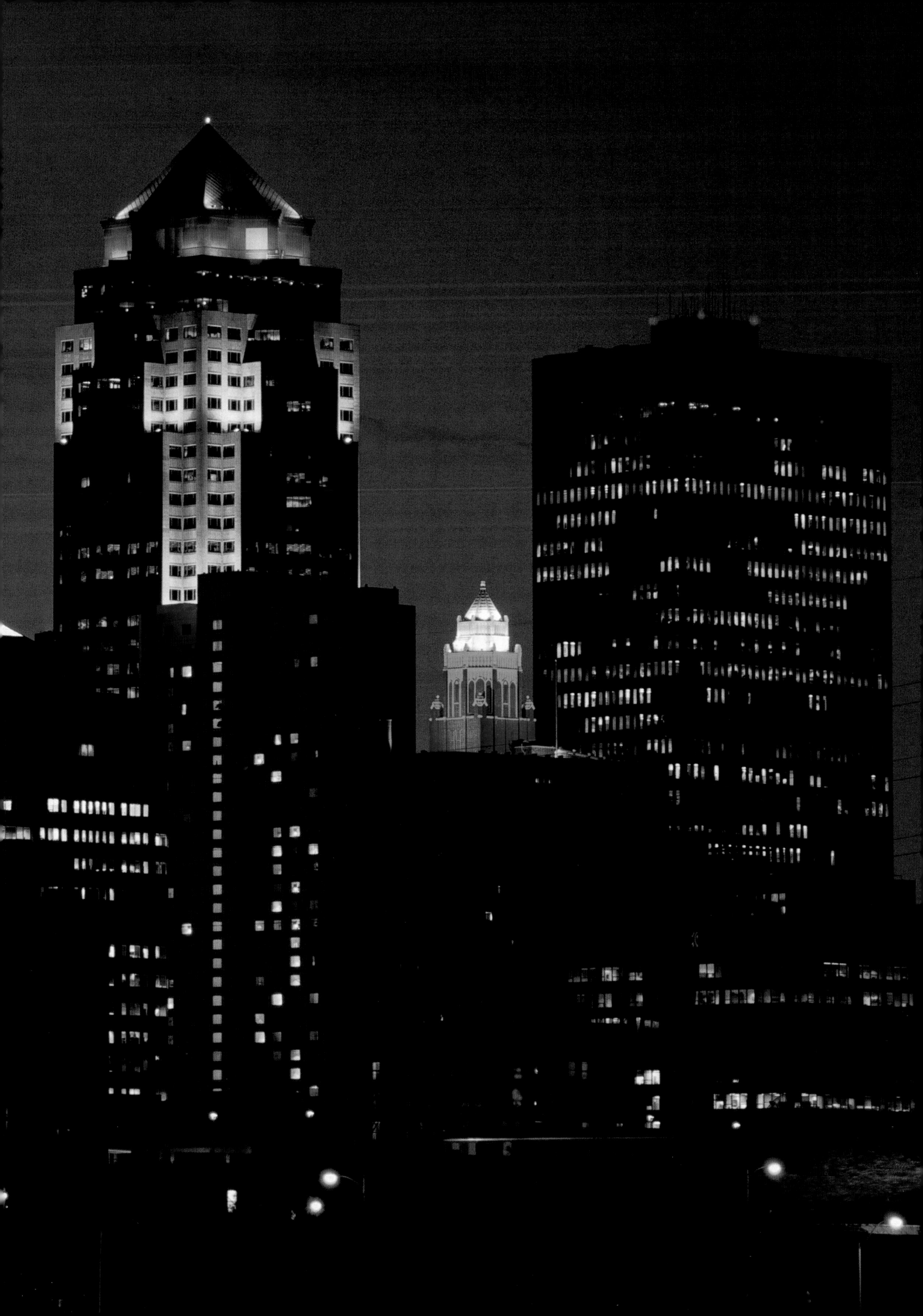

◆ © PAUL GATES BPC

Profiles in Excellence

A look at the corporations, businesses, professional groups, and community service organizations that have made this book possible. Their stories—offering an informal chronicle of the local business community—are arranged according to the date they were established in Des Moines.

AmerUs Group ■ Asgrow Seed Company LLC ■ The Associates Credit Card Center ■ Atlantic Coca-Cola Bottling Company ■ The Atlas Companies ■ August Home Publishing Company ■ Bankers Trust Company ■ Brenton Bank ■ Broadlawns Medical Center ■ Brooks Borg Skiles Architecture Engineering ■ Business Publications Corporation ■ Commercial Federal Corporation ■ Des Moines General Hospital ■ Des Moines Orthopaedic Surgeons ■ Des Moines Public Schools ■ The Des Moines Register ■ Diamond Animal Health, Inc. ■ Drake University ■ EMC Insurance Companies ■ Equitable Life Insurance Company of Iowa ■ Farm Bureau Financial Services ■ FIRST BANK ■ Firstar ■ Forrest & Associate, Inc. ■ Grand View College ■ Gratias Construction Inc. ■ Greater Des Moines Chamber of Commerce Federation ■ Holmes, Murphy & Associates, Inc. ■ Hotel Fort Des Moines ■ Hy-Vee, Inc. ■ Integra Health ■ Investors Management Group ■ The Iowa Clinic, P.C. ■ Iowa Heart Center ■ Iowa Kidney Stone Center/Laser Eye Center of Iowa ■ Iowa State University ■ John Deere Des Moines Works/John Deere Credit Worldwide ■ Karl Chevrolet Inc. ■ Kavanaugh Art Gallery ■ LaSalle National Bank ■ Manpower Inc., of Des Moines ■ Maytag Corporation ■ Mercy Hospital Medical Center ■ Meredith Corporation ■ Meyocks & Priebe Advertising, Inc. ■ The Mid-America Group ■ MidAmerican Energy Company ■ Mondo's of West Des Moines, Inc. ■ NCMIC Group, Inc. ■ Neumann Brothers, Inc. ■ Plumbers & Steamfitters Local No. 33 AFL-CIO ■ Polk County ■ Prairie Meadows Racetrack and Casino ■ The Principal Financial Group ■ QuikTrip Corporation-Des Moines Division ■ Relationship Marketing ■ Robertson Lowstuter ■ The Straub Corporation ■ Tone Brothers, Inc. ■ Triplett Companies ■ United States Cellular Corporation ■ University of Osteopathic Medicine and Health Sciences ■ Valley West Mall ■ Veterans Administration Central Iowa Health Care System ■ The Weitz Company, Inc. ■ Wells Fargo & Company ■ WHO-AM/KMXD-FM/KYSY-FM ■

◆ © CURTIS STAHR

1846-1934

1846 Polk County

1849 Des Moines Public Schools

1849 The Des Moines Register

1855 The Weitz Company, Inc.

1867 Equitable Life Insurance Company of Iowa

1868 Iowa State University

1872 Firstar

1873 Tone Brothers, Inc.

1879 The Principal Financial Group

1881 Brenton Bank

1881 Drake University

1885 MidAmerican Energy Company

1888 Greater Des Moines Chamber of Commerce Federation

1890 Plumbers & Steamfitters Local No. 33 AFL-CIO

1893 Maytag Corporation

1893 Mercy Hospital Medical Center

1895 Brooks Borg Skiles Architecture Engineering

1896 AmerUs Group

1896 Grand View College

1897 Wells Fargo & Company

1898 University of Osteopathic Medicine and Health Sciences

1901 FIRST BANK

1902 Meredith Corporation

1911 EMC Insurance Companies

1912 Neumann Brothers, Inc.

1916 Des Moines General Hospital

1917 Bankers Trust Company

1918 Farm Bureau Financial Services

1919 Hotel Fort Des Moines

1924 Broadlawns Medical Center

1924 WHO-AM/KMXD-FM/KYSY-FM

1932 Holmes, Murphy & Associates, Inc.

1934 Veterans Administration Central Iowa Health Care System

HEN IOWA BECAME A STATE IN 1846, THE EIGHTH Territorial Legislature established the county boundaries and named the area after President James K. Polk. By 1850, Polk County boasted a population of 4,513, and had 16 public schools, one church, a grist-

mill, and several sawmills. Today, Polk County has more than 350,000 residents in 17 cities and 17 unincorporated townships.

As the county grew in size and stature, its scope of services expanded. Today, Polk County enjoys one of the strongest financial positions of any county government in the nation, and employs more than 1,100 people to serve a range of community needs.

RESPONSIVE TO THE COMMUNITY

Like any successful organization, Polk County ensures responsiveness to a changing society. In addition to traditional services, from public works to law enforcement to congregate meals for the elderly, Polk County has entered new areas.

Polk County now provides central Iowa with meeting and entertainment facilities as the new owner of the Polk County Convention Complex, and has invested $600,000 to improve the facility for the tens of thousands of people who visit each year. In addition, Polk County is also the new owner of the landmark Veterans Memorial Auditorium.

Polk County is using technology to better serve the people of the community. The Information Technology Division was created to make the best use of state-of-the-art technology. In addition, citizens can access more and more public information through Polk County's Web site at www.co.polk.ia.us.

Education is an important issue at all levels of government. In 1997, Polk County became the first county government in Iowa to provide funding to local schools. With revenue earned from the Prairie Meadows Racetrack and Casino, Polk County provided $10.9 million in funds to help school districts improve their facilities.

LEADERSHIP FOR GREATER DES MOINES

Polk County leadership is a combination of elected and appointed officials. The board of supervisors is composed of five citizens who set priorities, enact local laws and policies, allocate resources, and maintain budgetary control.

The auditor oversees preparation and maintenance of all official records, and serves as the commissioner of elections. The county attorney ensures laws are

enforced within the county, and serves as counsel to all county offices.

The recorder maintains official real estate records, contracts, articles of incorporation, partnerships, state tax liens, military records, marriage licenses, and death and birth certificates. The sheriff provides law enforcement, manages and operates the Polk County Jail, and provides 911 emergency assistance. The treasurer is responsible for the management of all county funds, as well as for the issuance of vehicle titles and registrations, and the collection of property taxes.

The county manager and other appointed officials manage the departments that serve the public and provide for an efficient local government. Those departments are community and family services, conservation, general services, health, health services, human resources, public works, regional facilities, and veterans' affairs.

As Polk County continues to grow, it will face new challenges. To fulfill its mission to enhance the quality of life for the people in its communities, Polk County stands ready to respond to these growing and changing needs.

CLOCKWISE FROM TOP: MORE THAN 1,100 POLK COUNTY EMPLOYEES WORK TO MEET THE NEEDS OF THE COMMUNITY.

VETERANS MEMORIAL AUDITORIUM IS ONE OF THE REGIONAL FACILITIES OWNED AND OPERATED BY POLK COUNTY.

POLK COUNTY PROVIDES A WIDE RANGE OF SERVICES, FROM RECREATIONAL OPPORTUNITIES TO CHILD CARE ASSISTANCE.

MARK DAVITT, DAVITT PHOTOGRAPHY

ISTORIANS JOKINGLY SAY THAT THE FIRST NEWSPAPER IN Des Moines would have been called the *Fort Des Moines Star*, but there was a shortage of large type to compose the lengthy masthead. So, in 1849, Barlow Granger, working out of a log cabin, founded his newspaper as the *Iowa Star*.

The publication evolved through a variety of names and changes until 1903, when the *Register and Leader*, as it was then called, was purchased by Algona, Iowa, banker Gardner Cowles. While editor Harvey Ingham ran the paper's news side, Cowles concentrated on expanding its circulation to the entire state of Iowa, renaming it *The Des Moines Register* in 1915.

AN IOWA TRADITION IN A NEW ERA

In 1985, a year after *Time* magazine named *The Des Moines Register* among the 10 best newspapers in the country, Cowles Media sold it to Gannett Company, Inc., one of the nation's largest media holding companies. Still, *The Register* has remained a locally focused newspaper, maintaining its own management, editorial direction, and decision-making responsibilities. In addition, Charles Edwards Jr., Cowles' great-grandson, was the paper's president and publisher until 1996.

Within the Gannett family of newspapers, *The Register* has been designated the Best in Gannett in 1986, 1987, and 1990. Known as the Newspaper Iowa Depends Upon, *The Register* has garnered 15 Pulitzer prizes for excellence in covering agricultural issues, investigative reporting, and editorial writing and cartoons. *The Register*'s most recent Pulitzer was for meritorious public service for a provocative series on rape in 1990 by reporter Jane Schorer Meisner.

The paper has strong readership at all age, income, and educational levels, with more than 700,000 people each month reading the *Sunday Register*. It stays abreast of its readers' concerns through citizen advisory boards and meetings across the state. The NAACP has twice honored *The Register* as Merit Employer of the Year for the paper's support and advancement of women and people of color.

The Register annually recognizes top high school students through its Iowa Academic All-State Team. RAGBRAI®, *The Register*'s Annual Great Bicycle Ride Across Iowa™, which celebrated its 25th year in 1997, attracts more than 10,000 participants as well as local and national media attention each year.

AN EXCITING FUTURE

In April 1997, *The Register* debuted its World Wide Web site in an effort to meet the changing electronic needs of its readership. On the heels of that premiere, in April 1998, *The Register* broke ground for a $51 million, state-of-the-art production facility on a 16-acre site in a new business park south of the Des Moines airport. There,

new presses will be used to print *The Register* by midyear 2000, providing increased quality and quantity of color, limited ink rub-off, and greater flexibility in zoning. "The reproduction quality of the newspaper will improve so dramatically that people will be blown away by it," says *Register* president and publisher Barbara A. Henry.

While building excellence for the future, *The Register* celebrates the fact that it is the oldest operating business in Polk County, marking its 150th anniversary on July 26, 1999. With advancements and expansion in the area of on-line technology and the capabilities offered by faster, state-of-the-art presses, *The Register* is poised for success as an information company in the 21st century.

CLOCKWISE FROM TOP: RAGBRAI®, *THE REGISTER*'S ANNUAL GREAT BICYCLE RIDE ACROSS IOWA™, WHICH CELEBRATED ITS 25TH YEAR IN 1997, ATTRACTS MORE THAN 10,000 PARTICIPANTS AS WELL AS LOCAL AND NATIONAL MEDIA ATTENTION EACH YEAR.

WHILE BUILDING EXCELLENCE FOR THE FUTURE, *THE DES MOINES REGISTER* CELEBRATES THE FACT THAT IT IS THE OLDEST OPERATING BUSINESS IN POLK COUNTY, MARKING ITS 150TH ANNIVERSARY ON JULY 26, 1999.

IN APRIL 1998, *THE REGISTER* BROKE GROUND FOR A $51 MILLION, STATE-OF-THE-ART PRODUCTION FACILITY ON A 16-ACRE SITE IN A NEW BUSINESS PARK SOUTH OF THE DES MOINES AIRPORT. THERE, NEW PRESSES WILL BE USED TO PRINT *THE REGISTER* BY MIDYEAR 2000, PROVIDING INCREASED QUALITY AND QUANTITY OF COLOR, LIMITED INK RUB-OFF, AND GREATER FLEXIBILITY IN ZONING.

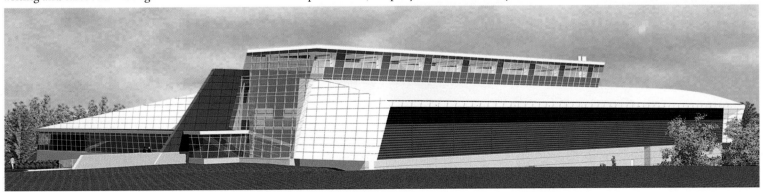

SINCE ITS ORGANIZATION 150 YEARS AGO, THE DES MOINES PUBLIC Schools has evolved from a collection of small school districts into a united, innovative district where all children are expected to learn. With more than 60 schools and numerous nationally recognized programs, 4,433 teachers and staff members work

together to meet the educational needs of 31,700 students.

The Des Moines Public Schools has its roots in a score of school districts that formed in and around the infant city. The first of these districts organized in 1849, with students attending school in a church and courthouse until a public schoolhouse was erected in 1856 at the present downtown intersection of Ninth and Locust streets. In 1907, 20 districts consolidated into the Independent School District of Des Moines. Together, they formed the core of what is now the largest school district in the state.

A TRADITION OF INNOVATIVE EXCELLENCE

The district's long history of innovation began in its early years. A Des Moines district formed the nation's second kindergarten program in 1884, and physical education classes began soon after. Classes for exceptional children began in 1914. A generous gift helped establish Smouse Opportunity School for health- and physically impaired children in 1931, a school that gained international attention when Des Moines

Superintendent of Schools John Studebaker served as U.S. commissioner of education for 15 years under Presidents Franklin D. Roosevelt and Harry S. Truman.

The district continues this tradition of excellence by promoting a strong core of basics while providing families with educational choices and forging partnerships with the community. As a result, Des Moines students score above the national average on Iowa Tests of Basic Skills. Average daily attendance across the district is about 95 percent. Class of 1998 graduates earned more than $4.8 million in scholarships and 75 percent planned to attend two- or four-year colleges.

Outstanding professionals instruct and serve the diverse student enrollment. More than 53 percent of the teachers in the school district hold advanced graduate degrees. And the district is home to top faculty, including the Iowa Teacher of the Year and national runner-up, the Iowa Secondary Principal of the Year and national runner-up, and two Milken Family Foundation award-winning teachers who each received $25,000 for exemplary success in the classroom.

Teachers make reading a top priority in elementary school, and all students are expected to read at or above grade level by fourth grade. Many teachers in

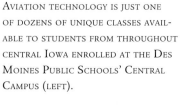

AVIATION TECHNOLOGY IS JUST ONE OF DOZENS OF UNIQUE CLASSES AVAILABLE TO STUDENTS FROM THROUGHOUT CENTRAL IOWA ENROLLED AT THE DES MOINES PUBLIC SCHOOLS' CENTRAL CAMPUS (LEFT).

A CARING STAFF WITH HIGH EXPECTATIONS FOR ALL STUDENTS IS ONE REASON STUDENTS IN THE DES MOINES PUBLIC SCHOOLS CONTINUE TO ACHIEVE AT HIGH LEVELS (RIGHT).

Des Moines are taking a new approach to education using a model created in Italy. The Reggio Emilia approach integrates several subject areas to facilitate high-level thinking skills and help students reach their highest potential. Using Reggio, art teachers become facilitators of children's learning, which is particularly useful in the early years when children's verbal and writing skills are less developed.

In a district that prizes diversity, families have several options when selecting schools for their children. For younger children, the district offers preschool, including Montessori instruction, which focuses on independent and hands-on learning. Montessori prekindergarten through sixth-grade instruction is also available at Cowles Elementary School.

Magnet schools provide other choices. King and Perkins elementary schools specialize in math and science, Edmunds Academy of Fine Arts offers a fine-arts curriculum, and Moulton Elementary School has an extended-year program. The district also offers two traditional elementary schools. One of them, Phillips Traditional Elementary School, provides a challenging curriculum based on the Core Knowledge Sequence developed by noted professor E.D. Hirsch Jr., author of *Cultural Literacy* and coauthor of *The Dictionary of Cultural Literacy*.

Enrollment in the district's Central Campus is highly prized by secondary school students from more than 50 school districts in central Iowa. It offers unique learning opportunities ranging from a nationally recognized Advanced Placement (AP) program to an impressive array of vocational-technical programs, including automotive technology and home building.

Enriching, Individualized Opportunities

The Des Moines Public Schools works hard to meet the individual needs of students and their families—from quality child care

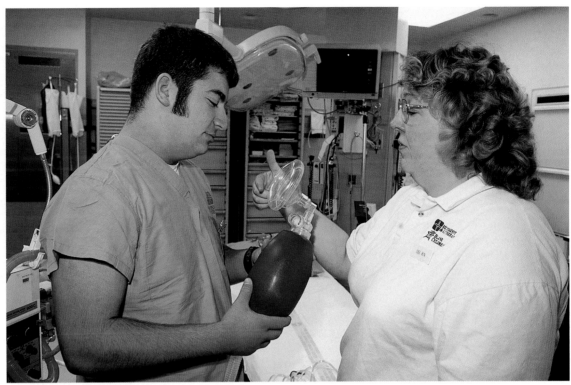

to a nationally recognized gifted-and-talented program.

The Des Moines Public Schools' gifted-and-talented program has been recognized as one of the best in the nation and serves students from across central Iowa. Participating students have the opportunity to learn material separate from the regular curriculum at an accelerated pace. The program runs in all schools, and serves 4,400 students based on their individual needs. In addition, Central Academy offers a host of AP courses and has been recognized as one of the top 100 AP programs in the nation.

The district is a recognized pioneer in the field of special education. Students find a comprehensive set of services—ranging from supplemental assistance to programs in specialized facilities—unavailable elsewhere in the state. Programs exist for students with a wide range of educational needs, including visual, physical, mental, and behavioral disabilities.

All elementary schools in the system offer Smoother Sailing, a nationally praised guidance program aimed at kindergartners through fifth graders. The program helps guide students

through childhood by building their problem-solving and decision-making skills. Smoother Sailing emphasizes education and prevention for all students.

Students can choose to participate in music, athletics, and other extracurricular activities. Certified teachers who are active participants in local, state, and national organizations teach the district's quality music-education program, and the district sponsors annual music festivals, summer camps, and an honor band. As for athlet-

The Iowa Methodist Hospital Emergency Room becomes an extension of the classroom and the nurse becomes a teacher for this health sciences student in the Corporate Academic Institute.

Technology is an integral part of preparing students in the Des Moines Public Schools for the 21st century.

ics, all public high schools in Des Moines belong to the Central Iowa Metropolitan League American Conference, which provides competition in football, soccer, volleyball, cross-country, basketball, swimming, wrestling, track, tennis, golf, softball, and baseball. Top-ranked Lincoln High School in Des Moines won the Class 4-A Baseball Championship in summer 1998.

The district's community, adult, and continuing education programs provide educational, cultural, and recreational opportunities to residents of all ages in the metro area. More than 150,000 participants benefit each year from school programs, buildings, and grounds.

STRONG COMMUNITY PARTNERSHIPS

The Des Moines Public Schools has developed partnerships with many local businesses and agencies to prepare students for postgraduate life. Throughout the system, the district incorporates school-to-work from prekindergarten through 12th grade—another example of the district leading the way in Iowa. One of the successful school-to-work

programs is the Corporate Academic Institute, which brings the district into partnership with several businesses to create learning opportunities unparalleled in most k-12 school districts. The institute works with students of all backgrounds and abilities to nurture talents and develop skills for success in the operating room or the boardroom.

The Downtown School opened in 1993 as a collaborative project between the Des Moines Public Schools and the business community. This nationally acclaimed learning program uses the entire

downtown area, connected by sky-walks, as its extended classroom. Students have access to unique learning resources from area businesses, the Civic Center, and working parents.

The Food, Fiber, and Environmental Sciences program, established with the help of Pioneer Hi-Bred International, is just one of the latest examples of innovation in Des Moines. It prepares students for careers in agriculture and veterinary care.

For its creative approach to addressing disadvantaged children's needs beyond the school day through a program called New Horizons, the district received the Award for Excellence in Community Collaboration for Children and Youth in 1997. The successful program, created three decades ago, provides supportive services and work experience to at-risk youth to ensure that they graduate. The award recognized the district's innovative work with a variety of community and support agencies in meeting the human-service needs of students and their families.

Planning for the future, the new superintendent of schools, Dr. Eric Witherspoon, wants to make the district the best in the nation. Since 1992, the district has budgeted approximately $25 million to improve school facilities, place technology in classrooms, and bring the district into the 21st century.

TIM TUTT, THIRD-GRADE TEACHER AND MILKEN FAMILY FOUNDATION NATIONAL EDUCATOR, IS REPRESENTATIVE OF THE OUTSTANDING, DEDICATED FACULTY IN THE DES MOINES PUBLIC SCHOOLS.

A HEAVY EMPHASIS ON READING LAYS THE GROUNDWORK FOR A SUCCESSFUL LEARNING CAREER IN THE DES MOINES PUBLIC SCHOOLS.

AT BRENTON BANK WHEN SOMEONE JOKES ABOUT "BANKER'S hours," the staff is quick with a response: Brenton's state-of-the-art systems have extended those hours to any time of the day or night. ■ For more than 117 years, Brenton has worked to know, understand, and gain the respect of the people it serves. The company's personal bankers have visited with customers in their homes and businesses, as well as in the bank's service locations. Now, through technology, Brenton offers even broader opportunities for convenient banking. In 1997, specialists in the Brenton Direct telephone center handled more than 1,500 calls per day—opening new deposit and consumer loan accounts, helping clients obtain new mortgages and consumer loans, or assisting customers in insuring their homes and cars.

Brenton Bank is Iowa's largest home-based bank holding company, with 46 service locations in metropolitan markets and regional economic centers across the state. The company offers retail, agricultural, and commercial banking; trust and investment management services; investment, insurance, and real estate brokerage; mortgage banking; cash management and international banking services; and proprietary mutual funds.

GENERATIONS OF BANKERS

The evolution of Brenton Bank began in 1853, when Dr. James Baird Brenton settled in Dallas County, Iowa. His son, William H. Brenton, started the first Brenton Bank in Dallas Center in 1881. In 1888, William's two sons, Charles R. and Clyde E., joined him in the banking business, and by 1891, their sister, Eva A. Brenton McColl, had also become involved. As three additional Brenton Banks opened over the years, the family continued operating the bank as a private institution until 1934.

Charles' son, W. Harold Brenton, started his banking career in 1920 and brought all the family's banks together in 1947 as Brenton Banks, Inc.—the first homegrown, multi-bank holding company in Iowa. William H. "Bill," C. Robert "Bob," and J.C. "Buz" Brenton, Harold's sons, have continued the Brenton tradition of banking, finance, and farming. Bob Brenton, then chairman of the board, retired from day-to-day management of the company in 1998, after more than four decades of leadership. The Brenton family remain as major shareholders, supporting the direction the bank is taking under the leadership of CEO Robert L. DeMeulenaere.

LEADING THE WAY

Brenton Bank has a history of firsts. During World War II, Brenton became the first Iowa bank to elect women as officers. Brenton also was the first to open neighborhood banks in the Des Moines area, where its lending policies helped the area's neighborhoods to prosper.

Brenton's mortgage loan-servicing portfolio has grown steadily—increasing by 24 percent in 1997—as the bank helped many Iowans buy their first homes through federal programs. Meanwhile, Brenton's century-old commitment to agriculture continues to grow even stronger as it sets its sights on being Iowa's premier agricultural banking organization by the turn of the century.

While every Brenton associate has specific sales and service goals and responsibilities, all the staff members work together in a partnership to achieve the organization's goals and to meet clients' objectives. Well into its second century of successful banking, Brenton's staff have proved what they can accomplish together—and even greater opportunities lie ahead.

BRENTON MEANS BUSINESS IN IOWA.

THROUGHOUT THE COMMUNITIES OF GREATER DES MOINES, certain rectangle-shaped, bronze plaques are a familiar site. Discreetly gracing hotels, office buildings, automobile showrooms, schools, YMCA buildings, and a new state prison, they simply read "The Weitz Company, Inc." In Iowa, and around

DALE PHOTOGRAPHICS

the country, these plaques have come to symbolize not only quality construction, but also the company's dedication to maximizing value to the customer.

As the oldest construction company west of the Mississippi River, The Weitz Company, Inc. began as a carpentry shop founded in 1855 by German immigrant Charles H. Weitz. For 140 years, descendants of the founder managed the company, making it the oldest family-managed business in Des Moines.

Charles Weitz's first job was installing windows in the basement of Des Moines' Old Savery House, but his reputation for quality craftsmanship and building excellence caused his business to grow steadily. When he retired in 1903 at age 77, three of his seven children—sons Fred W., Edward, and Charles H. Weitz—formed a partnership to operate as Charles Weitz Sons, General Contractors. With this partnership, the Weitz tradition of teamwork began. The company incorporated in 1929 and

changed its name to The Weitz Company, Inc. In 1935, Fred Weitz's sons, Rudolph and Heinrich, became the third generation to manage the firm. Rudolph's son, Frederick, became president in 1963 and assumed the chairman's post in 1974.

NEW LEADERSHIP TEAM: TRADITIONAL VALUES

On March 31, 1995, Frederick Weitz sold the company to a group of employees, who renewed the company's team commitment to be completely focused on meeting and exceeding customer needs. Today, Weitz is a sophisticated company that offers general contracting, design/build, and construction management services to a wide range of clients throughout the United States. Licensed

to do business in 35 states, it was listed in the July 1997 issue of *Building Design & Construction* as the 41st-largest nonresidential contractor in the country. The May 1998 issue of *Engineering News-Record* ranks Weitz as the nation's 40th-largest general building contractor, with revenues in 1997 of more than $410 million.

The Weitz Company has maintained its corporate headquarters, a divisional office, and a national division office in Des Moines. Other divisional offices are in Omaha, Denver, Phoenix, and West Palm Beach. The officers of the company are Glenn De Stigter, company president and CEO; Richard Oggero, chairman; and David Strutt, CFO and general counsel. Jerry Gosselink is

MANY PUBLIC AND COMMERCIAL PROJECTS HAVE BEEN CONSTRUCTED BY THE WEITZ COMPANY, INC. THESE INCLUDE (CLOCKWISE FROM TOP) THE PIONEER HI-BRED INTERNATIONAL BOARDROOM IN DES MOINES, PIONEER HI-BRED INTERNATIONAL RESEARCH CAMPUS IN JOHNSTON, AND HY-VEE CORPORATE HEADQUARTERS IN WEST DES MOINES.

COO; Larry Mohr is president of Weitz Arizona. James Simmons is president of Weitz Iowa and responsible for statewide operation.

LOCAL PROJECTS

Many landmark public and commercial buildings in Des Moines were constructed by the Weitz organization. Weitz built the original buildings at Fort Des Moines and the original Younkers store downtown in the 1890s. From 1910 to 1918, the company built the present-day City Hall, the Hubbell Building, the Valley Bank Building (now the Firstar Bank Building), Hotel Fort Des Moines, and Camp Dodge. During the 1920s, the firm constructed the Wallace Homestead Plant, the Hoyt Sherman Auditorium, and the Drake University field house and stadium.

Nationally, The Weitz Company has erected post offices and federal buildings in 42 states, as well as the Des Moines Ordnance Plant in Ankeny at the beginning of World War II. This facility now houses Deere & Co. Following the war, Weitz completed an addition to the Register and Tribune building, and constructed the Iowa Power and Light office building, dormitories at Drake University, and the solar plant later occupied by Massey-Ferguson.

In recent years, the company's long list of local projects has included Principal Financial Group's Z building, Hy-Vee corporate headquarters, Microware corporate headquarters, Color Converting Industries headquarters and manufacturing facility, Iowa Methodist Medical Center obstetrics expansion, Waukee High School, significant portions of the Des Moines Wastewater Treatment Plant, and Newton Prison. The Southside YMCA, Iowa State University Howe Hall, Clarinda Prison, and Candlewood Hotel comprise additional Iowa projects.

A special projects group is responsible for tenant improvement and building renovation work. Many long-term, repeat business relationships have been built with such clients as Pioneer Hi-Bred International, Norwest Bank Iowa, Mid-America Group, Central Iowa Health Systems, Draper and Kramer, and many others.

GUIDED BY CORE VALUES

Even with changes in a long-standing management structure and the evolution of The Weitz Company from a modest carpentry shop to a comprehensive, nationally prominent building contractor, the firm's core values have remained the same. Experience, integrity, and innovation are the foundation of all Weitz business relationships. The com-

pany will enter the 21st century guided by extensive expertise, dedication to professionalism, and continuing innovation.

The Weitz Company employs a team approach to project management in which the owner, architect, and builder meet on a regular basis to discuss budgets and scheduling, and to keep the lines of communication open for decision making and problem resolution.

The Weitz Company approach incorporates the latest in automated project management, scheduling, and cost control systems. Each job site is also linked to the home office via computer for instant, accurate communication. At Weitz, technology is employed to enhance project management efficiency.

The company also places a high priority on safety to eliminate injuries and increase productivity. As a result, its workers' compensation claim record is one-half the national average, meaning lower overhead costs and improved efficiency during construction.

In nearly a century and a half of business, The Weitz Company has grown from a one-man operation to a construction giant that builds millions of square feet of commercial, industrial, and institutional space each year. Yet the company's most important accomplishment is the building of strong customer relationships based on exceeding customer expectations through dedication to excellence, integrity, and innovation.

WEITZ HAS ALSO COMPLETED SUCH BUILDINGS AS (CLOCKWISE FROM TOP) THE PRINCIPAL FINANCIAL GROUP'S CORPORATE EXPANSION IN DES MOINES, DRAKE UNIVERSITY LAW LIBRARY IN DES MOINES, AND WAUKEE HIGH SCHOOL IN WAUKEE.

UNTIL THE MID-1800S, IOWA'S ECONOMY WAS BASED PRIMARILY on agriculture. But the formation of Equitable Life Insurance Company of Iowa in 1867 launched the state—and its capital city—into a new economic identity. By 1884, Des Moines was home to 18 insurance company home offices, and at the turn

of the 20th century, some industry leaders were calling Des Moines "the greatest insurance center of the United States."

F.M. Hubbell and 15 other prominent citizens of Des Moines are responsible for founding Equitable Life Insurance Company of Iowa. Equitable was the first business of its kind west of the Mississippi River. The effect of its presence was twofold: By establishing a life insurance company in Iowa to serve the needs of Iowans, the premium dollars remained in the state to be reinvested in its own economy. Consequently, Equitable was able to provide capital in the form of loans for the growth and expansion of commerce in Des Moines.

STEADY GROWTH, STRATEGIC CHANGES

From its inception, Equitable has been a leader in the establishment of Iowa's insurance industry. In 1868, under the guidance of Major Hoyt Sherman, it successfully sponsored the passage of Iowa's insurance deposit law, which required that an insurance company deposit with the State Insurance Commissioner interest-bearing securities equal in value to the full amount of the company's reserve on all contracts and policies in force.

By 1915, Equitable had achieved $100 million of life insurance in force. In 1949, it became the 31st company in the United States to attain $1 billion of life insurance in force. And in September 1994, Equitable's insurance operations reached another milestone, attaining $10 billion of life insurance in force.

In its second century, the company grew in other ways. E.I. Sales, Inc.—now known as Locust Street Securities, Inc.—was founded in 1968 to market investment-

oriented products for other companies. In 1972, the Hubbell family first sold shares of the company stock to the public. And in 1977, Equitable Life Insurance Company of Iowa became a wholly owned subsidiary of its newly formed public holding company, Equitable of Iowa Companies.

Equitable of Iowa Companies diversified in 1979, when it purchased the 123-year-old Younkers department store chain. In 1992, Younkers was sold, as Equitable shifted its focus on annuities and life insurance. Meanwhile, USG Annuity & Life Company was launched by Equitable in 1988, and soon became one of the fastest-growing annuity companies in the United States. In 1996, Equitable acquired Golden American Life Insurance Company to expand its presence in the variable annuity business and to add variable life insurance.

EQUITABLE LIFE INSURANCE COMPANY OF IOWA'S STATE-OF-THE-ART BUILDING MARKS EXCITING PROGRESS FOR THE HISTORIC COMPANY. AT THE SAME TIME, IT ALSO REPRESENTS A SOLID EQUITABLE TRADITION OF STRATEGIC MOVES TO REMAIN COMPETITIVE— AND TO CONTINUE AS A LEADER IN PRODUCTIVITY AND GROWTH WITHIN THE INSURANCE INDUSTRY.

ASSASSI PRODUCTIONS

ASSASSI PRODUCTIONS

Long and wide, spacious and light, and with built-in technological capabilities, Equitable's new headquarters on Locust Street is designed for efficiency, productivity, and profitability.

A new era began in 1997 with the acquisition of Equitable of Iowa Companies by ING Group, an integrated financial services company headquartered in the Netherlands. Equitable provides a strong platform for expanding ING's U.S. life insurance and annuity operations. The combination of Equitable's market presence and leadership experience with ING's financial strength and worldwide operations positions Equitable for a new round of growth and prosperity.

Part of Iowa History

Equitable's contributions to Des Moines have affected more than just the insurance industry. In 1878, Des Moines' first telephone was installed in the Equitable Life home office. The next day, the city's second telephone was installed in F.M. Hubbell's home.

Then, in 1971, heirs to the Hubbell estate gifted to the state Terrace Hill, the mansion home purchased by F.M. Hubbell in 1884. The following year, Terrace Hill became the official Iowa governor's mansion and public historical repository.

In addition, the 19-story Equitable Building, completed at 604 Locust Street in 1924, was the state's first skyscraper, and wore the distinction of being the city's tallest building until 1973. In July 1997, Equitable moved from the landmark building into its new facility on Locust Street. Long and wide, spacious and light, and with built-in technological capabilities, the new structure is designed for efficiency, productivity, and profitability. Its 200,000 square feet provide ample space for more than 20 departments and 600 employees, with room for continued future growth.

Equitable's state-of-the-art building marks exciting progress for the historic company. At the same time, it also represents a solid Equitable tradition of strategic moves to remain competitive—and to continue as a leader in productivity and growth within the insurance industry.

A Broad Portfolio

Today, the Des Moines operation is made up of USG Annuity & Life Company and Equitable Life Insurance Company of Iowa—both handling fixed annuity and life products. Golden American Life, an affiliate company headquartered in Wilmington, Delaware, handles variable annuities and variable life products.

Equitable has one of the largest independent agent networks in the country, selling products through more than 55,000 independent agents.

The company's current business strategy is to offer a wide portfolio of retirement savings and life insurance products that appeal to consumers throughout the United States. As the Des Moines operation focuses on becoming a world-class financial services provider, its priorities are to expand sales, provide premier customer service, and secure high productivity and efficiency. With a firm foundation and skills set in place, it strives to be adaptable in a changing retirement-savings market.

A CENTURY AGO, THEY WERE THREE VERY RADICAL IDEAS: Open universities to everyone. Teach students practical things, such as how to farm, build bridges, or manage homes. Share expertise on campus with the rest of the world. Built on these ideas, Iowa State University (ISU) opened its doors in 1868 as one of the nation's first land-grant colleges.

Located in Ames, Iowa State was the first state institution to establish a school of veterinary medicine, and it played a major role in the development of the field of engineering and the Cooperative Extension Service. Early graduates of Iowa State included George Washington Carver, who discovered hundreds of uses for crops, and Carrie Chapman Catt, who led American women to the ballot box.

Although Iowa State sprang from agricultural roots, it has since grown into a well-rounded research university with excellent programs in science and technology and the humanities and arts. ISU students can select from more than 100 undergraduate majors, numerous preprofessional programs, and nearly 200 fields of study leading to graduate and specialist degrees.

CAMPUS LIFE

Every state and more than 120 foreign countries are represented in the university's diverse student body. Nearly 50 percent of ISU's 25,000 students graduated in the top 20 percent of their high school classes, and for two years running, Iowa State has been ranked among the top six public universities in the number of freshman National Merit Scholars.

The ISU campus, a hub of arts and entertainment, has been named one of the 25 most beautiful in the nation. Sprawling over 2,000 acres, the campus provides a backdrop for a rich variety of art, including works by Grant Wood and Christian Petersen. The Iowa State Center, a four-building complex, draws major orchestras, theatrical performances, trade shows, and conferences, and is home to Big 12 athletic competition.

PUTTING KNOWLEDGE TO WORK

In the late 1930s and early 1940s, Professor John Vincent Atanasoff and graduate student Clifford Berry built the first electronic digital computer at Iowa State, helping to launch the computer age. Iowa State has a long tradition of educating individuals who put knowledge to practical use, and is the second-ranked university in the nation in the number of top technologies recognized by *Research & Development Magazine*. In classrooms and labs, ISU students rub shoulders with talented faculty and staff who are developing laser devices that can analyze a single blood cell, plastics that biodegrade, crops that are pest resistant, and lightweight aluminum for cars. They're also finding ways to reduce the fat in meat, identify food compounds that may fight cancer, increase accuracy in police lineups, improve airplane inspections, turn industry waste into fuel, and use virtual reality to test products.

Due in large part to the on-campus presence of the Ames Laboratory of the U.S. Department of Energy, Iowa State has emerged as an international leader

THE IOWA STATE UNIVERSITY CAMPANILE, A FAMOUS ISU LANDMARK, HOUSES THE CENTURY-OLD STANTON MEMORIAL CARILLON IN THE CENTER OF THE NEARLY 2,000-ACRE CAMPUS, WHICH IS RANKED AMONG THE TOP 25 MOST BEAUTIFUL CAMPUSES IN THE COUNTRY (LEFT).

THE IOWA COMMUNICATIONS NETWORK AND SATELLITE CONNECTIONS LINK IOWA STATE ACADEMIC RESEARCH STAFF TO PEOPLE ACROSS THE STATE, AND THE UNIVERSITY'S POPULAR WEB SITE PROVIDES A WORLDWIDE LINK (RIGHT).

in the materials science field. ISU also is a leader in developing new products from agricultural commodities. Recent products of ISU research are a low-saturated-fat soybean oil and an environmentally friendly lawn herbicide made from corn gluten. ISU researchers are leading the way in the use of irradiation to make meat and other food products safer, through work at the Linear Accelerator Facility, the nation's only commercial-sized irradiation facility for food research and demonstration.

Top Facilities

Among the high-tech facilities at Iowa State are the Molecular Biology Building, the center of the agricultural biotechnology program, and C2, one of the world's most advanced computer virtual reality rooms. Two more top facilities are in the works—the Livestock Teaching and Research Facility, where researchers will find ways to make animals healthier and meat safer, and the Engineering Teaching and Research Complex, where students will get hands-on lessons in 21st-century engineering.

At the Center for Advanced Technology Development (CATD), faculty and staff do the market research to move inventions from lab to marketplace. An outstanding success in tech transfer in recent years is Engineering Animation, a computer visualization company founded by ISU professors and graduate students. The firm now has hundreds of employees, several Fortune 500 clients, and a new facility in the ISU Research Park.

In a venture with the United Nations, Iowa State is extending knowledge beyond U.S. borders. The International Institute of Theoretical and Applied Physics puts scientists in developing countries in touch with their American counterparts to strengthen science in their home countries. Faculty and staff also are helping former Soviet countries build Western-style economies, and are collaborating with one of the top universities in China on faculty and student exchanges, research, and tech transfer projects.

Well Wired

Iowa State has one of the most extensive computer networks in the nation. The powerful Project Vincent system gives the campus community a speedy on-ramp to the Internet and access to high-speed computing centers on campus and to supercomputers and databases throughout the world. Iowa State's World Wide Web site, at http://www.iastate.edu, is one of the most lively and active in the country.

Becoming the Best

Iowa State aspires to become the best land-grant university in the nation. The university is supported in this lofty, but achievable, effort by the people of Iowa, alumni, and friends. A five-year capital campaign to raise $300 million by 2000 is the most ambitious campaign yet and is well ahead of schedule. That drive, which has provided Iowa State the confidence and momentum it needs to aspire to greatness, is aptly named Campaign Destiny: To Become the Best.

CLOCKWISE FROM TOP LEFT:
IOWA STATE UNIVERSITY RESEARCH PARK, LOCATED SOUTH OF THE MAIN CAMPUS, CONTRIBUTES TO IOWA'S ECONOMIC DEVELOPMENT BY HELPING COMPANIES TRANSFER UNIVERSITY-BASED RESEARCH INTO COMMERCIAL APPLICATIONS.

INTERNATIONALLY RENOWNED THEATER, DANCE, AND MUSIC PERFORMANCES ARE HELD EACH YEAR AT THE IOWA STATE CENTER.

IOWA STATE COMPETES IN 20 MEN'S AND WOMEN'S DIVISION I SPORTS AND RANKS FIRST IN THE BIG 12 CONFERENCE IN ATHLETIC GRADUATION RATE.

IOWA STATE IS HOME TO C2, ONE OF THE WORLD'S MOST ADVANCED COMPUTER VIRTUAL REALITY ROOMS, WHERE STUDENTS, RESEARCHERS, AND PROFESSIONAL ENGINEERS PURSUE ADVANCED SCIENTIFIC, ENGINEERING, AND DESIGN PROBLEMS.

T HE CORPORATE VISION STATEMENT OF FIRSTAR, A $38 BILLION financial company headquartered in Milwaukee, does not mention sponsoring New Year's Eve parties that have become community traditions. It says nothing about supporting local music concerts or redeveloping low-income

neighborhoods. Rather, it talks about becoming the most respected financial services provider in the markets it serves. But to achieve that goal, Firstar focuses on taking care of its customers—and their communities—as well as its employees and its shareholders. That's the Firstar way.

The Des Moines financial institution that became Firstar was founded in 1872 by J.J. Towne as Valley Savings Bank. In 1974, it was chartered as a national bank, and its name changed to Valley National Bank. The bank was sold in 1991, and became Firstar Bank Des Moines, N.A. In 1995, all Firstar banks in Iowa merged together to form one bank, Firstar Iowa.

The Firstar corporate family includes 720 banking offices in Indiana, Ohio, Kentucky, Tennessee, Wisconsin, Minnesota, Iowa, Illinois, Florida, and Arizona. Firstar Iowa operates 50 offices across the state—serving customers from Council Bluffs to Dubuque and from Sioux City to Burlington. In Des Moines, Firstar is headquartered in the prized Firstar Bank Building, which has been recognized by the Iowa State Historical Department as one of the finest examples of art deco architecture in the Midwest. Listed on the National Register of Historic Places, the building, completed in 1932 and restored in 1979, features fittings of Italian travertine marble, brass, bronze, Benedict nickel, and walnut wood. The bronze lantern at the entrance on Walnut Street weighs half a ton and repeats the chevron design found throughout the building. The four chandeliers on the second floor are Benedict nickel, each measuring seven feet in diameter and weighing 1,500 pounds. In addition to the main office, Firstar serves Des Moines customers through its five branch locations, including Highland Park, East Euclid, E.P. True Parkway, Westown, and the Kaleidoscope at the Hub Skywalk office.

MANY SERVICES UNDER ONE ROOF

A major Firstar focus is to be trustworthy, honest, and ethical. The company emphasizes a team approach to serving customers well, and strives to earn clients' business by providing financial solutions that create value for the customer.

Firstar has built a strong tradition of excellence in each of its three divisions, all offered under one roof: Commercial, Trust, and Community Banking. In the Community Banking—or retail financial services—division, Firstar maintains relationships with more than 3 million households and small businesses, handling $28 billion in consumer deposits and $25 billion in consumer loans. The division offers a growing selection of business and wealth management distribution channels, including its state-of-the-art, 24-hour-a-day, seven-day-a-week call center, and banking via personal computer,

FIRSTAR DES MOINES IS HEADQUARTERED IN THE HISTORIC FIRSTAR BANK BUILDING. THE BUILDING IS RECOGNIZED BY THE IOWA STATE HISTORICAL DEPARTMENT AS ONE OF THE FINEST EXAMPLES OF ART DECO ARCHITECTURE IN THE MIDWEST.

D.E. SMITH PHOTOGRAPHY

direct mail, and ATMs. The division also contains successful home mortgage and insurance subsidiaries in Firstar Home Mortgage Corporation and Firstar Insurance Services, and its credit card business, Elan Financial Services, is one of the most profitable in the United States.

Firstar's Commercial division helps businesses and other organizations manage their finances. Provided by an experienced team of professionals, available products include business loans and asset-based lending services, commercial real estate loans, and other capital market products. Additionally, Firstar provides correspondent banking, international banking, and cash management services to business clients. Firstar also operates one of the largest check collection operations in the Midwest.

The bank's Trust division handles personal trust services for individuals, probate and estate services, and institutional investment services for corporate retirement (401(k)) plans, endowments, and foundations. The division includes stock, bond, money market, and mutual fund investment services. Through various affiliates, the Trust division has $38 billion of assets under management. For the convenience of its customers, Firstar provides investment management and financial planning services in each branch office.

COMMUNITY SERVICE

Firstar actively supports the economic, social, and cultural well-being of all its communities by operating its business in a fashion that enables it to return significant financial and volunteer support to those communities. The organization consistently follows fair employment and business practices, reinvests customer deposits locally, and makes cash contributions exceeding $6 million annually to Firstar communities.

In addition, it is the sponsor of a host of art festivals, family picnics, and concerts and musical events—including the annual BIX Streetfest

D.E. SMITH PHOTOGRAPHY

THE CHANDELIERS AT FIRSTAR DES MOINES' MAIN OFFICE ARE AN EXAMPLE OF THE ATTENTION TO DETAIL THAT PLACED THE BUILDING ON THE NATIONAL REGISTER OF HISTORIC PLACES (TOP).

FIRSTAR IS DEDICATED TO HELPING ITS EMPLOYEES BUILD SATISFYING CAREERS (BOTTOM).

in Davenport. In Des Moines and around Iowa, Firstar Eve is an annual New Year's Eve event that focuses on a substance-free family evening. In 1997, more than 29,000 people attended the event statewide.

The Iowa State Fair has been the recipient of significant contributions from Firstar, including construction of the Firstar Building on the fairgrounds. The bank also sponsors the Iowa Paint-A-Thon, which provides home-painting assistance for low-income home owners who are over 60 or are permanently disabled.

KEY INGREDIENT: TALENTED PEOPLE

Because Firstar maintains that each of its employees is essential to its success, the bank is committed to helping those employees build satisfying careers. Firstar's policy is to recruit carefully and compensate competitively to attract talented personnel. The company strives to cultivate diversity, provide management encouragement and support, and invest in training and development for the advancement of employees.

Firstar's mission is to achieve sound, profitable growth, provide shareholders with a competitive return on their investment, and assure its future as one of the nation's most successful financial institutions. By pursuing this course, Firstar works to ensure that its employees and customers will achieve their financial and personal goals. As Firstar advises its customers, "To get there, start here."

AS CONSUMER TASTES HAVE CHANGED OVER THE YEARS, TONE Brothers, Inc. (Tone's)—a major processor and marketer of spices, extracts, and flavorings—has definitely adapted. In 1998, Tone Brothers, Inc. reached a milestone in its service to customers, celebrating 125 years of faithfully

offering high-quality spices, herbs, and extracts.

Founded in 1873 by brothers Jehiel and Isaac E. Tone as a coffee and spice business in Des Moines, the company flourished as a solid firm. The Tone brothers nurtured their budding business through growth driven by innovative packaging, new products, and geographic expansion.

LEADING THE SPICE TRADE

Tone's has been at the forefront of developing unique methods to ensure product freshness and quality to customers. For example, Tone's packaging made the transition from early tin containers to glass and airtight plastic that ensures long-lasting freshness. Today, the older glass and tin containers are prized among antique collectors and can be found at antique and flea markets. In 1982, Tone's developed a one-of-a-kind cryogenic grinding system with the help of Iowa State University research. During the process, certain spices are ground at subzero temperatures to pre-

serve their oil and aroma content, resulting in superior quality and freshness.

By 1985, Tone's was recognized as a spice leader in the food service industry, and it became the dominant supplier to U.S. membership warehouse club stores. Two years later, Tone's implemented a new, sophisticated logistics system that helped the company achieve a goal of 99.987 percent accuracy on its deliveries—a testament to its tradition of putting customer needs first.

From its humble beginnings at 207 Walnut Street in Des Moines, Tone's facilities have expanded notably over the years. In 1994, the company moved into its new 350,000-square-foot, high-tech plant in Ankeny. About one year later, construction was completed

on a new 360,000-square-foot warehouse facility that more than doubled Tone's storage capacity. In 1997, 20,000 square feet of existing space was remodeled to triple the laboratory space in the technology and research center in Ankeny.

Recently, Tone's focused on clarifying its brands' identities, streamlining brand lines, and eliminating unprofitable or duplicative products. It reduced its product line from 8,000 items to 3,500. Other products were revitalized by improving their formulations and changing their packaging. In the dry seasonings and mixes line, for example, 75 percent of the products underwent reformulation and taste panel testing to match current consumer taste preferences. Throughout the changes, new brands and products

TONE'S SPICES BRING OUT THE ARTISTRY IN EVERY COOK—AS IN THIS INDUSTRY ADVERTISEMENT CRAFTED FROM TONE'S MUSTARD POWDER, PAPRIKA, GARLIC SALT, POPPYSEED, AND FRESH PRODUCE (TOP).

TONE BROTHERS, INC. PROCESSES AND MARKETS A QUALITY ARRAY OF SPICES, FLAVORINGS, AND EXTRACTS (BOTTOM).

IOWA STATE FAIR CONTEST ENTRIES IN-
CLUDE MOUNDS OF MOUTHWATERING
PRIDE OF IOWA CINNAMON ROLLS
(LEFT).

DELECTABLE DIJON-GLAZED CHICKEN
WITH PEPPERS IS A FEATURED RECIPE IN
Easy Entertaining, TONE'S 125TH AN-
NIVERSARY COMMEMORATIVE COOK-
BOOK (RIGHT).

continued to be developed and marketed under the brand names Tone's®, Durkee®, Spice Islands®, French's®, DecACake®, Trader's Choice®, Dromedary®, and Blue Ribbon® (in Canada).

The company has worked to reengineer its product offerings and improve its ability to offer customers the right-sized, right-priced, right-packaged products they want with the greatest efficiencies in production, sales, and marketing. The results of the strategic business moves were stunning. In 1998, Tone Brothers, Inc. was a lean company of half the size it was in 1997, but twice as profitable.

Celebrating 125 Years

In commemoration of more than a century of service, Tone Brothers, Inc. significantly increased its participation in the 1998 Iowa State Fair. Tone's donated $24,250 for cash prizes in various competitions and sponsored the Pride of Iowa Cinnamon Roll Contest. Tone's awarded a total of $5,000 in the cinnamon roll contest alone. The top prize of $3,000 was the single-largest cash prize ever awarded in a culinary category in the fair's history, and it attracted a record number of cinnamon roll entries. Tone's distributed the winning cinnamon roll recipe to fairgoers during Tone's Day at the Iowa State Fair.

In addition, Tone Brothers, Inc. celebrated its 125th anniversary in

warehouse club stores by offering an impressive hardcover cookbook called *Easy Entertaining*. The cookbook features 84 tasty dishes prepared by using Tone's® spices, herbs, and flavorings, and is packaged with four selected spices.

A Look to the Future

As consumer scratch cooking continues to decline and meals prepared away from home increase, Tone's will concentrate on growing its food service customer base. A business channel to reach smaller food service providers is the membership club. The Tone's® brand already is represented in 443 units of the leading U.S. membership club.

Also in response to the decline of scratch cooking, Tone's will

focus on high-value, convenience-added products that meet consumer demands for more grilled foods in casual dining. Products such as grill seasonings, rubs, and ready-to-use mushrooms in shelf-stable cryovac packaging are high-value, high-impact accompaniments to the entrées consumers want today, and will want tomorrow.

Tone Brothers, Inc. is positioned to launch itself into the next millennium with zest. In the future, the company will maintain its uncompromising commitment to quality, service, and innovation in the food industry. Determined to continue meeting customer needs, Tone Brothers, Inc. is poised to help people eat healthier and spice up their foods for the next 125 years.

NANCY MACKLIN, MARKETING DIETICIAN,
CONDUCTS ONE OF MANY COOKING
DEMONSTRATIONS FOR TONE'S AT THE
1998 IOWA STATE FAIR (LEFT).

TONE'S DISPLAYS AT THE 1998 IOWA
STATE FAIR COMMEMORATE 125 YEARS
OF IOWA INNOVATION AND QUALITY
(RIGHT).

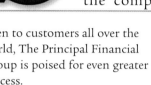

SINCE 1879, THE PRINCIPAL FINANCIAL GROUP HAS SERVED customers' financial needs from its home office in downtown Des Moines. Over the years, the customer base, number of employees, and office locations have grown immensely. Now, as the company approaches the next millennium with its doors open to customers all over the world, The Principal Financial Group is poised for even greater success.

For more than a century, The Principal Financial Group has practiced its philosophy—Plan Ahead. Get Ahead.—in growing from a small, midwestern company to a global financial services organization. Today, the firm is living proof of the success of its strategy: to get ahead, you have to plan.

PLANNING AHEAD

The Principal Financial Group began in 1879 as Bankers Life Assessment Company, offering an assessment insurance plan to bankers and their families. Soon that product was offered to other individuals as well, and in 1911, the company reorganized into a mutual legal reserve life insurance company, operating on behalf of its policyholders. The company's new name was Bankers Life Company.

Through the 1920s, the company increased its relationship with customers by establishing a field force and better utilizing the media.

MANY COUNTRIES ARE REORGANIZING THEIR RETIREMENT SYSTEMS, USING THE UNITED STATES AS A MODEL. THE PRINCIPAL FINANCIAL GROUP IS DEDICATED TO HELPING PEOPLE AROUND THE WORLD ACHIEVE THEIR RETIREMENT GOALS (RIGHT).

A VISIONARY GROUP OF PEOPLE FOUNDED THE COMPANY IN 1879. WHILE THE MEANS, METHODS, AND SIZE OF OPERATIONS HAVE CHANGED DRAMATICALLY OVER THE COURSE OF HISTORY, THE FOUNDERS' VISION OF HELPING CUSTOMERS MEET THEIR FINANCIAL GOALS HAS REMAINED AT THE CORE OF THE COMPANY (BOTTOM).

In 1940, Bankers Life opened its first company-owned office building on High Street. The next decades saw Bankers Life enter the group insurance, pension, individual health, and accident insurance fields. During the 1960s and 1970s, the company continued to expand, pioneering adjustable life insurance and the transition to defined contribution pension products such as 401(k) plans. The organization also acquired more member companies, broadening the company's offerings.

In the 1980s, the organization adopted a new corporate identity, The Principal Financial Group, to reflect its expanded financial services focus. The organization became a financial services leader, well positioned for a global marketplace. Products and services include pension plans; home mortgages; life, health, dental, and disability income insurance; annuities; and mutual funds. The home office in downtown Des Moines has grown to a corporate campus of seven buildings.

GETTING AHEAD

While The Principal Financial Group had experienced numerous changes over the years, the 1990s brought a flurry of activity related to the company's new vision: To be a global leader in retirement and related financial services for small and medium-sized businesses and employee groups while maintaining prominence and aggressive growth in diversified financial services in the United States.

This new focus for the future will require major shifts in the way

The Principal Financial Group operates, as well as in the scope of its business. What has not changed is the commitment to policyholders and the emphasis on customer service. Those traits that spring from the company's midwestern roots will remain at its core.

For many years, The Principal Financial Group has successfully developed and distributed new products. In the future, the company will seek new ways to learn about markets, to anticipate their needs, and to reach them. Principal Connection provides user-friendly technology customers can use to work directly with the company via the telephone or Internet. Principal Bank takes banking to a new level, as business is conducted via telephone, ATM machines, the Internet, and mail.

In one more step toward planning ahead, Principal Mutual Life Insurance Company, the flagship member company of The Principal Financial Group, became a mutual insurance holding company in the summer of 1998. The change preserved the rights of existing members, but allowed the company greater flexibility in organizing multiline businesses, and assured the ability to raise capital for additional growth, if desired.

Going Global

Many countries are reorganizing their retirement systems, using the United States as a model. As customers around the globe discover new ways to secure their retirement, The Principal Financial Group is there to fulfill their needs.

In 1998, the company operated in nine countries: Argentina, Chile, China, Hong Kong, India, Indonesia, Mexico, Spain, and the United States.

Not only is the company doing business internationally, but also it is creating a corporate culture and value system that will allow it to achieve the greatest competitive advantage anywhere in the world. Employees at all levels of the organization are encouraged to expand their diversity by studying other cultures, participating in company training courses on diversity and global awareness, and learning additional languages onsite. Changes are made with a global audience in mind, and competition comes from all corners of the world.

The Principal People

Employees at The Principal Financial Group are looking toward a future of continually

strengthened relationships with customers in the global marketplace. The company provides opportunities for this growth and encourages employees to create action plans for their futures by learning more about diversity, gaining greater business knowledge, and pursuing career goals. Together, the employees and their company are creating a workforce that thrives amid constant, exciting changes, but that retains the core values the company has focused on from its beginning: customer service, quality, strength, and integrity.

The company's 16,000 employees in more than 250 locations know the plans in place now will pave the way for future success. From Des Moines to Denver, Mexico to Mason City, Indianapolis to Indonesia, the company and its employees are focusing on great changes in the millennium. And they're planning ahead to get ahead.

In 1940, The Principal Financial Group moved into its new home office in Des Moines (top left). Since then, the company has grown into a global financial leader with operations in more than 250 locations worldwide, including offices in Europe, Asia, Latin America, and the United States. The corporate complex now makes a significant contribution to the Des Moines skyline (top right).

The Principal Financial Group is a diversified family of insurance and financial services companies that help more than 10 million customers meet their financial goals. In a dramatically changing world, the company relies on technology as an important tool for delivering unmatched service to its customers around the world.

DRAKE UNIVERSITY IS AN INDEPENDENT, PRIVATE UNIVERSITY with a mission to provide a student-centered learning environment that challenges and prepares students for productive careers, active leadership, and responsible citizenship. Founded in 1881, the university was named for Francis

Marion Drake, a Union general in the Civil War who later served as governor of Iowa. Drake University began offering graduate studies in 1883, and evening programs for adults in 1946.

A medium-sized university situated on a 120-acre campus 10 minutes from downtown Des Moines, Drake is consistently ranked by *U.S. News & World Report* magazine as being among the best regional universities in the Midwest, and is listed in both *Peterson's Guide to Competitive Colleges* and *Barron's 300 Best Buys in College Education*. More than 95 percent of all Drake graduates over the past five years have found professional employment or entered graduate schools within three months after receiving their degrees—and 90 percent of those graduates completed their degrees in four years.

A WIDE RANGE OF OPPORTUNITIES

Drake University offers 75 undergraduate majors and many graduate programs in its six colleges and schools: Arts and Sciences, including Fine Arts;

Business and Public Administration; Education; Journalism and Mass Communication; Law; and Pharmacy and Health Sciences.

Drake students enjoy both the personal attention of a small liberal arts college and the wide range of academic opportunities, professional programs, and internships commonly found at large universities. The average Drake class has 25 to 40 students, the ratio of students to faculty is 12-to-1, and 93 percent of the university's professors hold the highest degree in their fields. Approximately 3,100 full-time undergraduate students from 46 states and more than 50 countries are enrolled at the university.

Each year, Drake University awards more than 4,000 scholarships and a total of $40 million in financial aid to students. More than 90 percent of Drake's students receive some form of financial assistance, based on financial need, academic merit, or both. In 1997-1998, the average Drake financial aid package was $13,000.

Drake students can participate in more than 140 campus organizations, 13 men's and women's intercollegiate sports, 10 sports

clubs, and more than 20 intramural sports for men and women. Each April, more than 200 college and university track teams and more than 20,000 spectators attend the university's two-day Drake Relays. Launched in 1910, the event is now known as America's Athletic Classic and is one of the top track-and-field meets in the world. Michael Johnson, Gwen Torrence, Bruce Jenner, and Carl Lewis are among the past Olympians who have competed at the Relays.

Drake students also provide more than 13,000 hours of volunteer service to the Des Moines community each academic year. Volunteer efforts include working in homeless shelters, tutoring, reading to sightless persons, and sponsoring blood drives.

The university's reputation for quality academic programs continues to grow. To ensure Drake's position as a leader in higher education into the next century, the university has launched Campaign Drake, with a goal of raising $190 million, to further enhance the intellectual transformation of its students and the exceptional quality of its faculty.

DRAKE UNIVERSITY'S BEAUTIFUL, 120-ACRE CAMPUS IN THE HEART OF DES MOINES FEATURES AWARD-WINNING, STATE-OF-THE-ART FACILITIES AS WELL AS BUILDINGS ON THE NATIONAL REGISTER OF HISTORIC PLACES. THE STEEPLED OLD MAIN WAS BUILT SHORTLY AFTER THE UNIVERSITY WAS FOUNDED IN 1881.

COWLES LIBRARY, DRAKE UNIVERSITY'S MAIN LIBRARY, OFFERS A RICH VARIETY OF BOOKS, JOURNALS, PERIODICALS, AND ON-LINE RESOURCES TO HELP PATRONS DISCOVER KNOWLEDGE AND ACHIEVE ACADEMIC SUCCESS.

Iowa natives William T. Proudfoot and George W. Bird developed a taste for classic styles during their architectural studies on the East Coast in the late 1800s. When they returned to Iowa in 1895, they brought that style with them, beginning a remarkable evolution of architecture and designing some of the state's most significant buildings.

Proudfoot and Bird developed a solid reputation for quality. This led to many successful long-term relationships with Iowa public school systems, universities, government, insurance and banking companies, and hospitals. As it expanded to include new partners, the firm underwent a series of seven name changes in its first century of business, ultimately becoming known as Brooks Borg Skiles after former partners John Woolson Brooks, Elmer H. Borg, and Paul Skiles. The current partners—Robert J. Mathieu, Rod R. Nelson, William L. Anderson, Donald L. Swanson, and Stephen J. Stimmel—later revised the name to its present form, Brooks Borg Skiles Architecture Engineering.

A Tradition of Excellence

Proudfoot and Bird's original architectural practice reflected the midwestern values of intelligent practicality, fine craftsmanship, and financial responsibility. From the beginning, the firm's philosophy has revolved around determining common grounds between its talented personnel and its clients. Today, Brooks Borg Skiles Architecture Engineering

believes every project should satisfy its clients' functional and financial aims, while achieving the highest aspiration for beauty. Exceeding expectations while creating lasting quality is the company's objective.

Since its first project for the Iowa Board of Regents in 1898, the firm has designed thousands of impressive projects, including more than 70 buildings at Iowa State University, the University of Iowa, and the University of Northern Iowa. The Polk County Courthouse, built just after the turn of the 20th century, is one of more than 30 buildings designed by the firm that are listed on the National Register of Historic Places.

In more recent years, the firm has designed major facilities for several corporations including Farm Bureau Insurance, Pioneer Hi-Bred International, Inc., the EMC Insurance Companies, and Principal Financial Group. In 1997, the innovative, 20-story EMC Insurance Companies expansion was completed, as was the 750-bed Newton Correctional Facility, the College of Pharmacy Research Building at the University of Iowa, and the stadium press box on the Iowa State University campus. Also, construction was begun on the Fort Dodge Correctional Facility, the Engineering Teaching and Research Complex at Iowa State University, and the Biological Sciences Complex and the Levitt Center for University Advancement—both at the University of Iowa.

Brooks Borg Skiles Architecture Engineering enters its second century of business as a leader in the use of computer technology for engineering and architectural design. The company also embraces important elements that originally inspired its founders.

The firm's talented and diverse team of more than 60 licensed architects, engineers, and support staff continues to offer clients a thoughtful, purposeful, and collaborative process of translating ideas to physical reality.

The heritage of Brooks Borg Skiles Architecture Engineering rests on its proud tradition of service and design excellence, which are as familiar to Iowans as the more than 4,000 building projects the company has produced. The current partners are unwavering in their commitment to continue that tradition in serving ongoing generations of clients.

FARSHID ASSASSI

BROOKS BORG SKILES COMPUTER IMAGE

The heritage of Brooks Borg Skiles Architecture Engineering rests on its proud tradition of service and design excellence, which are as familiar to Iowans as the more than 4,000 building projects the company has produced.

Clockwise from top: The EMC corporate high-rise, Levitt Center for University Advancement, and Lakewood Cemetery Memorial Chapel all represent the collaborative process of translating ideas to physical reality.

MidAmerican Energy Company, Iowa's largest utility, is a multifaceted corporation that provides service to 648,000 electric customers and 619,000 natural gas customers in 500 communities in Iowa and portions of Illinois, Nebraska, and South Dakota. Founded in 1885 as Des Moines Edison Light & Power Company, it became MidAmerican Energy Company after a 1995 merger of Midwest Resources Inc. and Iowa-Illinois Gas and Electric Company.

MidAmerican is a subsidiary of MidAmerican Energy Holdings Company, which has assets of $4.3 billion, and has 60,000 shareholders in 50 states and 33 foreign countries. It is unique in its focus on improving the quality of its customers' lives by delivering comfort and convenience to their homes and enhancing the profitability of their businesses. During 1997, the firm reorganized its operations into four new distinct business units: energy delivery, transmission, generation, and retail.

More than just a provider of gas and electric energy, MidAmerican also offers complimentary economic development consulting, manufacturing technology services, and financial packaging for businesses planning to relocate or expand in its service area. In 1998, it also became the first energy company in the country to diversify into the residential real estate business.

Benefiting Its Customers

MidAmerican has long pledged to its customers that, "We're satisfied only when you are." In June 1998, it unveiled a new company slogan, "Obsessively, Relentlessly At Your Service." The company reinforces its pledges with five distinct promises: "To do the job right . . . and then some; to be here when you need us; to respect your property as if it were our own; to respect your time and not waste it; and to teach you and your children about energy safety and help us all stay safe."

MidAmerican is investing more in training and technology to improve customer services, and has made a firm commitment to listening to its customers in order to determine and exceed their expectations. With its purchase of highly recognizable names in the real estate industry, MidAmerican has expanded in the consumer market to become the leading regional provider of not only energy, but also related services to benefit home owners.

Competitive Prices

Before electricity can be delivered to homes and businesses, it must travel from key generation sites. Thousands of miles of transmission lines connect MidAmerican's generation facilities with distribution substations and provide interconnections with five surrounding states. The geographic position of the transmission system is a valuable asset for MidAmerican when retail markets are restructured to offer customer choice.

Sixty-five percent of MidAmerican's generating capacity is fueled by coal, 18 percent is fueled by nuclear power, and the remainder is fueled by natural gas and oil. According to Federal Energy Regulatory Commission data, MidAmerican's electric generation production costs rank eighth lowest among the 100 largest investor-owned utilities in the nation. Also, a 1997 Utility Data Institute report placed five of MidAmerican's coal-fired steam generating units among the 25 lowest cost of the country's 777 fossil-fueled facilities.

Promoting Economic Development

Most residential customers of MidAmerican Energy readily identify it as the local supplier of gas and electric energy. But many Des Moines-area industrial and commercial customers also recognize MidAmerican as a key provider of economic development assistance.

MidAmerican's Economic Development group delivers site selection services to expanding Des Moines-area businesses to accommodate planned growth in the area cities served by MidAmerican. Using MidAmerican's CyberSites site selection database, Economic Development consultants respond to current and prospective customers' requests for detailed building and site reports and tours. Once the optimum location for growth is identified, the Economic Development group assists growing businesses to include all available local and state incentives in their project financing strategies to reduce project costs. Working in close cooperation with Des Moines-area economic development organizations, MidAmerican helps its customers navigate local government requirements.

MidAmerican Economic Development also provides access to

Kent Wills, gas serviceman for MidAmerican Energy Company, checks on the status of an order from a mobile data terminal (MDT). MDTs are portable computers, similar to laptops, mounted in service vehicles between the driver and passenger front seats. The units decrease response time and provide for more efficient scheduling of work.

energy and process-related products and services. Often packaged in customer growth strategies are MidAmerican's commercial energy efficiency programs, leading-edge services such as Total Managed Solutions, and Economic Development rates. Through area providers, assistance in workforce recruitment and training, new product development, technical production, and industrial engineering are delivered through MidAmerican's Economic Development group. For ongoing assistance, MidAmerican sponsors the Iowa Business Network, an Internet site devoted to delivering information resources to Iowa's small businesses (located at www.iabusnet.org).

MidAmerican's economic development assistance extends to Des Moines-area development groups and real estate professionals, as well. Local business job creation and tax base retention and recruitment programs are increased through MidAmerican's local partner's financial and technical assistance programs.

DEVELOPING NEW OPPORTUNITIES

On May 27, 1998, MidAmerican Holdings Company purchased the nation's third-largest real estate brokerage organization, expanding the company's market reach across the Midwest and providing new channels for its products and services throughout the region. The acquisition of AmerUs Home Services, Inc. included real estate operations in five states: Iowa Realty—the state's largest—and First Realty/Better Homes & Gardens based in Des Moines; Edina Realty in Minnesota, North Dakota, and Wisconsin; and Carol Jones, Realtors, in Springfield, Missouri. In addition, on August 18, 1998, MidAmerican announced its purchase of the number one and number two residential brokerages in Omaha—HOME Real Estate and CBS Real Estate—and JC Nichols in Kansas City, making MidAmerican the nation's largest real estate brokerage organization.

Other services provided by MidAmerican and its subsidiaries contribute to its role as a gateway to the home. In late 1997, AAA Security Systems, Inc., one of the largest security companies in the Midwest, acquired the assets of Strauss Security Systems, Inc. AAA is controlled by MidAmerican Capital, a subsidiary of MidAmerican Energy Holdings Company. This acquisition enabled MidAmerican to conveniently provide burglar and fire alarm systems, closed-circuit television, intercom systems, multiroom stereo systems, and telephone systems for homes and businesses to more than 12,000 security customers in Des Moines, Kansas City, and Minneapolis. MidAmerican Capital also owns A/C Security in the Omaha area.

Customers who enroll in MidAmerican Service's Extended Service Protection (ESP) plan pay one simple monthly fee, then receive timely appliance repair from local, highly trained technicians. Because there is no charge for the service call, home owners avoid unexpected repair bills and lock into long-term savings.

Under MidAmerican's Safety Link™ program, drivers of the company's service vehicles are equipped with radios and cell phones to alert authorities when they spot a motorist or other person in distress within the service territory. Many MidAmerican line-crew members are certified in cardiopulmonary resuscitation and other first aid, and lend assistance if possible and appropriate. Safety Link also provides distribution of tips on home safety, as well as information on how to avoid power lines, transmission towers, and electric substations, and how to recognize a natural gas leak.

AT YOUR SERVICE

At MidAmerican, the future is bright with opportunities to achieve higher levels of business growth, continued cost reductions, and improved effectiveness of management. As the utility industry has undergone significant transformations, MidAmerican Energy has built a foundation for competitiveness. It focuses on customer loyalty and shareholder value to make its vision a reality: To become the leading regional provider of energy and complementary services.

MIDAMERICAN ENERGY COMPANY IS A MULTIFACETED CORPORATION THAT PROVIDES SERVICE TO 648,000 ELECTRIC CUSTOMERS AND 619,000 NATURAL GAS CUSTOMERS IN 500 COMMUNITIES IN IOWA AND PORTIONS OF ILLINOIS, NEBRASKA, AND SOUTH DAKOTA.

BUILT UPON THE RICHEST SOIL IN AMERICA'S HEARTLAND, GREATER Des Moines has flourished from a military post on the prairie to a sophisticated metropolis. Greater Des Moines is the best of both worlds: cosmopolitan yet typically American, modern yet historic, sophisticated yet sincere. The area is a diverse community of more than a half-million people who are living the "smart life."

CLOCKWISE FROM TOP:
THE DOWNTOWN DES MOINES SKYLINE AT DUSK SHOWS THE CITY'S VIBRANCY. THE PRINCIPAL FINANCIAL BUILDING IS THE TALLEST POINT BETWEEN CHICAGO AND DENVER, AND THE BRIGHT EMC BUILDING HAS RECEIVED NATIONAL ACCLAIM.

APPROXIMATELY 1 MILLION PEOPLE ANNUALLY VISIT THE IOWA STATE FAIR IN DES MOINES.

THE STATE CAPITOL BUILDING IS LOCATED IN EAST DES MOINES. THIS RECENTLY REFURBISHED, 114-YEAR-OLD BUILDING IS PART OF A MULTI-STRUCTURE CAPITOL COMPLEX.

A SMART PLACE TO LIVE

Greater Des Moines is the political, economic, and cultural capital of Iowa. Morgan Quitno Press named Iowa one of the most livable states. Iowa topped the publisher's survey in 1996 and has been in the top 10 every year since 1992. Des Moines is also a gracious and safe place to raise a family. The Children's Rights Council rated Iowa as the number one state in which to raise children, due to its low crime, infant mortality, and teen pregnancy rates.

Des Moines offers diverse and beautiful neighborhoods alive with leadership and volunteerism. Whether it's a Victorian "painted lady" in the historic Sherman Hill district, a renovated downtown loft, a charming Beaverdale brick home, or a suburban country club estate, there is a home to suit any lifestyle. The National Association of Homebuilders includes Des Moines in the 25 most affordable metro areas to buy a home, and *USA Today* ranked Des Moines second in the nation among the five hottest housing markets.

Iowa has long been considered a leader in education with a very strong public school system, having long held the distinction of having the nation's highest literacy rate and lowest high school drop-out rate. Iowa's graduating seniors earn the highest average test score in the nation on the ACT and SAT college entrance exams.

Greater Des Moines is also a regional health center, with seven hospitals providing all levels of patient care. It is also home to a number of quality nursing programs, Drake University's College of Pharmacy, and the University of Osteopathic Medicine and Health Sciences.

Central Iowa is the vital center of social life in Iowa, offering a historic entertainment district with restaurants, microbreweries, and a variety of live music. There is also nearby Prairie Meadows Racetrack and Casino, and a host of nightclubs. Sports activities include professional basketball, hockey, soccer, AAA baseball, arena football, sprint-car racing, and motorcycle racing. The internationally recognized Drake Relays is held each spring. Greater Des Moines is the site of the 1999 Senior U.S. Golf Open.

A SMART PLACE TO WORK

Once a military post, Greater Des Moines is now a vibrant community with an ever expanding business climate. The region's economic base continues to diversify with industries including biotechnology, agribusiness, telecommunications, financial services, insurance, and publishing. It is the third-largest insurance center in the world, and is regarded as America's seed capital, biotech capital, and test market capital.

Des Moines' signature skywalk system links parking, offices, restaurants, and retail stores. It also connects the Polk County Conven-

GREATER DES MOINES CONVENTION AND VISITORS BUREAU

GREATER DES MOINES CONVENTION AND VISITORS BUREAU

GREATER DES MOINES CONVENTION AND VISITORS BUREAU

tion Complex, the Civic Center, and a three-story retail mall to both office and residential spaces. Downtown serves as an employment center for 25 percent of the area's workforce. Their average daily commute is under 17 minutes.

Des Moines' many suburban communities offer dozens of modern corporate office parks that boast large campuses, elaborate landscaping, and public art. They cut the daily commute to just minutes, and are still a short drive from downtown and the Des Moines International Airport.

The area ranks fourth in the nation in overall financial security, according to ReliaStar Financial Corporation, making it one of the best cities in the country to earn and save money, and a very smart place to work.

A Smart Place to Grow

Greater Des Moines has experienced an ever broadening business base that promises sustained growth. Each year, new companies join the area's impressive corporate community, which includes Pioneer Hi-Bred International, Principal Financial Group, MidAmerican Energy Company, AmerUs Companies, Meredith Corporation, Farm Bureau Financial Services, U S WEST Communications, Hy-Vee Food Stores, the Norwest companies, Wellmark, and *The Des Moines Register*, among many others. New business growth outpaced the nation in 1997 with a 2.3 percent increase. The area

also outpaced the nation in per capita income growth, mean household income, and total household income during the 1990s. More than $3.5 billion in new construction and renovation has taken place in downtown Des Moines over the past decade. *Sales and Marketing Management* magazine included Des Moines in the top 20 hottest domestic markets for business in 1998.

Economic watchdogs anticipate more growth in the years to come. *Area Development* magazine calls Iowa a distribution stronghold, thanks to its location on the proposed Trade Corridor Super Highway. *BF Express*, a publication of *Business Facilities* magazine, tagged Des Moines as one of the Up-and-Coming Four cities for logistics and named the city among its Hot Five and Steady Seven cities.

A Smart Place for Business

At the center of Greater Des Moines' growth is the Greater Des Moines Chamber of Commerce Federation. Representing 2,100 area companies and 5,000 business leaders, The Chamber is the voice for business. Its mission is to help existing companies grow, attract new business, and help shape the necessary infrastructure to support them.

The Chamber provides networking tools, educational resources, business referrals and marketing opportunities, workforce development, international consulting, leadership programs, and a lobby-

ing voice for business-friendly legislation. The organization continually promotes issues relating to economic development, education, food and agriculture, health and human services, regulation and taxation, transportation, and urban affairs to local, state, and federal government.

The Chamber's regional approach to economic development capitalizes on the strengths of central Iowa's economy. Its membership includes 17 affiliate organizations and alliances with more than 35 development groups and organizations, all working toward the same goal. The Chamber's primary economic development initiative, Project 21, played an integral role in bringing 9,241 jobs to the area, accounting for more than $425 million in new economic activity in less than five years and helping to assure Greater Des Moines' economic growth well into the next millennium.

CLOCKWISE FROM TOP LEFT: DES MOINES' SIGNATURE SKYWALK SYSTEM CONNECTS MORE THAN THREE AND A HALF MILES OF BUSINESSES AND DOWNTOWN HOUSING IN A SMOKE-FREE, CLIMATE-CONTROLLED ENVIRONMENT.

DESIGNED BY ARCHITECTS ELIEL SAARINEN, I.M. PEI, AND RICHARD MEIER, THE DES MOINES ART CENTER IS SOMETHING TO LOOK AT BOTH OUTSIDE AND INSIDE. ONE OF THE MIDWEST'S PREMIER ART CENTERS, IT IS BEST KNOWN FOR ITS THOUSANDS OF PERMANENT WORKS OF 20TH-CENTURY ART.

FROM MAY THROUGH OCTOBER EACH YEAR, MORE THAN 75,000 PEOPLE BUY FRESH PRODUCE AND OTHER GOODS FROM MORE THAN 120 VENDORS AT THE DES MOINES FARMERS MARKET.

GREATER DES MOINES CONVENTION AND VISITORS BUREAU

SINCE 1890, SUCCESSFUL DEVELOPERS WHO BUILD IN DES MOINES have consistently relied on the skilled craftsmanship of the United Association of Plumbers & Steamfitters Local 33 AFL-CIO's members. One of the first building trades to organize in Des Moines, Local 33 earned its national reputation for

building and construction excellence by continuously providing contractors, builders, and developers exceptionally well-trained journeymen for more than a century. This achievement is made possible by Local 33's early dedication to creating and maintaining a superior apprenticeship training and journeyman upgrading program.

ONE OF THE FIRST BUILDING TRADES TO ORGANIZE IN DES MOINES, THE UNITED ASSOCIATION OF PLUMBERS & STEAMFITTERS LOCAL 33, AFL-CIO EARNED ITS NATIONAL REPUTATION FOR BUILDING AND CONSTRUCTION EXCELLENCE BY CONTINUOUSLY PROVIDING CONTRACTORS, BUILDERS, AND DEVELOPERS EXCEPTIONALLY WELL-TRAINED JOURNEYMEN FOR MORE THAN A CENTURY.

SETTING THE STANDARDS

While today's building and construction technology may be a far cry from the methods and standards of a 100 years ago, there is a certain consistency with regard to a professional work ethic that Local 33's members pass on from generation to generation. Many current members can claim that their great-grandfathers were original Local 33 members. They proudly point to buildings constructed by preceding generations as part of their individual family's legacy. These buildings have become landmarks that symbolize

Des Moines' rich heritage. The members' pride is not by chance: They live and raise their families here and care about the quality of their work to the extent that they expect it to last for generations. In fact, due to their recognized expertise, a large portion of Local 33's membership is currently

engaged in the retrofitting and maintenance of the area's most significant structures.

SUPERIOR TRAINING MARKS THE DIFFERENCE

A quick tour of Local 33's Education and Training Center provides considerable insight into the degree of value instructors place on mastering the technological depth and skill levels today's building designs demand. Utilizing state-of-the-art, computer-assisted programs, apprentices and journeymen alike are exposed to a constantly evolving construction technology. In addition to a full spectrum of basic craft skills, the education program includes a complete OSHA safety and first-aid curriculum certified by the U.S. Department of Labor's Apprenticeship Bureau.

BUILDING UNION IS GOOD BUSINESS

As the demand for skilled workers increases across America, Local 33's members and their contractors enjoy a particular

UTILIZING STATE-OF-THE-ART, COMPUTER-ASSISTED PROGRAMS, APPRENTICES AND JOURNEYMEN ALIKE ARE EXPOSED TO A CONSTANTLY EVOLVING CONSTRUCTION TECHNOLOGY.

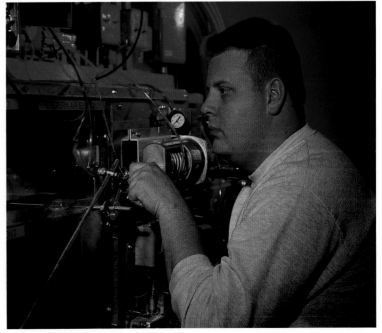

competitive edge within the marketplace. Construction and building experience confirms that superb labor skills translate into peak efficiencies, specifically when dealing with fast-track projects. Having the job done right the first time not only saves a developer time and money, but serves to provide substantial peace of mind in the future, a factor to consider when formulating the cost of skilled labor within a building project's total budget. By eliminating wasted resources resulting from on-the-job training of unskilled workers, developers maximize their initial return on their labor investment.

The net economic result verifies the added value of employing skilled union members and their contractors. Ensuring a well-planned, well-executed building project is as simple as hiring the area's most productive construction team: Local 33's skilled union journeymen and experienced union contractors. The benefits of the organization's stabilized teamwork, combined with more than a century of experience, provide builders and developers the greatest value for their investment dollars. An investment in quality, Local 33 truly believes building union is just good business.

A Legacy of Commitment

From its beginning, Local 33 assumed a leadership role within the building trades of central Iowa. Active participants in community and civic affairs, Local 33's membership includes a former Des Moines' city councilman and mayor, in addition to numerous volunteers serving local charitable institutions and PTAs. They are citizens who participate in the political fabric of their community, who serve on phone banks and vote regularly, and who provide a structure of stability to their industry. Thanks to their outstanding education and training programs, health insurance, and pension coverage, Local 33 members are able to make a life commitment to the construction business. Therein lies a legacy of commitment and stability, and of giving employers a fair day's work for a fair day's pay, passed on from generation to generation.

As Local 33 has anticipated and planned for its future, builders and developers have continuous access to a skilled workforce armed with technological expertise and an unrivaled work ethic. Entering its second century, Local 33 will continue its long tradition of providing leadership for its industry and community.

AS THE DEMAND FOR SKILLED WORKERS INCREASES ACROSS AMERICA, LOCAL 33'S MEMBERS AND THEIR CONTRACTORS ENJOY A COMPETITIVE EDGE WITHIN THE MARKETPLACE (LEFT).

ENSURING A WELL-PLANNED, WELL-EXECUTED BUILDING PROJECT IS AS SIMPLE AS HIRING THE AREA'S MOST PRODUCTIVE CONSTRUCTION TEAM: LOCAL 33'S SKILLED UNION JOURNEYMEN AND EXPERIENCED UNION CONTRACTORS (RIGHT).

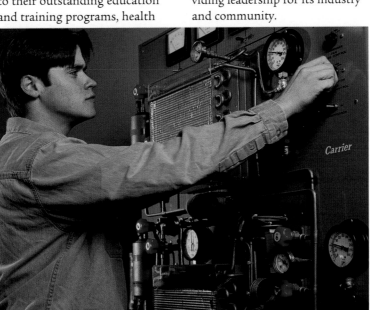

THE BENEFITS OF LOCAL 33'S STABILIZED TEAMWORK, COMBINED WITH MORE THAN A CENTURY OF EXPERIENCE, PROVIDE BUILDERS AND DEVELOPERS THE GREATEST VALUE FOR THEIR INVESTMENT DOLLARS.

BUILDING ON ITS HERITAGE OF HOME APPLIANCES, TRADITIONAL values, and brand strengths, Maytag Corporation is growing in new dimensions. The central-Iowa-based, Fortune 500 corporation—best known for laundry equipment—is more diversified than it has ever been, with home and commercial

appliances sold to a wider range of customers than ever in North America and targeted international markets.

Acquisitions within the past two decades have extended Maytag's heritage and core strengths. The corporation's balanced earnings stream now cuts across five different product lines: major appliances, floor care products, commercial laundry, commercial cooking, and vending. These product lines involve diverse customers, and nearly 50 percent of the corporation's earnings now come from outside the traditional major appliance industry.

WASHING MACHINE BEGINNINGS

Maytag Corporation traces its roots to 1893, when F.L. Maytag began manufacturing farm implements in Newton, Iowa. In an effort to offset seasonal slumps in business, Maytag introduced a wooden-tub washing machine in 1907.

In 1915, Maytag filled a vital need in the home-laundry business by introducing the first gasoline-powered washer, specially targeted for areas where electricity was not yet available. Four years later, the company made the transition from wooden to metal tub machines by casting its first aluminum tub. The washing machines proved so popular that by the mid-

1920s, Maytag dropped its farm implement business and focused its full attention on production and sales of the aluminum tub washer, which catapulted the company toward a leadership position in the washing machine industry.

In 1949, Maytag introduced its first automatic washer and

THE PASTIME, BUILT IN 1907, WAS MAYTAG'S FIRST WASHER. IT IS HOUSED IN THE JASPER COUNTY MUSEUM IN NEWTON (TOP).

MAYTAG'S CORPORATE HEADQUARTERS AND THE HEADQUARTERS OF MAYTAG APPLIANCES, THE CORPORATION'S LARGEST BUSINESS UNIT, ARE LOCATED IN NEWTON, IOWA, 40 MILES EAST OF DES MOINES (BOTTOM).

experimented shortly thereafter with an electric dryer. During the 1950s, one Maytag innovation followed another. As the world began to move faster, the industry expanded beyond the home. Commercial laundries sprung up, and Maytag moved aggressively into this burgeoning market, which continues today to be a successful revenue source for the corporation.

The advertising concept for Ol' Lonely®, the Maytag repairman with nothing to do, planted the seed in the 1960s for one of the most powerful print and television ad campaigns ever created. The universal appeal of the lonely repairman continues today to stand for product performance and dependability.

THE POWER OF BRANDS℠

During the early- to mid-1980s, the corporation acquired the Jenn-Air, Magic Chef, and Admiral brands of major appliances, and the Dixie-Narco brand of vending machines. Jenn-Air brand is synonymous with distinctive styling and innovation through a full line of major appliances. Magic Chef, known as a reliable and affordable brand, is a leading supplier to the recreational vehicle industry. Dixie-Narco, the leading producer of soft-drink vending equipment, recently began manufacturing

FALK DESIGN, ST. LOUIS

Maytag Dishwasher

Jenn-Air Range

Hoover Wind Tunnel™ Upright

Maytag Neptune™ Washer

Maytag Side-by-Side Refrigerator

Maytag. Growing in new dimensions.

Dixie-Narco Hershey® Vender

MagiKitch'n Grill

Maytag Dependable Care® Dryer

WAGMAN PHOTOGRAPHY, INC.

specialty-snack venders to extend its product line.

In 1989, Maytag Corporation expanded again by acquiring Hoover, the most recognized brand name in floor care products. The brand, which dates back to 1908, has earned consumer preference through its dedication to market research and innovation.

In 1996, the corporation entered a joint venture with Hefei Rongshida (Group) Company Ltd., a leading manufacturer of washing machines in China, which added RSD brand. RSD brand automatic and semi-automatic washers are sold by department stores and wholesalers throughout China. The Rongshida-Maytag joint venture will manufacture refrigerators for the Chinese market. Maytag International, the international sales and marketing division of Maytag Corporation, oversees the joint venture in China, as well as direct sales operations and area and regional offices throughout the world.

In the second half of 1997, Maytag acquired the G.S. Blodgett Corporation, a commercial-cooking

equipment manufacturer, which added commercial-quality ovens, grills, charbroilers, and fryers to Maytag's product lineup. Blodgett commercial-cooking equipment, manufactured under the brand names Blodgett Ovens, Pitco Frialator, MagiKitch'n, and Blodgett Combi, is supplied to all major hotel and restaurant chains around the world.

CONTINUED PRODUCT INNOVATION

These new dimensions of Maytag Corporation open opportunities to accelerate the intelligent product innovation and superior performance associated with the corporation's reputation in each of its core businesses.

Maytag Corporation steps into the 21st century with a heritage deeply rooted in Iowa; with brand names among the best known in home appliances, commercial appliances, and vending; and with customers in homes and businesses throughout the world.

A DISPLAY AT DES MOINES INTERNATIONAL AIRPORT ILLUSTRATES THE DIVERSITY OF MAYTAG'S BUSINESSES AND PRODUCT LINES.

EVER SINCE MERCY HOSPITAL MEDICAL CENTER WAS FOUNDED, more than a century ago, its health care experts have been guided by the belief that a healing mission is essential in contemporary society. Compassionate care emphasizing Christian values, respect, and concern for the sanctity of

life is critical in patient care and in Mercy's commitment to the Des Moines community.

The commitment began in 1893 when six Catholic Sisters of Mercy from Davenport traveled across the state to establish the first Mercy Hospital in Des Moines. Their mission was simple: "To promote the dignity of all persons and to serve the needs of the sick, the poor, and the uneducated." Mercy opened as a seven-bed facility. From this humble start emerged the foundation for the caring and stewardship that embody Mercy's mission today and have forged a medical center among the finest in the nation.

Today, Mercy is a 673-bed medical center with two Des Moines campuses, more than 4,800 employees, and a highly skilled medical staff of nearly 700 family medicine and specialty physicians. In July 1998, Mercy became part of the Mercy Health Network, a statewide health organization comprised of other Mercy hospi-

MERCY HOSPITAL MEDICAL CENTER IS A LEADING MEDICAL CENTER IN THE MIDWEST (TOP).

MERCY'S HEART SPECIALISTS ARE RECOGNIZED NATIONWIDE FOR THEIR INNOVATIVE CARDIAC TREATMENTS, INCLUDING A SPECIALIZED CARDIAC CATHETERIZATION LABORATORY, A CARDIAC TRANSPLANT PROGRAM, AND THE ONLY PEDIATRIC HEART SURGERY PROGRAM IN CENTRAL IOWA (BOTTOM).

tals throughout the state that offer Iowans medical coverage right in their own neighborhoods.

MEETING THE REGION'S NEEDS

Mercy's reputation in cardiac care can be traced to 1905, when a Mercy physician revived a man by manually manipulating his heart. Since then, the hospital's cardiac program has developed into one of the Midwest's premier heart centers.

In 1971, heart surgeons performed central Iowa's first openheart surgery. Fourteen years later, Mercy surgeons performed central Iowa's first heart transplant and, in 1988, the state's first artificial heart transplant.

Annually, Mercy's cardiac catheterization laboratory team performs nearly 20,000 procedures, including clearing clogged coronary arteries. With the only children's heart program in central Iowa, Mercy is the destination for hundreds of children who come for treatment by pediatric cardiac specialists, and Mercy's comprehensive heart rehabilitation program helps recovering patients return to active lives.

In 1992, Mercy opened the state's first chest pain center. This special unit of the Emergency Department is specifically designated to treat patients who arrive with chest pain. Mercy Heart Checks help diagnose potential problems in hundreds of people, and reassure those who are on the track to good health.

Mercy and the Iowa Heart Center were among the first three sites in the nation to offer the Dr. Dean Ornish Program for Reversing Heart Disease, aimed at reversing the effects of heart disease through proper diet, exercise, and living well.

More babies are born every year at Mercy than at any other hospital in Iowa. In 1997, the Birthing Center staff delivered 3,743 babies—a record for Mercy. The hospital added the Perinatal Diagnostic Center in 1997, one of only three such centers in Iowa approved by the state, where mothers with high-risk pregnancies receive unsurpassed care. An expanded Level III Neonatal Intensive Care Unit can treat 32 infants at a time, with the latest in equipment and specialized nursing and physician techniques. The medical center's

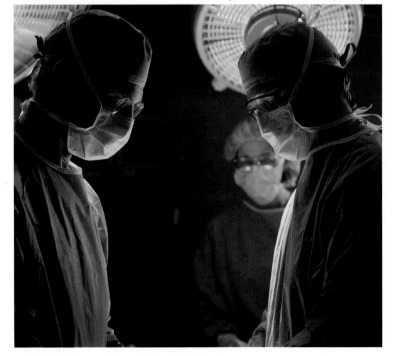

programs and care for mothers and babies have become hallmarks of excellence in Iowa.

The Mercy Cancer Center was the first cancer radiation treatment center in Iowa—and one of the first in the nation—accredited by the American College of Radiology. With one of Iowa's few libraries solely dedicated to cancer resources and with a direct computer link with the National Cancer Institute, the Mercy Cancer Center offers area patients cancer information to enhance their lives. Mercy oncologists also maintain a crucial link with the world-renowned Mayo Clinic and other cancer centers that share research and treatment expertise.

Mercy cancer prevention specialists annually reach out through schools, workplaces, and group meetings to bring a strong message of cancer prevention and early detection. Its affiliation with the American Lung Association and Iowa Heart Center offers a community smoking cessation program. The Mercy Cancer Center provides breast cancer detection instruction with three nationally accredited mammography centers, screenings for skin and prostate cancer, and education regarding how nutrition can lower cancer risk. Once cancer is diagnosed, the hospital's cancer experts provide some of the finest care possible.

More than 51,000 persons seek emergency treatment at Mercy every year. In 1995, Mercy was verified as a Level II trauma center. Mercy Air Life, the hospital's air ambulance, averages more than 55 flights each month and can reach any location in Iowa within one hour.

To complement its lifesaving services, Mercy established the School of Emergency Medical Services in 1979, which instructs nearly 11,200 emergency personnel annually in numerous emergency-related courses.

Other areas of specialization for Mercy include pediatrics, critical care, behavioral medicine, neu-

rology, orthopedics, and senior services.

OUTSIDE THE WALLS

Annually, the hospital's 23 family practice and specialty clinics provide care to more than 500,000 patients, and Mercy's home health nurses, aides, and rehabilitation experts make nearly 60,000 patient home visits.

Through the Midwest Rural Telemedicine Consortium, Mercy has helped link 38 hospitals, long-term care centers, and clinics in rural communities to Mercy medical experts and to each other. Now, without leaving their own communities, rural Iowans and physicians are able to consult with Mercy specialists.

A COMMUNITY LEADER

It takes much more to create a healthy community than making health care services available. Environment, lifestyle, education, nutrition, employment, and security all impact the well-being of a community.

Mercy is making every effort to meet this challenge head-on. The House of Mercy, opened in 1987 in Des Moines' inner city, provided care for 254 homeless women and their children in 1997. It offers teen pregnancy and substance abuse programs, foster care, and day care for children.

KNOWN STATEWIDE FOR ITS MATERNAL AND CHILD SERVICES, MERCY'S BIRTHING CENTER STAFF ANNUALLY CELEBRATES THE BEGINNING OF LIFE WITH MORE PARENTS AND NEWBORNS THAN ANY OTHER IOWA HOSPITAL.

Also, young women receive a second chance to enhance the lives of their children by improving their parenting, education, and job skills, and returning to productive lives in the community.

Likewise, Mercy employees are busy throughout the community—volunteering to paint neighborhood homes, working with the Des Moines Police Department to provide community activities for at-risk youngsters, or offering a special home ownership program to help revitalize a Des Moines neighborhood.

It's the Mercy mission. For as long as there are people in need, Mercy will be in Des Moines.

A UNIQUE BLEND OF TRADITION, INNOVATION, AND GROWTH is a key part of the AmerUs Group distinguished heritage. The tradition of two outstanding life insurance companies forms the core of AmerUs' success. Central Life Assurance and American Mutual Life—each with a century of excel-

lent service—merged in 1994 and retained the American Mutual name. When the AmerUs brand identity was adopted in 1996, the AmerUs Group (then consisting of insurance, mortgage, banking, and real estate companies) was born, and American Mutual was renamed AmerUs Life Insurance Company.

A History of Growth
The first mutual insurance holding company in the nation, and a widely regarded leader in the industry, AmerUs has earned a well-deserved reputation for innovation. As a result, growth has played a significant part in the company's history, especially in recent years. For example, AmerUs Life Holdings, the holding company for the corporation's life insurance and annuity operations, went public on January 29, 1997, with a subscription stock offering to policy

owners and a subsequent initial public offering.

What happened during the remainder of 1997 is nothing short of amazing: AmerUs Life Holdings enjoyed a 123 percent increase in its stock price, four straight quarters of record operating earnings, and an increase in

assets from $4.4 billion to $10.3 billion. The increase in assets came through internal growth and the acquisition of two highly respected annuity companies: Delta Life Corporation in Memphis, Tennessee, and AmVestors Financial Corporation in Topeka, Kansas. AmerUs Life Holdings culminated that year of growth and profitability with its move from the Nasdaq to the New York Stock Exchange on February 20, 1998.

"AmerUs has generated a tremendous amount of momentum with the success of its public company," says Roger Brooks, chairman and chief executive officer of AmerUs Group. "We're working to continue that momentum in the years ahead, as we grow our business and enhance the value and strength of our company for our shareholders, customers, and employees."

The future of AmerUs Group lies in the continued growth in its

MEMBERS OF AMERUS GROUP'S SENIOR MANAGEMENT, THE BOARD OF DIRECTORS, AND OTHER EMPLOYEES WERE THE CENTER OF ATTENTION AS AMERUS LIFE HOLDINGS DEBUTED ON THE NEW YORK STOCK EXCHANGE IN EARLY 1998.

LEIGH CHARLTON

AmerUs associates spend countless hours assisting in volunteer activities, such as the tutoring program with Willkie House. Through this program, AmerUs tutors meet with 15 students for one hour each week on-site at AmerUs Life.

life insurance and annuity businesses and in the further development of its niche businesses, such as AmerUs Home Equity. The home equity lending portion of AmerUs Bank's business grew by almost 800 percent from 1993 to 1998.

After the sale of the bank to Commercial Federal in 1998, AmerUs Home Equity was formed to take advantage of the management expertise, technology, and risk management perspective developed by AmerUs Bank.

"With the success of our current businesses—AmerUs Life, Delta, and AmVestors—and the tremendous potential of AmerUs Home Equity," Brooks concludes, "our future remains very bright."

A GOOD CORPORATE CITIZEN

Committed to being a good corporate citizen, AmerUs recognizes its responsibility to support the social, civic, and educational initiatives that make its communities better places to live.

Employees spend countless hours assisting in volunteer activities, including several projects with area schools. Possibly the best example of the volunteer spirit is the tutoring program that exists between AmerUs and

LEIGH CHARLTON

Willkie House. Through this program, AmerUs tutors meet with 15 students—all central-city children in second through eighth grade—for one hour each week at AmerUs Life. The program is considered a model program by central Iowa businesses and schools.

In addition, for each of the past several years, the AmerUs Group and its Charitable Foundation have donated more than $1 million to various nonprofit agencies to improve the overall quality of life. And every year, AmerUs employees open their hearts and wallets during the United Way fund-raising drive, establishing the company as one of the three largest contributors in central Iowa.

In recognition of its community service, the AmerUs Group received the 1997 Outstanding Corporation/Foundation Philanthropy Award from the National Society of Fund Raising Executives. The corporation also received the Awards for Excellence in Corporate Community Service from the Points of Light Foundation.

For more than 100 years, the principals of AmerUs Group have been committed to outstanding corporate service—to its customers and to the community. Such dedication—and the resulting success—has made the organization an industry leader that is sure to see many more years of prosperity.

FOR MORE THAN 100 YEARS, GRAND VIEW COLLEGE HAS BEEN dedicated to a distinct vision of helping each student develop the innate qualities and abilities that lead to a rewarding and fulfilling life. The independent, four-year, liberal arts college, founded by Danish immigrants in 1896, is affiliated with the

CLOCKWISE FROM TOP: GRAND VIEW COLLEGE STUDENTS ENJOY A BREAK BETWEEN CLASSES ON A WARM SPRING DAY.

GRAND VIEW COLLEGE MEMORABILIA REFLECT THE RICH HISTORY AND CHARACTER OF THE INSTITUTION THAT HAS BEEN SERVING STUDENTS FOR MORE THAN A CENTURY.

GRAND VIEW'S HUMPHREY CENTER, MOST COMMONLY KNOWN AS OLD MAIN, HAS BEEN THE HEART AND SOUL OF THE CAMPUS FOR GENERATIONS OF STUDENTS. THE ROCK, OUTSIDE THE FRONT DOOR OF THE SPLENDID BUILDING, IS AN EQUALLY FAMOUS CAMPUS LANDMARK.

Evangelical Lutheran Church in America and has prepared thousands of students for responsible citizenship in their communities and the world.

Grand View College offers 26 baccalaureate degree majors, including nursing, accounting, business administration, information services, education, biology, communication, art, and criminal justice, to mention only a few. Students can take advantage of day, evening, weekend, and summer classes at any or all of three locations in the Des Moines metropolitan area: the main campus, Grand View West at Valley High School, and Camp Dodge in Johnston. At each campus, they find the Grand View trademark of quality programs, personal attention, affordability, and flexibility.

Grand View College is accredited by the North Central Association of Colleges and Schools. The nursing program is accredited by the Iowa State Board of Nursing and by the National League for Nursing, and the teacher education program is approved by the Iowa Department of Education. With these credentials, and the dedication of its faculty and staff,

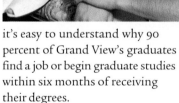

it's easy to understand why 90 percent of Grand View's graduates find a job or begin graduate studies within six months of receiving their degrees.

Grand View has an enrollment of close to 1,400 students. Classes are always taught by professors, rather than by graduate students, and the student/faculty ratio is 14-to-1. In addition to classes, students can take advantage of an outstanding and respected internship program that the college has with schools, hospitals, and corporations in Des Moines. Students also benefit from athletic programs, student government associations, and clubs that stimulate intellectual, social, emotional, vocational, and spiritual growth. They also enjoy

the advantage of many entertainment and cultural activities available in the Des Moines area.

Grand View College is a beloved mainstay in the community. The heart and soul of campus, Old Main is on the National Register of Historic Places. The majestic building was renovated in 1998 and renamed the Humphrey Center, in honor of the alumna who donated the funds for the renovation—52 years after attending the college. Such generosity, combined with the ongoing commitment of the faculty, staff, and administration to educate and prepare students for the future, ensures that the college will continue to enrich the lives of generations of students to come.

MEREDITH CORPORATION TOUCHES THE LIVES OF MILLIONS of American families through its magazines, books, and television stations. Headquartered in Des Moines, it is one of America's leading media and marketing companies. ■ Meredith is the country's foremost home-and-

family publisher. Each year its magazines reach one-sixth of the U.S. adult population. Its flagship magazine, *Better Homes and Gardens*, is the third-largest magazine in the country.

The group continues to grow by increasing circulation and adding new magazine and book titles. In addition to *Better Homes and Gardens*, the Publishing Group produces magazines such as *Ladies' Home Journal, MORE, Country Home, Country Gardens, Midwest Living, Traditional Home, Renovation Style, WOOD, Family Money, American Patchwork & Quilting, Decorative Woodcrafts, Cross Stitch & Needlework, Successful Farming, Mature Outlook, Crayola Kids*, and *Golf for Women*.

Playing off the success of its most popular magazine, Meredith also publishes more than 45 *Better Homes and Gardens* special-interest publications. It also has more than 300 Meredith-trademarked consumer books in print, including the popular *Better Homes and Gardens New Cook Book*. The familiar red-plaid cookbook has sold more than 32 million copies since its introduction in 1930. Other publishing group products include the American Park Network, a collection of 21 visitor guide magazines, and integrated marketing programs for clients such as

Nestlé, MetLife, and the Home Depot.

Meredith Corporation's reach extends beyond the printed page to broadcasting and television programming. Having entered the television market 50 years ago, the Meredith Broadcasting Group today includes 12 television stations—five CBS affiliates, one NBC affiliate, and six Fox affiliates— in some of the fastest-growing markets across the continental United States. Meredith Broadcasting Group also produces the weekly syndicated show *Better Homes and Gardens Television*, which is broadcast on more than 140 stations across the country.

COMMITTED TO DES MOINES

Through product development and strong management, Meredith Corporation revenues and profits have maintained a strong pattern of growth, reaching record levels in recent years. Meredith Corporation has been in Des Moines since 1902, when Edwin Thomas Meredith began publishing *Successful Farming* magazine. In 1912, the 200-employee company moved into the core of the corporate headquarters building on Locust Street in Des Moines. A decade later, Meredith began publishing *Fruit, Garden and Home*

magazine, a home-and-family service publication that in 1924 would be renamed *Better Homes and Gardens* magazine. Over the years, seven additions have been made to the original headquarters. The most recent, a $40 million campus addition completed in 1998, includes the *Better Homes and Gardens* Test Gardens. Today, the company employs more than 2,400 people throughout the country, including approximately 1,000 in Des Moines.

Meredith Corporation takes pride in being a part of downtown Des Moines. The corporation's position as an anchor for the Gateway downtown redevelopment project demonstrates its support for the community. Meredith also encourages employee volunteerism, and funds local charitable causes focused on the arts, education, and human services. Meredith's strong tradition and growth ensure that it will be an important part of Des Moines for many years to come.

MEREDITH CORPORATION TOUCHES THE LIVES OF MILLIONS OF AMERICAN FAMILIES THROUGH ITS MAGAZINES, BOOKS, AND TELEVISION STATIONS.

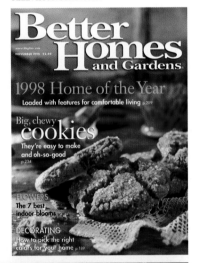

LTHOUGH WELLS FARGO & COMPANY (FORMERLY NORWEST Corporation) is based in San Francisco, Des Moines is home to four of the company's core businesses: Norwest Mortgage, Inc., Norwest Financial, Inc., Norwest Bank Iowa, N.A., and Norwest Card Services. Combined, nearly 5,000 team

members in Des Moines contribute to the strong customer service orientation and business acumen that have helped the organization emerge as one of America's most admired companies.

In 1998, these Des Moines companies had not yet completed name changes to reflect their relationship with parent Wells Fargo & Company.

Des Moines and numerous other communities nationwide are benefactors of the rich tradition of charitable giving practiced by Norwest entities. The company looks at charitable giving as an investment in the future and, combined, the Des Moines-based Norwest organizations support hundreds of important local and national causes. These include the United Way, Habitat for Humanity, and Toys for Tots, to name a few.

NORWEST MORTGAGE

With Iowa roots stretching back to 1908, Norwest Mortgage has become the nation's leading mortgage lender, funding nearly one of every 15 homes financed in the United States through its 850 stores nationwide. In recognition of the company's efforts to make it possible for all Americans to own their homes, Norwest Mortgage is consistently recognized as the nation's leading lender to minority first-time home buyers by the Department of Housing and Urban Development (HUD).

Norwest Mortgage is proud of the service its more than 14,000 team members nationwide provide. Using Norwest's state of-the art technology and broad array of products, Norwest Mortgage is able to serve its customers when, where, and how they choose—in their home or business, over the phone, via the Internet, or at one of its retail locations. As a result, Norwest Mortgage has been able

CLOCKWISE FROM TOP RIGHT: LOCATED IN THE HEART OF DOWNTOWN DES MOINES, THE NORWEST FINANCIAL CENTER HOLDS AN IMPRESSIVE PRESENCE IN THE CITY'S SKYLINE.

LEADING WELLS FARGO'S OPERATIONS BASED IN DES MOINES ARE (FROM LEFT) BEN AEILTS, VICE PRESIDENT AND REGIONAL MANAGER, NORWEST FINANCIAL; DEB MOORE, PRESIDENT, NORWEST CARD SERVICES; LYNN HORAK, PRESIDENT, NORWEST BANK, IOWA, N.A.; AND MARK OMAN, GROUP EXECUTIVE VICE PRESIDENT, WELLS FARGO & COMPANY, AND CHAIRMAN AND CEO, NORWEST MORTGAGE, INC.

THROUGH ITS WEB PAGE, NORWEST PROVIDES PC BANKING TO ITS CUSTOMERS SO THEIR BANKING NEEDS CAN BE PERFORMED FROM THE COMFORT OF HOME.

to help more Americans realize their dreams of home ownership than any other lender in the country.

NORWEST CARD SERVICES

As one of the nation's leading credit card issuers, Norwest Card Services (NCS) serves approximately two million cardholders. Because of its strong commitment to customer service, a high-quality portfolio, and competitive pricing, NCS maintains a strong market position.

Since NCS issued its first credit card in 1969, the business has expanded dramatically to encompass consumer credit cards, commercial credit cards, transaction processing services for merchants, and Instant Cash® services, including 1,800 ATMs and more than 1.25 million debit cards nationally. For NCS, the most important business strategy—and one of its key competitive advantages—is the dedication of more than 700 talented team members, most of whom are based in Des Moines.

NORWEST FINANCIAL, INC.

While only a select few companies are able to survive for more than 100 years, fewer still can say they have earned a profit in each of those years. Norwest Financial, Inc. (NFI) has done both. Today, NFI's primary business is the same as it was more than a century ago: making loans to consumers.

In 1897, Jacob Levitt opened the company's first lending office in Des Moines under the name of State Loan Company. Recognizing the working class's need for accessible credit, the fledgling business prospered, and in 1924, its second office opened in Sioux City. The company grew steadily, first changing its name to State Finance Company, then to Dial Finance Company. In 1960, the company's common stock was first offered to the public, and in 1968, it was first listed on the New York Stock Exchange. In 1992, Dial merged with Norwest Corporation (then Northwest Bancorporation) and changed its name to Norwest Financial in 1983.

Geographic growth and diversification continued during the 1990s. Today, NFI provides direct loans to consumers and financing for the customers of retailers through more than 1,100 branch offices in 47 states, Guam, Canada, Puerto Rico, Panama, Netherlands Antilles, U.S. Virgin Islands, Aruba, Costa Rica, and Argentina. The company also offers bank credit cards, insurance premium financing, automobile financing, lease and private-label financing programs for businesses, and information systems for the North American consumer finance industry.

Norwest Financial and its subsidiary companies have more than 12,000 team members, with more than 1,200 team members in the Des Moines area. It has been recognized by the National Federation of Business and Professional Women and the National Association for the Advancement of Colored People (NAACP) for its commitment to hiring, training, and retaining women and minorities.

NORWEST BANK IOWA, N.A.

Norwest Bank Iowa, N.A. has been serving Iowans since 1929, when the company (then Northwest Bancorporation) opened one of its first branches in Mason City. Today, Norwest is the state's largest bank, providing financial services to one in every six Iowa households.

Norwest has grown into a diversified financial services company dedicated to selling and servicing all the financial products needed by consumers, small businesses, farmers, and large corporations. Norwest Bank Iowa's philosophy is to manage locally, operate regionally, and strategize globally. To do this, the bank strives to offer better products and a broader product line than local competitors. In addition, Norwest also competes directly with national banks by staying closer to local customers, understanding community and customer needs, and providing professional, personalized, and timely service.

While many banking products—such as checking and savings accounts, mutual funds, and home equity loans, as well as high-tech services like automated telephone banking and on-line banking—can be widely duplicated by competitors, caring, knowledgeable professionals cannot be so readily copied. The Norwest Bank professional team strives to be the best at what they do, to care the most, and to be the best trained to provide customers with financial solutions—this is the Norwest way.

As Iowa's leading banking company, Norwest Bank's top priority is its customers. Norwest Bank tellers are an integral part of its commitment to serve customers when, where, and how they want to bank (top).

In 1993, the Norwest Housing Foundation (NHF) was created to help meet affordable housing needs in Norwest communities nationwide through financial contributions and the volunteer support of Norwest team members. Since its inception, NHF has partnered with Habitat for Humanity on hundreds of home builds across the country, including this home for a Des Moines-area family (bottom).

THE UNIVERSITY OF OSTEOPATHIC MEDICINE AND HEALTH Sciences (UOMHS) boasts some impressive numbers. One hundred years old in 1998, the university contains the second-oldest and second-largest college of osteopathic medicine in the country. During the 1997-1998 school year, the university

had an enrollment of 1,327 students in its three colleges. The university includes 288 full-time and 36 part-time employees on its payroll, has an annual operating budget of $27 million, and produces approximately $75 million annually in local economic impact. Yet, for those who assess the value of an organization not only with numbers or with dollar signs, but also in contributions to the community, the worth of UOMHS to central Iowa may be immeasurable.

Des Moines: An Ideal Location

The University of Osteopathic Medicine and Health Sciences was founded in 1898 as the Dr. S.S. Still College and Infirmary of Osteopathy. Originally located on West Locust Street, it was named after its first president, who was a nephew of Dr. Andrew Taylor Still, the founder of osteopathy. A trade newspaper of the time described Des Moines as an ideal location for the nation's second osteopathic college, citing the city's good streets, low incidence of disease, relatively low death rate, excellent libraries, three large hos-

DAVID KRAUSE

CLOCKWISE FROM TOP:
THE UNIVERSITY OF OSTEOPATHIC MEDICINE AND HEALTH SCIENCES (UOMHS) CAMPUS IS CENTRALLY LOCATED IN DES MOINES ON GRAND AVENUE.

DR. S.S. STILL WAS ONE OF THE FOUNDERS AND THE FIRST PRESIDENT OF UOMHS.

UOMHS WAS FOUNDED IN 1898 AS THE DR. S.S. STILL COLLEGE AND INFIRMARY OF OSTEOPATHY.

pitals, and many parks and other facilities "for developing life to its best usefulness."

The city also provided a spirit of community that contributed to the school's survival in the early years. In 1904, $50,000 was raised by the people of Des Moines in support of the college. The school's 1906-1907 catalog stated, "The college exists solely as a direct result of activity of the people of Des Moines." In return, the university has provided hundreds of trained health care professionals to the community and the state.

From its inception, UOMHS' policy was that women would be admitted on the same terms as men, that there would be no distinction as to sex, and that students would have the same opportunities and be held to the same requirements. In 1943, the university graduated its first racial minority students, and it now includes students from several foreign countries.

UOMHS moved in 1927 to Sixth Avenue, where it remained until relocating to its present campus on Grand Avenue in 1972. The university's name was modified several times through the years and, with the addition of

the College of Podiatric Medicine and Surgery, and the College of Health Sciences in 1981, the institution gained university status, becoming the University of Osteopathic Medicine and Health Sciences.

Treating the Whole Person

Osteopathy is based on the guiding philosophy that good health is an outgrowth of the proper alignment of bones, muscles, and joints, along with the body's innate ability to heal itself. Therefore, the University of Osteopathic Medicine and Health Sciences has traditionally emphasized primary care—including general and family practice, general internal medicine, pediatrics, and osteopathic manipulative medicine. Approximately 60 percent of all graduates practice primary care, and more than 70 percent of UOMHS alumni in Iowa today are primary care practitioners.

UOMHS offers degree programs through its three colleges: the College of Osteopathic Medicine and Surgery, the College of Podiatric Medicine and Surgery, and the College of Health Sciences. The university offers the Doctor of Osteopathic Medicine degree, as well as Doctor of Podiatric Medicine; Master of Science, Physical Therapy; Master of Health Care Administration; and Bachelor of Science, Physician Assistant degrees.

In Iowa, one in every 10 physicians is a graduate of UOMHS. Approximately 700 alumni practice in some 150 Iowa communities. The university operates the on-campus, multispecialty Tower Medical Clinic and the Southeast Family Practice Clinic. UOMHS is also affiliated with selected rural and urban clinics in Iowa and communities throughout the United States, and operates a mobile health clinic.

In response to the health care needs of the unemployed in central Iowa, UOMHS offers a program of free primary medical care called We DO Care. The program provides health care to temporarily unemployed individuals and their families through the university's clinics.

Students in Des Moines-area schools—elementary through college—benefit from UOMHS' Community Ambassador Program. The program offers educational presentations on scientific, medical, and health-related topics as a free service. Students are invited to tour the university's facilities, including medical laboratories, an EKG laboratory, a medical library, and lecture halls. The program's goals are to educate students in the areas of anatomy, physiology, and wellness. It also serves to promote and nurture a commitment

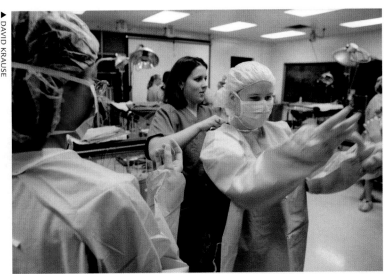

▶ DAVID KRAUSE

to community service among UOMHS students.

TRAINING HEALTH CARE PROFESSIONALS

UOMHS provides students with the knowledge and skills needed to become health care professionals dedicated to maintaining and restoring the health of their patients. Classroom instruction and clinical training are presented in an atmosphere where humanitarian concerns, scholarly activity, and health care

delivery are a primary focus. Affirming its osteopathic commitment to meeting basic health care needs, the university serves as a local, state, and national resource for primary care physicians and associated health care providers.

As it begins its second century of operation, UOMHS will continue to prepare physicians and allied health personnel for careers in the ever changing field of medicine, while developing innovative programs to serve students and the community.

UOMHS STUDENTS PROVIDE COMMUNITY SERVICE BY WORKING WITH A MEDICAL EXPLORER POST THAT MEETS ON CAMPUS.

STUDENTS RECEIVE PART OF THEIR MEDICAL EDUCATION IN LABORATORY SETTINGS.

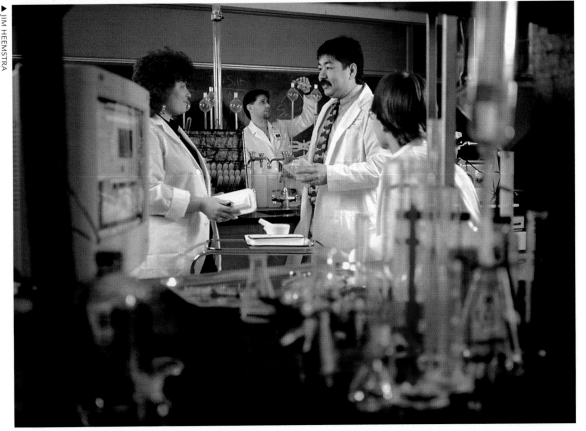

▶ JIM HEEMSTRA

I N 1900, VETERAN BANKERS LELAND WINDSOR AND SIMON CASSADY joined forces to organize a private bank in a small town outside Des Moines. Their business was named Windsor & Cassady Bankers; the town was known as Valley Junction. ■ Within a year, the bank had recorded deposits of some $40,000. The owners then decided to

make the business a national bank, obtaining a charter from the U.S. government authorizing the bank to issue notes acceptable as legal tender. Thus, on July 1, 1901, the First National Bank of Valley Junction was founded.

Nearly a century later, the small town has grown into the thriving metropolitan community of West Des Moines. The bank, whose name was changed in 1938 to First National Bank of West Des Moines, now has three locations and assets totaling nearly $56 million. Yet, despite the changes, one distinction remains the same: FIRST BANK is still a locally owned bank.

TWO GENERATIONS OF MESSERSCHMIDTS CURRENTLY MANAGE FIRST BANK. ROY, CHAIRMAN (SEATED); RICK, PRESIDENT/CEO (LEFT); AND BILL, CASHIER (RIGHT), REPRESENT MORE THAN 80 YEARS OF COMBINED BANKING EXPERIENCE.

THE MESSERSCHMIDT LEADERSHIP

On June 19, 1939, Roy M. Messerschmidt of Des Moines bought the controlling interest in First National Bank of West Des Moines, took immediate possession, and became president. His wife, Mable O. Messerschmidt, became vice president. Counting its officers, the bank had only six employees. But within the next decade, the bank grew in personnel and in physical stature.

Roy W. Messerschmidt joined his parents in the business in June 1949. That same year, the bank constructed a two-story addition onto its west end. As the bank continued to grow and prosper through the 1950s and early 1960s, it was again necessary to expand. In 1964, the bank purchased the neighboring building to the north and expanded the lobby.

By 1969, Roy W. Messerschmidt had become president of the bank and Roy M. Messerschmidt had taken on the role of chairman. Total assets had grown to $3.9 million. One of the first tasks of the new president was to plan and build a new bank building, and, after much study, land was purchased in the northeast corner of the proposed Westown Shopping Center on 22nd Street. Construction of the new bank began in August 1971, and the building was the first in the shopping center to be completed. With construction completed in March of 1972, First National Bank of West Des Moines moved its main office to the new site. The old facility became a branch office in the downtown West Des Moines business district

FIRST BANK PROVIDES COMPLETE BANKING SERVICES TO COMMERCIAL ACCOUNTS OF ALL TYPES. PICTURED IS AMERICA'S BEST, A LOCAL COMPANY INVOLVED IN BUSINESS INTERNATIONALLY.

THE NEWEST OFFICE OF FIRST BANK, LOCATED ON SOUTHWEST NINTH STREET, SERVES THE SOUTH DES MOINES MARKET AREA.

called Valley Junction. At the time of the move, the bank had grown to 15 employees, including officers, and its total assets were more than $7 million.

In July 1991, the bank moved the location of its historic office from its original location to Fifth Street in West Des Moines. While it was very difficult to leave the original location, rich in tradition and history, the move was necessary in order to provide customers with modern banking services. The new location—still within Valley Junction—provides drive-up facilities and an ATM, as well as convenient parking for bank customers.

On December 31, 1993, the bank converted its national charter to a state charter and changed its legal name to FIRST BANK, consistent with what its customers and the community had been calling the bank for the preceding 25 years.

In 1995, FIRST BANK purchased property located on Southwest Ninth Street in Des Moines with the intent of bringing locally owned full-service banking to another area of Des Moines. The former office of American Federal Savings and Loan opened on

October 14, 1996, as FIRST BANK's newest office. The office is designed and staffed to bring high-quality, friendly, hometown banking service to south-side people and businesses.

Now led by President and CEO Rick R. Messerschmidt, the financial institution is proud of its tradition of local ownership and of its slogan: "FIRST BANK—the bank Des Moines calls first!" FIRST BANK prides itself in serving a

diverse group of customers ranging from individual consumers to commercial accounts in various businesses. A large portion of its loan portfolio is vested in commercial real estate and development projects. As it approaches the 21st century, FIRST BANK looks forward to continuing to provide the same high-quality, personalized financial services to its customers that it became noted for nearly a century ago.

FIRST BANK IS ACTIVE IN THE REAL ESTATE MARKET, PROVIDING FINANCING FOR BOTH INDIVIDUALS AND DEVELOPERS IN THE RESIDENTIAL AND COMMERCIAL ARENA. PICTURED IS A NEW DEVELOPMENT IN THE SOUTHEAST SECTOR OF DES MOINES.

THE UNIQUE SHAPE AND DRAMATIC LIGHTING OF EMC INSURANCE Companies' 20-story office tower are immediately recognizable in downtown Des Moines. The company that built this singular structure is also recognized by independent insurance agents and consumers throughout the country who seek the values

of service, integrity, and stability in their insurance company.

Organized in 1911 to provide workers' compensation coverage to Iowa manufacturers, Employers Mutual Casualty Company grew into a group of companies that currently markets a wide array of insurance products and services through a nationwide network of branch offices and independent agents. To accommodate its growth into the 21st century, the company, along with its subsidiaries and affiliates, now called EMC Insurance Companies (EMC), completed the construction of its distinctive office tower in 1997 as an addition to its home office. This massive project signaled EMC's belief in a healthy and profitable future for the company and for the city it is proud to call home.

EMC INSURANCE COMPANIES GREW UP IN DOWNTOWN DES MOINES. THE COMPANY'S FIRST OFFICES WERE LOCATED JUST A FEW BLOCKS AWAY FROM THE 20-STORY OFFICE TOWER COMPLETED IN 1997 (TOP).

PICTURED IN FRONT OF THE LATEST ADDITION TO EMC'S HOME OFFICE IN DOWNTOWN DES MOINES ARE (FROM LEFT): BRUCE KELLEY, PRESIDENT AND CEO; FRED SCHIEK, EXECUTIVE VICE PRESIDENT AND COO; AND JIM FONTANINI, RESIDENT VICE PRESIDENT AND DES MOINES BRANCH MANANGER (BOTTOM).

STRONG LOCAL ROOTS WITH BROAD NATIONAL PRESENCE

What do a home owner in Arizona, a printer in Kansas, a family in Pennsylvania, a school in Iowa, and a bank in Mississippi have in common? They are all insured through EMC Insurance Companies of Des Moines.

With assets of nearly $2 billion and more than 1,900 employees across the country, EMC is ranked as one of Iowa's largest property and casualty insurance companies and among the top 80 insurance companies nationwide. The more than one dozen separate and distinct companies of EMC are represented by more than

2,700 independent insurance agencies in 39 states.

Since opening its first branch office in Wichita in 1934, EMC's competitive strength has been, and continues to be, the responsive service the company provides agents and policyholders through a network of strategically located branch offices. Each branch responds to its own geographic market, changing and enhancing its marketing emphasis to be of greater value and service to its customers. The company's long-term and ongoing commitment to the agents and customers in these regions sets EMC Insurance Companies apart.

As geographic opportunities present themselves, EMC will con-

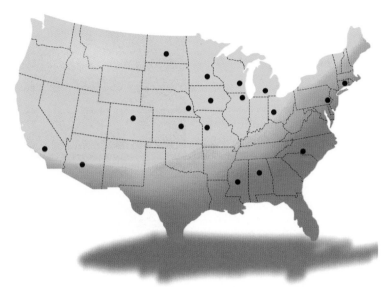

tinue its successful pattern of growth—region by region. In 1997, an affiliation with Hamilton Mutual Insurance Company in Cincinnati allowed EMC to make its products and services available to individuals and businesses in Ohio and Kentucky, while expanding its presence in Michigan.

Protecting Policyholders' Assets

I nsurance is our business and we intend to stay in it," reads a sign in the office of the president and chief executive officer of EMC Insurance Companies. To achieve this singular mission, the company provides its customers with a high degree of financial stability and a comprehensive range of insurance coverages.

EMC's sound underwriting practices and successful investment strategies offer the peace of mind important to insurance buyers. The company's financial statement consistently demonstrates a strong financial position. It has an A (Excellent) rating from A.M. Best company, the oldest and most respected independent organization to rate the financial stability of insurance companies. The company also enjoys a rating of exceptional claim-paying ability from Standard & Poor's.

Although the history of EMC Insurance Companies is firmly rooted in Iowa and downtown Des Moines, its unique branch office structure has made the company one of the preferred choices of independent agents and their customers across the country.

Agents and their customers turn to EMC for a comprehensive range of insurance coverages—from traditional to progressive—a list that continues to grow as new risks are identified and new services are introduced. EMC's comprehensive commercial property and casualty insurance programs are tailored to the needs of various sizes and types of businesses and trade associations. In Iowa, EMC insures all public school districts.

Competitive personal lines policies offer numerous premium discounts, including a special Customer Plus program for preferred home owners and automobile owners. EMC has a complete line of life insurance products for individuals, businesses, and their employees—including a special Youth Plus policy designed to provide a lifetime of life insurance coverage for newborns.

EMC is also a trusted and reliable source of fidelity and surety bonds, a product line it has underwritten since 1942. Its technical expertise and the capabilities of

A NETWORK OF 18 STRATEGICALLY LOCATED BRANCH OFFICES PROVIDES EMC INSURANCE COMPANIES WITH THE FLEXIBILITY TO RESPOND MORE APPROPRIATELY TO THE NEEDS OF AGENTS AND CUSTOMERS THROUGHOUT THE COUNTRY.

EMPLOYEES FROM VARIOUS EMC DEPARTMENTS MEET TO ADDRESS THE CHALLENGES FACING THE COMPANY AND ITS CUSTOMERS.

a fully staffed risk improvement department help policyholders reduce the incidence and severity of workplace injuries. It offers the flexibility of a multiline, third-party administrator to complement any company's self-insurance program. For hard-to-insure drivers and other extraordinary risks that are occasionally faced by individuals, organizations, and companies, EMC Insurance Companies provides access to nonstandard risk auto insurance, as well as excess and surplus lines of insurance.

EMC maintains a professional countrywide claim service, incorporating the latest in communica-

WHETHER THEY'RE DONATING FOOD, WORKING WITH YOUNG PEOPLE, CLEANING UP NEIGHBORHOODS, OR CONTRIBUTING TO LOCAL CHARITIES, EMC AND ITS EMPLOYEES REALIZE THE RESPONSIBILITY THEY HAVE TO IMPROVE THE QUALITY OF LIFE IN THE COMMUNITIES IN WHICH THEY LIVE AND WORK (TOP RIGHT).

EMC OFFERS A FULL RANGE OF INSURANCE PRODUCTS AND SERVICES FOR HOMEOWNERS, BUSINESSES, AND ORGANIZATIONS SUCH AS SCHOOLS, CITIES, AND OTHER SPECIALIZED RISKS (RIGHT AND BELOW).

tion technologies to assure that claims are handled in a timely and accurate manner. The firm also offers convenient and flexible financing options to fit various cash flow situations.

EMC realizes that its customers have a regular opportunity to review their insurance options. By continually developing and enhancing products and services, the company is able to retain its customers' confidence and trust.

Through almost a century of growth and stability, EMC Insurance Companies has demonstrated its ability to respond to the changing needs of the marketplace. As the firm approaches the 21st century, every EMC department and branch office is investigating ways to be of even greater value and service as the company pursues its mission of protecting policyholders' assets.

BUILDING STRONGER RELATIONSHIPS FOR A STRONGER FUTURE

EMC Insurance Companies' continuing success is dependent on the quality of the relationships it maintains with agents, policyholders, and employees. By building stronger relationships with these groups, the company

continues to build a stronger future for itself, its community, and the people it serves.

More than ever, independent insurance agents are important in today's complex insurance marketplace. They provide clients with objective, professional counsel in the area of insurance coverages. By supporting agents with technology, products, and services, EMC is assured of a steady stream of quality business today and in the future. It is not unusual to find agencies throughout the country that have represented EMC Insurance Companies for 50 years or longer.

In 1997, EMC was among a handful of companies recognized by the National Association of Professional Insurance Agents for their efforts in developing innovative, caring programs and projects that benefit insurance consumers. When agents or policyholders call EMC, they know they are dealing with insurance professionals—people who understand insurance and know how to serve. Having highly trained and motivated people throughout the company enhances the quality of relationships EMC enjoys with agents and policyholders. EMC's management team is proud of these professionals who serve its various customers every day. The company is committed to supporting their professional and personal goals with technology, training, and attractive benefit programs.

WHETHER A SITUATION INVOLVES ON-THE-SCENE RESPONSE TO NATURAL DISASTERS, A JOB SITE INJURY, A HOUSE FIRE, OR A CAR ACCIDENT, EMC IS THERE WITH THE PEOPLE AND TECHNOLOGY TO SATISFY POLICYHOLDERS' NEEDS.

A LEADER IN THE INDUSTRY AND THE COMMUNITY

Since its early beginnings, EMC Insurance Companies has played an active role in improving and enhancing the insurance industry. Key company executives serve on national boards and committees involved with legislation and with policy issues of importance to the insurance industry. The company is also a strong supporter of personal development programs offered through various insurance institutes and associations.

As a major employer in central Iowa, EMC has taken a leadership role in civic activities and charitable giving, most notably through the United Way of Greater Des Moines, Drake University's Kelley Insurance Center (named for the former chairman and CEO of EMC, Robb B. Kelley), Salisbury House Foundation, Living History Farms, Des Moines Symphony, Science Center of Iowa, State Historical Society of Iowa, and a variety of other organizations that enhance the quality of life in central Iowa.

EMC and its employees provide more than financial resources to these organizations. An active volunteer committee is constantly providing human resources to goodwill programs throughout the community—delivering meals to local shut-ins every workday; collecting food during the holiday season and throughout the year; and supporting children's programs and youth projects, such as a Boy Scout Explorer Post. EMC branch offices mirror this community-minded spirit of the company by supporting local initiatives and organizations in their individual areas.

CHANGING THE SHAPE OF THE FUTURE

Throughout the construction of its 20-story office tower, EMC used the phrase Shaping The Future to bring attention to its new and uniquely shaped building. The building definitely has changed the shape of the Des Moines skyline. At the same time, EMC remains committed to shaping the future for its agents, policy-

holders, and employees. It will continue to do that by providing competitive products, value-added services, and a work environment that encourages employees to seek higher levels of professionalism. For individuals, businesses, and organizations associated with EMC Insurance Companies, the future promises continued growth and success.

DOWNLOADING OF POLICY INFORMATION TO EMC'S AGENTS AND OTHER INFORMATION MANAGEMENT SYSTEMS CONTINUES TO ENHANCE SERVICE LEVELS FOR POLICYHOLDERS. AN INTERNET DELIVERY SYSTEM WILL FURTHER IMPROVE SERVICE AND COMMUNICATIONS TO AGENTS IN THE YEARS AHEAD.

NEUMANN BROTHERS, INC. WAS FOUNDED IN 1912 WHEN 28-YEAR-old Arthur H. Neumann began A.H. Neumann Company. Childs Hall at Des Moines College was the first major commission in a long list of projects completed by his company. ■ After the founder's three brothers completed their college

training in engineering, they came to work for the firm. In 1932, the company was incorporated under the name of Arthur H. Neumann and Brothers. In 1976, the firm's name was shortened to Neumann Brothers, Inc.

The second generation of Neumann leadership continued the building tradition into the mid-1980s. Upon their retirement, the third generation of Neumann builders, C. Arthur Wittmack, Marshall Linn, Scott Linn, and John Neumann, assumed the responsibility for operations.

While Neumann Brothers has always provided its clients with a competitive advantage, the family-oriented philosophies of personal commitment, pride, and integrity have been passed through each generation and remain fundamental hallmarks of the company today.

From its inception, the company has been involved in a wide spectrum of construction projects, including commercial construction; renovation and restoration; construction management; and industrial work such as heavy equipment setting, rigging, and millwright work. Neumann also continues to offer pre-engineered buildings as a Butler Building Systems dealer/builder.

Des Moines is Neumann Brothers' home. Although the company has completed projects in California, Louisiana, Florida, and other states, the company's efforts have always been focused in central Iowa.

As Barbara Beving Long writes in her book *Des Moines and Polk County: Flag on the Prairie*, "Neumann Brothers, Inc. has given Des Moines its skyline—starting in 1924 with the state's first 'sky scraper,' the 19-story Equitable Building, to the 36-story Ruan Center, the Marriott Hotel, American Republic Insurance Company, and the domed Botanical Center." The firm's history of shaping Des Moines' skyline continues today, with the recently completed, $54 million EMC Insurance Company's 700 Walnut building and Meredith Corporation's $26 million 1615 Locust corporate expansion project. This landmark entrance or "gateway" to downtown Des Moines

NEUMANN BROTHERS, INC.'S HISTORY OF SHAPING DES MOINES' SKYLINE CONTINUES TODAY, WITH THE RECENTLY COMPLETED, $54 MILLION EMC INSURANCE COMPANY'S 700 WALNUT BUILDING (TOP) AND MEREDITH CORPORATION'S $26 MILLION 1615 LOCUST CORPORATE EXPANSION PROJECT (BOTTOM).

from the west was completed in spring 1998. Both of these Neumann Brothers projects are innovative in their design, materials, applications, and construction techniques.

Evidence of Neumann Brothers' growth and diversity can be seen not only in downtown Des Moines, but throughout the metropolitan area and beyond. Jobs with Maytag Corporation in Newton and Central College in Pella, as well as projects in Leon, Fort Dodge, Ames, Ankeny, Dallas Center, Dubuque, and other Iowa towns, show Neumann's ability to be competitive in all Iowa markets.

Neumann Brothers continues as one of Iowa's premier renovation and restoration contractors, with projects including Grand View College Old Main, Terrace Hill (the governor's mansion), and Drake University. The Iowa State Capitol Building 17-year, multiphased, $60 million restoration project has drawn attention and praise from across the nation.

Neumann Brothers is at the forefront of the industry in utilizing innovative delivery systems, from design/build to program management. The company's approach to projects creates a win-win environment through partnering to maximize overall project success.

Neumann Brothers' expertise in construction management has led to many successful projects, including consecutive, multi-million-dollar construction management contracts with the Des Moines Public Schools.

Jobs from under $50,000 to more than $50 million get the same attention from the builders on the Neumann Brothers team. Architects and clients alike benefit from the firm's use of Timberline estimating and Primavera scheduling. These state-of-the-art systems ensure that accurate and complete information is used on every project.

Author Long writes, "Since 1912, Neumann Brothers, Inc. has kept pace with the demands of changing times. Neumann Brothers is a 'new' company with a proud Des Moines heritage." As always, Neumann Brothers offers its clients advantages that become benefits.

As Barbara Beving Long writes in her book *Des Moines and Polk County: Flag on the Prairie*, "Neumann Brothers, Inc. has given Des Moines its skyline—starting in 1924 with the state's first 'sky scraper,' the 19-story Equitable Building, to the 36-story Ruan Center [left], the Marriott Hotel, American Republic Insurance Company, and the domed Botanical Center [right]."

The Iowa State Capitol Building 17-year, multiphased, $60 million restoration project has drawn attention and praise from across the nation (left).

Neumann Brothers is at the forefront of the industry in utilizing innovative delivery systems, from design/build to program management, such as in the Prairie Meadows casino project (right).

FTER MORE THAN 80 YEARS OF PROVIDING CARE, DES MOINES General Hospital continues its mission to provide the best-quality health care services for the community. Located near the Iowa State Capitol Building, the private, nonprofit hospital is a health care leader in central Iowa. Today,

CLOCKWISE FROM TOP:
LOCATED NEAR THE IOWA STATE CAPITOL BUILDING, DES MOINES GENERAL HOSPITAL IS A HEALTH CARE LEADER IN CENTRAL IOWA.

PATIENTS ARE MONITORED THROUGHOUT THEIR HYPERBARIC OXYGEN THERAPY, AN EFFECTIVE TREATMENT FOR HARD-TO-HEAL WOUNDS.

THE NEWLY REMODELED NURSES STATION SERVING THE MEDICAL/SURGICAL/PEDIATRIC UNIT PROVIDES STATE-OF-THE-ART WORK AREAS FOR PROFESSIONALS AND OPEN ACCESSS TO CAREGIVERS FOR PATIENTS AND THEIR FAMILIES.

TERRANCE KURTZ, D.O., MEDICAL DIRECTOR OF THE HYPERBARIC MEDICINE CENTER OF IOWA, AND JULIE ROONEY, R.N., PREPARE A PATIENT TO RECEIVE HYPERBARIC OXYGEN THERAPY AT DES MOINES GENERAL HOSPITAL.

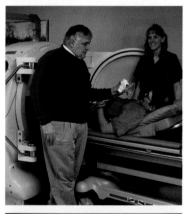

the teaching hospital offers a comprehensive range of medical services through a staff of caring professionals.

National Reputation for Excellence

Des Moines General's reputation as a nationally recognized teaching institution began soon after its inception in 1916. The hospital represents the second organized osteopathic hospital in the nation. Currently it is affiliated with the University of Osteopathic Medicine and Health Sciences in Des Moines, and attracts medical professionals from across the country.

The 226-bed hospital offers a complete range of services, from emergency room to obstetrics to open-heart surgery. Patients stay in newly remodeled private rooms and suites, and the obstetrics wing includes private childbirth rooms. A variety of inpatient and outpatient services are available, including cardiac diagnostic and rehabilitation services. The hospital backs up its medical procedures with the latest in technology, ensuring that patients receive individualized attention while experiencing the best care. Most recently, the hospital has expanded its specialty programs and added family medical clinics

to provide more locations for complete and convenient health care around the Des Moines metropolitan area.

Strong Specialty Programs

Des Moines General offers a wide selection of care options to older Iowans. The Geropsychiatric Partial Hospitalization Program allows patients to participate in intensive therapy and support systems while continuing to live at home. Professionals trained to assist with difficulties common to older adults—such as the loss of a loved one and physical limitations—staff the program. Connections, a 20-bed unit within the hospital, is designed to help patients with mental health problems return to a normal lifestyle. In addition, the Memory Diagnostic Center provides evaluation of chronic forgetfulness, which can be caused by more than 70 medical conditions. The comprehensive evaluation includes diagnosis and recommendations from the neurologist and evaluation team.

The Lil' General Sick Bay serves younger patients. Since 1985, the hospital has operated a progressive licensed facility that offers short-term care for children aged six weeks to 16 years who are too sick to attend school or day care, but not sick enough to be in the hospital.

Another specialty program, BetterCare Diabetes Center, provides comprehensive inpatient and outpatient care for people with the disease. BetterCare patients have access to the hospital's renowned Wound Care Center® of Iowa, which treats hard-to-heal wounds. The Hyperbaric Medicine Center provides hyperbaric oxygen therapy, which promotes healing, to patients of the Wound Care Center and other hospital patients.

Gateway Centers provide drug, alcohol, and gambling addiction treatment programs to more than 1,200 patients a year. The comprehensive program assists family members with addiction-related issues. Former Governor and U.S. Senator Harold Hughes, who founded the center, first introduced separate men's and women's recovery units. Additionally, Gateway provides separate-sex halfway houses to help patients who are dealing with addictions.

Des Moines General plans to continue its legacy of excellence through ongoing reinvestment in high-tech equipment, quality facilities, and niche programs. With its staff of dedicated health care professionals and its extensive range of programs, the hospital will serve Iowans and their families with superior health care services well into the new millennium.

BROADLAWNS MEDICAL CENTER'S HISTORY DATES BACK TO 1913, when the Iowa legislature authorized Polk County, among other counties, to care for tuberculosis patients residing within that county. With the encouragement of the Iowa State Tuberculosis Association (now the American Lung Association of Iowa), Polk County residents approved the bond issue needed to build a new hospital. A tract of land at 18th Street and Hickman Road was purchased for $64,000. Construction began in 1922, and the hospital opened in April 1924. The first buildings consisted of a 60-bed tuberculosis unit and a 30-bed nurses' dormitory.

Seventy-five years later, the small hospital has evolved into Broadlawns Medical Center, a general medical and psychiatric hospital with a licensed bed capacity of 200. During the 1996-1997 fiscal year, the hospital admitted more than 5,000 inpatients and treated nearly 200,000 outpatients. The pharmacy filled almost 300,000 prescriptions, more than 500 babies were born, and more than $30 million in free services were provided to people with limited financial resources.

COMPASSION FOR THE NEEDY

Today, 18 percent of Broadlawns' revenue is derived from Medicare or Medicaid, while 36 percent comes from Polk County taxes in response to health care needs of residents otherwise unable to afford care. Among the many services the center provides are primary and family health care, a homeless outreach program, telephone and walk-in crisis care, family planning, a nutritional program that supplies grocery vouchers for women and children, and a full range of specialty clinics.

The hospital's dental clinic offers both routine and emergency dental care, as well as specialized services for patients with AIDS. In 1979, Broadlawns opened a federally funded community health center to serve the growing number of people using the hospital's emergency department as their main source of medical care.

REACHING OUT TO POLK COUNTY

Broadlawns' extensive mental health services include programs of crisis intervention; intensive case management; and inpatient, day, and outpatient programs for adults and adolescents. Chemical dependency services are available through a walk-in center or outpatient treatment programs.

Medical graduates from around the world vie each year for 30 positions in Broadlawns Medical Center's Family Practice Residency Program and four positions in its Transition Residency Programs. In addition, each year, nearly 300 health professional students from more than 20 colleges and universities receive applied instruction in nursing, music therapy, social work, psychology, dentistry, and other health care professions.

Broadlawns Medical Center is administered by a volunteer, seven-member, nonpartisan governing board elected by and accountable to the citizens of Polk County.

The center is fully accredited by the Joint Commission on Accreditation of Healthcare Organizations (JCAHO) and the American Council on Graduate Medical Education.

As a public hospital, Broadlawns is challenged to use its resources efficiently while dealing with an increasing number of patients with complex health concerns. The administration, physicians, and staff are committed to working even harder in the future to serve Polk County residents who choose Broadlawns Medical Center as their source for health care.

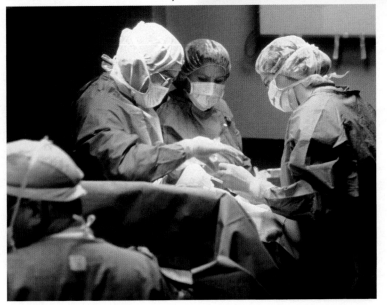

DURING THE 1996-1997 FISCAL YEAR, BROADLAWNS ADMITTED MORE THAN 5,000 INPATIENTS AND TREATED NEARLY 200,000 OUTPATIENTS. THE PHARMACY FILLED ALMOST 300,000 PRESCRIPTIONS, MORE THAN 500 BABIES WERE BORN, AND MORE THAN $30 MILLION IN FREE SERVICES WERE PROVIDED TO PEOPLE WITH LIMITED FINANCIAL RESOURCES.

AS A PUBLIC HOSPITAL, BROADLAWNS IS CHALLENGED TO USE ITS RESOURCES EFFICIENTLY WHILE DEALING WITH AN INCREASING NUMBER OF PATIENTS WITH COMPLEX HEALTH CONCERNS.

IN A WORLD OF BANKING MEGA-MERGERS AND RESULTANT NAME CHANGES, one Des Moines financial institution is standing firm—and remaining independent. Bankers Trust Company, Iowa's oldest and largest autonomous bank, offers its customers a bold guarantee: It will never change its name. In fact, its conviction is so strong that the

company has vowed to pay each account holder $100 if it ever does alter its moniker. But that's typical of Bankers Trust and its efforts to promote commitment and pride in the Iowa region.

For more than 80 years, Bankers Trust has cultivated an image to match its name: a bank customers can trust. Because of that ongoing feeling of security, more than 100 current account holders have been customers for 50 years or longer. Founded in 1917, Bankers Trust Company originally opened for business at the southwest corner of Fifth and Walnut streets. The bank moved to the northwest corner of Sixth and Locust streets

in 1920, and remained in that location until establishing its present office in the Ruan Center in 1975.

Eight branches now serve Bankers Trust customers in the Greater Des Moines area. They include locations on the downtown skywalk and a downtown motor bank, as well as sites in Grimes, Windsor Heights, and Clive, and offices on Merle Hay Road, East Euclid Avenue, and East Army Post Road.

EIGHT DECADES OF TRUST

Bankers Trust's reputation for reliability has been well earned. In 1933, in the wake of widespread bank failures, President Franklin D. Roosevelt ordered a one-week, nationwide moratorium on banking. During that time, Bankers Trust arranged for an examination of its records by federal authorities and became one of only two banks in the state given immediate clearance from officials to reopen.

The Federal Reserve continually awards the bank an Outstanding rating for its Community Rein-

vestment Act programs, and Bauer Financial Reports has assigned it a Five Star Superior rating. Sheshunoff Information Services includes Bankers Trust in its *Highest-Rated Banks in America*, a nationally recognized measurement of a bank's safety and soundness. The *Wall Street Journal*'s *Smart Money* ranked Bankers Trust as one of the Country's Best Banking Deals, comparing the fees of 800 banks nationwide and choosing the 20 best deals for consumers.

Bankers Trust's solid stature remains an attractive asset to customers seeking stability in the fast changing world of banking. As a result, in 1997, Bankers Trust opened 2,300 new accounts in a 10-month span.

While Bankers Trust is a local bank with local management, it is linked to international networks that give customers access to investment and electronic funds transfer services. Customers can use its automated teller machines (ATMs) at thousands of Cirrus network stations internationally. Bankers Trust's International

BANKERS TRUST COMPANY'S EXECUTIVE OFFICES AND SKYWALK BRANCH ARE LOCATED DOWNTOWN IN THE RUAN CENTER (LEFT).

THE BANKERS TRUST SENIOR MANAGEMENT TEAM INCLUDES (FROM LEFT, STANDING) ROBERT DEWAAY, PAUL ERICKSON, DARRELL HUGHES, RENEE HARDMAN, KIP ALBERTSON, AND (SEATED) J. MICHAEL EARLEY (RIGHT).

BANKERS TRUST REACHES BEYOND
PROVIDING VALUABLE, HIGH-QUALITY FI-
NANCIAL SERVICES TO ITS CUSTOMERS
BY PARTICIPATING IN COMMUNITY OR-
GANIZATIONS THROUGH ITS CORPORATE
CONTRIBUTIONS PROGRAM.

Department helps customers manage foreign currency transactions throughout the world. Its Trust Division works with a constant flow of information from local and international investment centers so trust officers can track the value of an investment minute by minute.

Community Activity

Bankers Trust reaches beyond providing valuable, high-quality financial services to its customers by participating in community organizations through its corporate contributions program.

In 1996, Bankers Trust, in partnership with the Oakridge Neighborhood, created a summer jobs program. During the eight-week program, eight Des Moines teens spent their mornings learning better communication, computer, and interviewing skills,

and their afternoons working for various businesses. The program earned an Excellence in Community Service Award from the Iowa Bankers Association.

Based on the bank's accomplishments in recruiting and promoting minority employees, the National Association for the Advancement of Colored People (NAACP) named Bankers Trust its 1996 Merit Employer of the Year, and the company earned the Employer of the Year Award from the Business and Professional Women of Des Moines. In addition, the Des Moines Better Business Bureau presented Bankers Trust its inaugural Integrity Award for the bank's ethical business practices, and the company finished as one of the top three finalists in the nation for the Better Business Bureau's Torch Award for Marketplace Ethics.

Redefining Banking

Customers of Bankers Trust have grown accustomed to the friendly, reliable, personal service that is the bank's trademark. But those methods have evolved into a new concept that Bankers Trust hopes will redefine banking in the Midwest and set the tone for the entire banking industry. Called "relationship banking," it means traditional teller lines are being replaced with account representatives at individual desks who personally handle all transactions, from simple deposits to consumer loans and investments.

From a strong, proud past, Bankers Trust has emerged as a leader in the future of Des Moines' banking industry. More than ever before, the company's efforts toward and commitment to high-quality service have defined it as a bank customers can trust.

O NE OF THE MOST WIDELY RECOGNIZED AND RESPECTED business names in Iowa, Farm Bureau takes on a variety of meanings for the people it serves. To more than 158,000 farm member families throughout the state, Farm Bureau first signifies a general farm organization that

was formed in 1918 and remains dedicated to improving net farm income and quality of life. To these member families, Farm Bureau also means a voluntary, grassroots organization that represents the interests and concerns of farmers, and offers members access to a wide variety of programs and services. These include leadership development, marketing education/information, and state and national affairs.

To sharp investors, analysts, and stockbrokers, Farm Bureau may mean the New York Stock Exchange symbol FFG. It represents this dynamic organization's holding company, FBL Financial Group, Inc., whose stock was made public in 1996.

And for hundreds of thousands of families throughout Iowa and 14 other states, Farm Bureau may mean a relationship with Farm Bureau Financial Services, the affiliated insurance companies that

Since 1974, the headquarters for more than 1,200 Farm Bureau employees and 1,800 Farm Bureau Financial Services agents and managers has been just off Interstate 80/35 on University Avenue in West Des Moines.

function as a servicing organization for the Farm Bureau Federation. Over the past half century, Farm Bureau Financial Services has grown in breadth and scope to serve the members of the Farm Bureau with life insurance, disability income insurance, mutual funds, annuities, and property-casualty insurance.

In any case, the companies affiliated with the Iowa Farm

Bureau Federation have earned widespread respect.

WEST DES MOINES HEADQUARTERS

S ince 1974, the headquarters for more than 1,200 Farm Bureau employees and 1,800 Farm Bureau Financial Services agents and managers has been just off Interstate 80/35 on University Avenue in West Des Moines. Its 430,000-square-foot office is located on a 70-acre campus, and includes an 8,235-square-foot conference center with a 146-seat auditorium, a day care center that can accommodate up to 135 children, and a wellness facility with exercise equipment, a running track, and basketball and volleyball courts. A 243,000-square-foot addition to the original structure was completed in 1989 to allow for planned growth.

STRENGTH AND STABILITY FOR THE FUTURE

F arm Bureau Financial Services is comprised of seven insurance companies, including the original provider of property-casualty protection to farmers, Farm Bureau Mutual Insurance Company. Other property-casualty operations include South Dakota

Over the past half century, Farm Bureau Financial Services has grown in breadth and scope to serve members and customers with property-casualty insurance, life insurance, disability income insurance, annuities, and mutual funds.

MAXIMIZING GROWTH THROUGH STRONG ALLIANCES

Building quality relationships—whether they involve employees, customers, or outside financial organizations—has been a standard for Farm Bureau Financial Services since its inception. It is also the organization's focus for the future. Farm Bureau Financial Services assumes a proactive posture in seeking ways to secure and retain Farm Bureau members, while supporting the goals of the organization and enhancing the quality of life for its customers. It takes care to recognize the dignity and value, as well as the needs, of each participating individual—members, policyholders, shareholders, agents, and employees.

Teamwork is essential to the success of the Farm Bureau companies and to the success of its associates. They are knowledgeable and competent, and conduct themselves with integrity as representatives of the Farm Bureau companies and the insurance and financial services industries. They also demonstrate leadership as responsive and reliable corporate citizens within their communities.

Farm Bureau Financial Services is proud of its long tradition of dependability and service. In a dynamic financial services marketplace that is increasingly competitive, the company's focus on its core competencies, and its ability to leverage those strengths, postures it well for continued vitality and growth.

Farm Bureau Mutual Insurance Company, Utah Farm Bureau Insurance Company, Western Agricultural Insurance Company, and Western Farm Bureau Mutual Insurance Company. On a statutory basis, total assets for the five property-casualty companies exceed $656 million, and funds for the protection of policyholders have grown to $320 million.

Farm Bureau Financial Services also includes Farm Bureau Life Insurance Company and Western Farm Bureau Life Insurance Company. These companies sell universal life insurance, variable universal life insurance, traditional life insurance, disability income insurance, and traditional and variable annuity products to Farm Bureau members and other individuals and businesses. Together, on a statutory basis, these companies have assets exceeding $3.1 billion and represent life insurance in force of more than $18 billion. In 1997, policyholder benefits totaled $261.2 million, and dividends totaled $35.6 million.

Originally called Iowa Life, Farm Bureau Life Insurance Company was founded in 1945 after the

Iowa Farm Bureau Federation had witnessed the early success of its property and casualty lines. With a part-time sales force of local member farmers known and trusted in their communities, the life insurance company set early sales records.

Since that time, the company has given consistent and careful attention to the development of a diverse product portfolio. Meeting the needs of members and customers with innovative products and services that can help them plan for a future that is financially secure has been, and continues to be, the highest priority.

FROM A SETTING WHERE BUSINESS HAS LONG BEEN CONDUCTED ON A HANDSHAKE, THIS COMPANY HAS DEVELOPED A REPUTATION THAT IT CHERISHES AND PROTECTS—A REPUTATION BASED ON HONESTY, INTEGRITY, AND FAIR DEALING.

TO MORE THAN 158,000 FARM MEMBER FAMILIES THROUGHOUT THE STATE, FARM BUREAU FIRST SIGNIFIES A GENERAL FARM ORGANIZATION THAT WAS FORMED IN 1918 AND REMAINS DEDICATED TO IMPROVING NET FARM INCOME AND QUALITY OF LIFE.

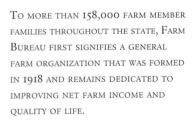

SECURITIES PRODUCTS OFFERED THROUGH EQUITRUST MARKETING SERVICE, INC.

WHEN THE HOTEL FORT DES MOINES OPENED IN 1919, *Hotel World* magazine observed that it included "absolutely everything that could add to the comfort and convenience of guests and promote ease and efficiency in operation." Named for a military fort

built in 1843 near the junction of the Des Moines and Raccoon rivers, the 11-story hotel cost $1.5 million to construct and $350,000 to furnish. Designed by the Des Moines architectural firm of Proudfoot, Bird, and Rawson, it was built by Charles Weitz Sons, General Contractors. The original group of owners included Clyde Herring, later Iowa's governor and a U.S. senator; and Edwin T. Meredith, who went on to become the U.S. secretary of agriculture.

When first constructed, the Hotel Fort Des Moines represented the most modern ideas in American hotel construction and equip-ment. Immediately, it assumed a position as one of the leading hotels of the Middle West.

A CELEBRITY FAVORITE

Within two months of its opening, the Hotel Fort Des Moines hosted Woodrow Wilson, who was the first of 12 presidents to visit the hotel. Through the decades, it has been a favorite overnight stop of government officials, politicians, royalty, and celebrities, including Harry and Bess Truman, John F. Kennedy, Louis Armstrong, Tallulah Bankhead, Count Basie, Tom Brokaw, Yul Brenner, Walter Cronkite, Henry Fonda, Averell Harriman, Helen Hayes, Bob Hope, Sinclair Lewis, Charles Lindbergh, Glenn Miller, Eleanor Roosevelt, Isaac Stern, Ed Sullivan, Elizabeth Taylor, Mae West, and Prince William of Sweden.

Now nearly 80 years old, it is the only Des Moines hotel listed on the National Register of Historic Places. Today, the hotel is locally owned by the Hunter family, who have long been prominent in Des Moines business and real estate. After extensive renovations, the facility now proudly showcases its old-world elegance, which includes rich walnut paneling in the main lobby and the original marble baseboards throughout the hotel. The main marble staircase from the lobby to the second-floor conference rooms is accented with curving brass banisters and intricate wrought iron railings.

It was in the hotel's Grand Ballroom in November 1969 that then-Vice President Spiro Agnew made his famous speech attacking opponents of the Vietnam War as disloyal and accusing television networks of biased news coverage. The Iowa State Democratic Party had its headquarters in the hotel from the mid-1930s to the late 1950s. It was also there that former U.S. ambassador, and later president, George Bush stayed while preparing for his 1980 Iowa presidential caucus, only to be upset by the Republican party favorite, Ronald Reagan. In addition, Nikita Krushchev stayed in the hotel while visiting Iowa to study agricultural methods.

A HISTORY OF HOSPITALITY

Despite its rich heritage, the staff and management of the hotel don't live in the past. Continuing its "history of hospitality," the

THE HOTEL FORT DES MOINES' GRAND STAIRCASE FEATURES THE SAME MARBLE AND WALNUT THAT IS USED THROUGHOUT THE HOTEL'S LOBBY.

facility today offers 240 guest rooms and 55 spacious suites, complete with in-room movies, cable television, room service, valet service, a newsstand, and gift shop. Free shuttle service is available to and from the airport, the downtown Court Avenue area, and the central business district.

Hotel guests have a variety of dining choices, including Landmark Grille, which serves lunch and dinner. The Landmark Grille menu features the finest fresh and seasonal ingredients from the Heartland with international and bistro notes catering to contemporary tastes. The stunning bar restoration features the original cast plaster ceiling, cherry paneling, and a comfortably clubby wine cellar.

The Hotel's coffee shop offers a breakfast buffet with coffee, espresso, cappuccino, and lighter fare available all day in the adjoining coffee bar/newsstand. Patrons can enjoy a quiet cocktail in Chequers Lounge or join the crowd next door to the hotel at Raccoon River Brewing Company for hearty pub fare and a selection of handcrafted beers brewed at the pub.

The Hotel Fort Des Moines also houses an 8,000-square-foot health club that features an indoor lap pool, sauna, whirlpool, and fitness equipment. The hotel's main, second, and third floors are wheelchair accessible, as are additional selected guest rooms.

BALLROOMS TO MEETING ROOMS

In addition to accommodating interesting guests—from movie stars to Iowa high school girls' basketball teams to state dart-throwing champions—the Hotel Fort Des Moines also is a popular place for business meetings and social events. More than 30,000 square feet of meeting and conference space is located on the second and third floors of the hotel. Hundreds of brides and grooms have danced through wedding receptions in its two beautiful ballrooms—each capable of seating up to 800 people or providing banquet accommodations for more than 500 guests. The convention floor also has a 7,000-square-foot exhibit hall, while the state-of-the-art conference level provides more than 9,000 square feet of meeting space with 13 conference rooms and breakout rooms for smaller conferences ranging in size from five to 50 attendees.

Explaining the lasting appeal of the historic establishment, Hotel Fort Des Moines owner Jeff Hunter says, "Not many buildings of our vintage survive in a useful fashion to this day. When you're this old, you'd better be good or you're history. This building has the best of yesterday and today."

THE HOTEL FORT DES MOINES IS IOWA'S LANDMARK HOTEL (LEFT).

THE HOTEL'S 7,000-SQUARE-FOOT FITNESS FACILITY HAS RECEIVED RECOGNITION FOR ITS EXQUISITE DESIGN (RIGHT).

I N 1999, NEWS RADIO WHO-AM 1040 MARKED ITS 75TH ANNIVERSARY as a 50,000-watt powerhouse in the radio industry. The Big Stick has covered most of Iowa during the day, and most of the 48 continental states at night. Known widely as The Voice of the Middle West, WHO has earned far-reaching credibility as an

information source for news, current agricultural data, and Iowa sports coverage.

WHO Radio's long history began in 1924, when it was founded as a 5,000-watt radio station. Originally owned by the Banker's Life Company, the station's unusual call letters were chosen by the company's manager in response to inquiries of "Who is this?" and "Who are we listening to?"

The station was purchased in 1930 by Colonel B.J. Palmer and his son, Dr. David D. Palmer, members of one of America's pioneer broadcasting families. Plans were made for expansion, and in 1933, the FCC allowed WHO to boost its operating power to 50,000 watts, enabling WHO to reach the entire Midwest and far beyond—one of the few

stations in the country to broadcast to such a wide range of listeners. To better serve its enormous new audience, the station created the WHO Radio News Bureau. During World War II, members of the Radio News Bureau brought Iowans on-the-scene accounts of major events, and at night, Iowa soldiers stationed around the world could dial in WHO for a familiar voice from home.

WHO-AM was joined in 1948 by sister station WHO-FM, which played an adult contemporary format. In 1973, the station's old broadcasting equipment was replaced with new, all-stereo equipment, and WHO-FM's call letters were changed to KLYF. Broadcasting at 100,000 watts, KLYF-FM became KMXD in 1998, with its New Mix format featuring ex-

panded music lists (including top hits of the 1970s); local personalities like Kenn McCloud, Rob Olson, Kate Austin, and Greg Chance; frequent remote programs; and popular promotions and contests.

The programming resources of both stations were supplemented by the creation of the Palmer Radio Network in the late 1980s by parent company Palmer Broadcasting Company. With WHO-TV, an NBC affiliate that began telecasting on Channel 13 in 1954, the stations, along with Palmer Broadcasting's corporate headquarters, moved to new facilities on Grand Avenue in 1981. In 1997, Jacor Communications purchased WHO and KMXD. In 1998, WHO and KMXD Mix Radio welcomed KYSY Sunny 106.3 as a third radio station under the same roof.

DECADES OF CREDIBILITY

In the early 1990s, WHO Radio won six Marconi Awards— radio's most prestigious recognition. Determined by peer vote, the Marconi Awards twice cited WHO as Station of the Year for medium-size markets, and once as a Legendary Station.

WHO Radio has a long-standing reputation for providing agricultural news and information. In a state known throughout the world for agriculture, WHO has built a long-term relationship with farmers and related farm industries, and counts farm clients among its top advertisers. Its award-winning Farm Service Department was radio's first full-time organization specializing in agricultural information and service. Today, the National Association of Farm Broadcasters ranks WHO number one among

VAN HARDEN (LEFT) AND BONNIE LUCAS HOST WHO-AM'S POPULAR MORNING SHOW.

all stations and networks with farm audiences.

The station's strong daytime programming includes the locally hosted morning show *Van and Bonnie*; a noontime farm show, *Mark and Gary*; a local call-in talk show with Jan Mickelson; and WHO's original news and feature show, *Drive Time Des Moines with Jerry and Sue*. WHO also features *Dr. Laura* and *Rush Limbaugh*.

WHO continues a long tradition of sports broadcasting, such as play-by-play coverage of the University of Iowa's football and basketball games, the Iowa Barnstormers, and area high-school play-offs.

Parade of Personalities

WHO is proud of its long lists of award-winning broadcast journalists and on-air personalities. In the 1930s, former President Ronald Reagan was the station's first sports director. Reagan did play-by-play broadcasts of college football, and is an Iowa legend for his in-studio re-creations of professional baseball games. The late U.S. Representative H.R. Gross served as one of WHO's news directors. Andy Williams and Roger Williams both won national fame after their early days on WHO.

Today, General Manager Mark Halverson says, like himself, many of WHO's personnel are native Iowans who grew up depending on the station for information and entertainment, and who appreciate the tradition.

Listener Loyalty

WHO Radio enjoys a solid foundation of longtime listeners, and plans to expand in response to that loyalty. Halverson says that six years of record financial performance were made possible by a great programming team and a sales force that sells custom ideas and solutions rather than just great ratings. Growth in the areas of news and sports franchises and the further establishment of KMXD as Des Moines' personality-

driven music station and KYSY Sunny 106.3 as the premier, Soft Favorites-format station are part of the company's future.

The stations are developing databases that will help provide more effective results for advertisers. Advertising airtime is sold by the stations' marketing consultants, who are trained to consult with clients, providing their expertise in advertising. Focusing on the creative elements of good commercials, they encourage advertisers to describe their unique features. As a result, the sale of airtime from 1992 to 1997 increased by at least $3 million in total revenue growth. The employees know they make a difference and contribute to the stations' goals.

As more Iowa cornfields turn into housing subdivisions, and as

Greater Des Moines continues to prosper, radio stations WHO-AM 1040, KMXD-FM 100.3, and KYSY-FM 106.3 will remain as flagships, serving residents as a dependable source for local, world, and agricultural news; sports coverage; and locally produced entertainment.

Known widely as The Voice of the Middle West, WHO Radio has earned far-reaching credibility as an information source for news, current agricultural data, and Iowa sports coverage (top).

Ronald "Dutch" Reagan was sports director at WHO Radio from 1932 to 1937 (bottom).

THE LAST THING HOLMES, MURPHY & ASSOCIATES, INC., SETS OUT to do is to simply sell insurance. Rather, the company takes a partnership approach to serving the risk-management needs of a long list of blue-chip companies. The approach has been so successful that it has propelled the Des Moines-based

firm into the top 40 insurance brokers in North America, based on *Business Insurance* magazine's ranking. Holmes Murphy is the largest independent broker of insurance in the state.

Thousands of companies throughout the nation turn to Holmes Murphy for commercial property and casualty insurance, loss-control consulting, contract surety bonds, group employee benefits, and employment and personnel practices. As a result, the firm has grown to include offices in three states—Iowa, Illinois, and Texas.

BORN OF OPTIMISM

Company founder Max L. Holmes was an optimist and an idealist. In 1932, at the height of the Great Depression, he opened his own insurance agency in Des Moines, determined that hard work and dedicated customer service would sustain his business. Within a decade, the Max L. Holmes Agency was known as an authority in the property and casualty insurance field.

J. Raymond Murphy Jr., a former member of The University of Iowa's famous Ironmen football team of 1939, joined the agency as a salesman in 1948. By 1951, Murphy had become a partner in the firm, which then operated under the name Holmes Murphy.

During the 1950s, the company broadened its base and became proficient in bonding and construction insurance. In connection with the Iowa State Bar Association, Holmes Murphy provided a benefits package designed for the law association. The firm also launched the development of its

Employee Benefit Department, which became an integral part of Holmes Murphy's business.

The thriving agency continued to grow, handling the insurance needs of several of Des Moines' largest employers. During the 1960s, four new partners were brought into the firm: Harry S. Barrows and Robert A. Dee in 1962; Roy L. Heggen in 1967; and Richard J. Noyce in 1969.

In 1971, the firm incorporated under the name Holmes, Murphy & Associates. Ownership rests with 10 shareholders, who earned their positions through years of service as successful sales representatives and leaders. The average age of the current shareholders, who also serve as the board of directors, is just over 40. Clients will benefit from this consistent, committed leadership team for many years to come.

EXPECTATION OF EXCELLENCE

Before Holmes Murphy writes an insurance plan, a team is assembled that specializes in the client's industry. That team, which includes an account executive, an account manager, a claim consultant, and a loss-control specialist, closely examines client needs to determine the most appropriate means of insurance protection. The team then partners with the client to correct unsafe workplace procedures, negate potential injuries, and organize safe, efficient company operations.

Holmes Murphy's reach goes far beyond central Iowa. The firm's clients own large manufacturing facilities and have permanently stationed employees on every continent of the world. Holmes Murphy's world network includes more than a dozen international experts, each with an area of

LEADING THE WAY ARE HOLMES MURPHY'S TOP EXECUTIVE OFFICERS (FROM LEFT): J. DOUGLAS REICHARDT, CHAIRMAN AND CEO, HOLMES, MURPHY & ASSOCIATES, INC.; JAMES S. SWIFT, PRESIDENT, HOLMES MURPHY/IOWA; AND NICKOLAS J. HENDERSON, PRESIDENT AND CHIEF OPERATING OFFICER, HOLMES, MURPHY & ASSOCIATES, INC.

specialization, and a network of 161 affiliate brokers in 91 countries around the globe. These professionals, with more than 200 years of international risk-management experience, are available at any time to help clients with their account management issues. The affiliate brokers provide on-the-ground professionals in foreign countries to help clients solve local problems with local experts, while the firm's Des Moines account executives and account managers coordinate the process to build consistent coverage worldwide at a lower cost for customers.

For more than 60 percent of its clients, Holmes Murphy not only handles risk management, but also designs and implements employee benefit programs. The agency also specializes in the issuance of contractors' surety bonds, largely to Iowa-based highway construction and building trades clients, and is among the top 10 percent of surety bond producers in the United States. The most recent addition to Holmes Murphy was the formation of the Business & Financial Services department. Through HMA Financial Services, Inc., the agency addresses the financial security needs of the firm's business and personal clients using investment and insurance solutions. Holmes Murphy's desire to proactively diversify and grow this dynamic area led to the firm's alliance with one of the largest life insurance agencies in the country, Principal Financial Group-Des Moines Agency.

COMMUNITY COMMITMENT

Holmes Murphy's corporate culture is based on a feeling of family among its staff and a commitment to the community. In late 1996, the company announced an ambitious goal of doubling agency revenue within five years, while reinforcing its position as a closely held private firm.

Holmes Murphy's 250 employees eagerly follow the example of community involvement set long ago by its founders and participate in Big Brother programs, school activities, and numerous church and civic boards. Holmes Murphy sponsors needy families and prepares meals for the homeless on an ongoing basis. The United Way has awarded Holmes Murphy its highest recognition as an employee group that best exemplifies a spirit of community commitment and leadership. Holmes Murphy was also honored as the 1997 Outstanding Company of the Year by Junior Achievement of Central Iowa, Inc.

In relationships with clients, employees, and the community, Holmes Murphy champions the philosophy established by its founders and enhanced by its current leaders: Dedicated people serving people, partners helping partners. Its success in serving and helping is best chronicled by its long-running testimonial campaign, in which "Leaders Acknowledge The Leader: Holmes Murphy."

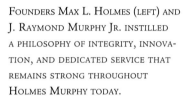

FOUNDERS MAX L. HOLMES (LEFT) AND J. RAYMOND MURPHY JR. INSTILLED A PHILOSOPHY OF INTEGRITY, INNOVATION, AND DEDICATED SERVICE THAT REMAINS STRONG THROUGHOUT HOLMES MURPHY TODAY.

HOLMES MURPHY'S LONG-RUNNING LEADERS CAMPAIGN FEATURES THE TESTIMONIALS OF INDUSTRY LEADERS, INCLUDING DAVID HOAK, CHAIRMAN AND CEO OF WHEELER CONSOLIDATED, INC.; LARRY REELITZ, GENERAL MANAGER OF THE DES MOINES AGENCY OF THE PRINCIPAL FINANCIAL GROUP; AND MARVIN A. POMERANTZ, CHAIRMAN OF GAYLORD CONTAINER CORPORATION.

SIMPLY STATED, THE BUSINESS OF THE VETERANS ADMINISTRATION (VA) Central Iowa Health Care System is to provide health care services to central Iowa veterans who served their country in the armed services. VA Central Iowa Health Care System is the result of the 1997 merger of the Des Moines and Knoxville,

Iowa, VA Medical Centers. This integrated health care system brings two previously separate organizational structures, located 50 miles apart, into one cohesive entity. The system provides a full continuum of health care services to veterans. The Des Moines Division provides acute and specialized medical and surgical services, as well as intensive outpatient treatment programs in substance abuse and post-traumatic stress. The Knoxville Division offers a full range of mental health and long-term care services. Programs are accredited by JCAHO and CARF (rehabilitation).

DEEP ROOTS IN THE GREATER DES MOINES AREA

The Des Moines Veterans Administration Hospital opened in 1934 as a 300-bed facility built on 33 acres of natural timberland on 30th Street. Initially, the staff cared for veterans of the Spanish-American War and World War I with service-connected disabilities.

During World War II, the number of veterans seeking care increased, and the hospital reached its peak employment of 1,801 staff members. Residency training programs were established, and eventually the hospital's educational services grew to compete with surrounding university programs. Today, the center looks for ways to cooperate rather than compete, and is affiliated with other local medical centers in order to provide the most comprehensive range of services possible.

The present site of the Knoxville Veterans Administration Medical Center was first occupied in 1892 as a state-run home for the blind. In 1922, the federal government purchased the 345-acre hos-

pital site from the state, and established the Veterans Hospital as a 125-bed facility. Three years later, 14 new brick buildings and a modern dairy barn were constructed. Two older buildings—now listed on the National Register of Historic Buildings—were remodeled and are still in use today.

By 1944, the Veterans Hospital had grown to 1,540 beds. Much of the original grounds was sold in the 1960s. The site has an award-winning fire station, an education building that was dedicated in 1996, and a new laundry that also provides services for other medical centers in the network.

COMMUNITY NETWORKING

VA Central Iowa Health Care System maintains a close working relationship with other medical facilities, within both the VA and the local community. Every medical skill and diagnostic tool available is accessible by VA patients.

One of the guiding concepts of VA Central Iowa Health Care System is that the hospital is no

longer the hub of activity. In the past, all patients were admitted, and the bed count was the primary measure of the system's complexity. New medical techniques allow shorter lengths of stay, so the focus was shifted to outpatient services. The goal is to care for patients when and where treatment is needed. The VA Clinic-Mason City is an example of this shift in focus. The physician-staffed Primary Medical Care Clinic is a component of VA Central Iowa Health Care System.

A STATE-OF-THE-ART MEDICAL CENTER

Medical science has put new diagnostic tools and treatments in the hands of VA physicians. Computers make medical histories, lab results, and digitally scanned X rays instantly available to specialists at both divisions of the Veterans Administration Central Iowa Health Care System. Video cameras let doctors see patients at both facilities and share diagnoses with consulting physicians.

CLOCKWISE FROM TOP:
MEDICAL SCIENCE HAS PUT NEW DIAGNOSTIC TOOLS AND TREATMENTS IN THE HANDS OF VETERANS ADMINISTRATION (VA) CENTRAL IOWA HEALTH CARE SYSTEM PHYSICIANS. COMPUTERS DIGITALLY SCAN X RAYS INSTANTLY, WHICH ARE THEN AVAILABLE TO SPECIALISTS AT BOTH DIVISIONS.

OUTREACH HEALTH CLINICS ARE CONDUCTED REGULARLY IN AN EFFORT TO TAKE CARE OF VETERANS.

THE BUSINESS OF THE VA CENTRAL IOWA HEALTH CARE SYSTEM IS TO PROVIDE HEALTH CARE SERVICES TO CENTRAL IOWA VETERANS WHO SERVED THEIR COUNTRY IN THE ARMED SERVICES.

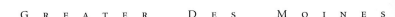

© WAYNE GRITTON | PHOTOGRIFF

◆ © DAMON G. BULLOCK / DIAMOND STAR PHOTOGRAPHY

1935-1997

1946 NCMIC Group, Inc.
1947 John Deere Des Moines Works/John Deere Credit Worldwide
1952 Diamond Animal Health, Inc.
1953 Manpower Inc., of Des Moines
1955 Des Moines Orthopaedic Surgeons
1959 Hy-Vee, Inc.
1960 Forrest & Associate, Inc.
1961 The Mid-America Group
1962 The Atlas Companies
1970 Iowa Heart Center
1971 The Straub Corporation
1972 Gratias Construction Inc.
1973 Triplett Companies
1974 The Associates Credit Card Center
1974 QuikTrip Corporation-Des Moines Division
1975 Atlantic Coca-Cola Bottling Company
1975 Valley West Mall
1978 August Home Publishing Company
1978 Karl Chevrolet Inc.
1981 Business Publications Corporation
1982 Investors Management Group
1984 Meyocks & Priebe Advertising, Inc.
1986 Iowa Kidney Stone Center/Laser Eye Center of Iowa
1988 Kavanaugh Art Gallery
1989 Prairie Meadows Racetrack and Casino
1992 Relationship Marketing
1992 United States Cellular Corporation
1993 The Iowa Clinic, P.C.
1993 Integra Health
1994 Robertson Lowstuter
1996 Commercial Federal Corporation
1997 Asgrow Seed Company LLC
1997 LaSalle National Bank
1997 Mondo's of West Des Moines, Inc.

◆ © MIKE WHYE

STABILITY, EXPERIENCE . . . AND CHANGE. NCMIC GROUP, INC. has changed significantly since National Chiropractic Insurance Company was established by a group of prominent Webster City, Iowa, chiropractors in 1946. More than 50 years later, their legacy continues. ■ Located in West Des

Moines, NCMIC Group has evolved from a mutual insurance company to a mutual holding company that is poised to meet the challenges and expectations of a changing industry and market. National Chiropractic Mutual Holding Company (NCMHC) is the parent company for NCMIC Group and its several subsidiaries, including NCMIC Insurance Company (NCMIC), NFC Finance Corporation (NFC), and TRIAD Healthcare, Inc.

RESPONDING TO CLIENT NEEDS

NCMIC is the nation's oldest provider of chiropractic malpractice insurance, insuring almost one-half of all doctors of chiropractic (D.C.s)—the largest market share in the industry. NCMIC offers malpractice insurance products and services that help to protect and inform practitioners as they provide quality care to their patients. At NCMIC, policyholders can select the type of malpractice coverage that best fits their practice and budget, and NCMIC maintains a nationwide network of highly respected defense attorneys with experience in defending chiropractic malpractice cases. Clients rest easier knowing they're protected by an NCMIC policy.

Another NCMIC Group subsidiary, NFC, has introduced products or nurtured partnerships since 1991 in response to NCMIC policyholders' need to manage their finances. Enterprising products such as credit cards, equipment financing, and NCMIC insurance premium financing have all joined the list of competitive offerings from NFC. In short, NFC's mission is to provide its clients with the credit they deserve.

TRIAD Healthcare, Inc., another NCMIC Group subsidiary, began setting the pace in 1996 with an efficient and accessible managed care network for the chiropractic profession. Focusing on providing quality, access, and choice in managed care, this independent practice association (IPA) network provides the potential for the development of national contracts, covering millions of people, and assures access to chiropractic care for more individuals.

While the company's primary focus remains on providing chiropractic malpractice insurance, NCMIC Group has achieved strategically planned diversification to respond to client needs by pro-

viding cutting-edge insurance, financial, and practice-oriented products and services.

EXCEEDING CLIENT EXPECTATIONS

A progressive, nine-member board of directors, all licensed doctors of chiropractic, directs the organization's efforts that are focused on the team concept. In this unique work environment, employee teams have the authority and skills to make work-flow decisions, allowing them to respond quickly to a client's needs.

In short, NCMIC Group is focused on meeting the competition and exceeding clients' expectations. Altogether, the company's efforts are backed by NCMIC's 50-plus years of experience and service to the chiropractic profession, as well as the confidence of the largest policyholder base in the industry—one that has trusted this company to provide quality malpractice insurance and financial products.

Truly, the company's philosophy and culture relates back to the organization's mission, "We take care of our own," within the chiropractic and health care communities.

NCMIC GROUP IS LOCATED IN WEST DES MOINES. AS THE PARENT COMPANY FOR A GROUP OF DYNAMIC AND INNOVATIVE SUBSIDIARIES, IT IS POISED TO MEET THE CHALLENGES AND EXPECTATIONS OF A CHANGING INSURANCE INDUSTRY AND MARKET (TOP).

A GROWING AND INNOVATIVE COMPANY, NCMIC GROUP'S SUBSIDIARIES PROVIDE CHIROPRACTORS WITH QUALITY INSURANCE PRODUCTS AND FINANCIAL SERVICES. BACKED BY AN OUTSTANDING TEAM OF EMPLOYEES, MANAGEMENT PERSONNEL, AND BOARD OF DIRECTORS, THE COMPANY MISSION IS "WE TAKE CARE OF OUR OWN," WITHIN THE CHIROPRACTIC AND HEALTH CARE COMMUNITIES (BOTTOM).

AFTER WORLD WAR II, THE U.S. GOVERNMENT WAS SADDLED with a surplus of property and equipment that was once essential to the manufacture of wartime goods. To help alleviate the problem, in 1947, the government put up for sale a large ordnance manufacturing plant located

10 miles north of Des Moines.

At the time, Moline-based Deere & Company needed another factory to meet the heavy postwar demand for its farm equipment. So, in September 1947, the company paid the War Assets Administration $4,154,565 for 590 acres of land that included five large buildings, a power plant, a sewage disposal plant, and various smaller structures. The company renamed the facility, now part of Ankeny, the John Deere Des Moines Works.

IMPLEMENTS AND INNOVATION

Deere & Company, founded in 1837 in Grand Detour, Illinois, grew from the one-man shop of a young blacksmith named John Deere into a worldwide corporation that today conducts business in more than 160 countries, manufactures products in 11 countries, and employs more than 35,500 people. It manufactures, distributes, and finances a full line of agricultural equipment, as well as a broad range of construction, forestry, commercial, and consumer equipment. Support operations include parts and engines. Additionally, the company's financial services organization offers

credit, insurance products, and managed health care plans.

A 226 Corn Picker was the first implement off the assembly line at the John Deere Des Moines Works, and several years later, the redesigned 227 Corn Picker became the first machine completely designed and built at the plant. During the 1950s, the facility added cotton pickers, beet harvesters, sorting carts, cultivators, rotary hoes, rod weeders, potato planters, and diggers to its list of products.

After 1980, the Des Moines Works' most profitable year, a downturn in the overall farm economy and the advent of personal computers brought an era of downsizing for the factory. Even so, by 1989, it had designed and produced a state-of-the-art, self-propelled cotton picker, as well as grain drills, grinder mixers, rotary hoes, seeders, field cultivators, disks, plows, and other farm equipment. Today, the factory manufactures all of Deere's tillage implements, grain drills, and cotton harvesting equipment, and has design responsibility for a line of self-propelled sprayers.

A MAJOR EMPLOYER

When the Des Moines Works began operation in 1947, it had 546 employees. By the end of 1948, the number of wage employees had grown to nearly 1,000. Little more than a decade later, in 1960, the plant was the area's largest employer, with 2,700 employees from 120 communities in central Iowa. Today, the factory employs 1,171 people.

John Deere provides more than a place to work for many employees. Through the years, the company has sponsored athletic leagues for men's softball, women's bowling, women's basketball, and golf.

The Des Moines Works also takes pride in being a good neighbor to the community. After a 1974 tornado struck Ankeny, the factory lent personnel and machines to help with the cleanup operation. In 1991, during the Persian Gulf War, the company's loading dock was used to ship 134 pieces of military equipment being sent from Camp Dodge in Johnston, Iowa, to Fort Irwin, California.

JOHN DEERE DES MOINES WORKS CONTINUES TO EMPHASIZE ITS PURPOSE OF BEING A WORLD-CLASS MANUFACTURER. ITS MISSION IS TO BETTER SERVE ITS CUSTOMERS BY ENGINEERING, MANUFACTURING, AND MARKETING THE HIGHEST-QUALITY PRODUCTS WITH VALUE-ADDED FEATURES, AND TO PROVIDE SUPERIOR CUSTOMER SERVICE (TOP).

JOHN DEERE PRODUCTS—SUCH AS THE 12-ROW, SELF-PROPELLED SPRAYER SHOWN HERE—DEMONSTRATE THE COMPANY'S GOAL TO BE A WORLD-CLASS MANUFACTURER (BOTTOM).

FINANCIAL SERVICES

Most Iowans recognize Deere's familiar slogan, Nothing Runs Like a Deere, and identify it as an agricultural implement manufacturer. But fewer people realize that the firm has another business unit located in the Des Moines area. Des Moines is worldwide headquarters of John Deere Credit (JDC), employing more than 800 Iowans at its facility on 28th Street in West Des Moines, and a total of 1,300 in the United States and five foreign countries.

With nearly $10 billion in assets administered, JDC is one of the leading nonbank providers of equipment financing, and serves more than 500,000 customers annually. JDC also provides financing for recreational vehicles, yachts, manufactured housing, transportation, and equipment manufactured by other companies.

Since 1995, total JDC worldwide revenues have increased by nearly 34 percent, swelling to $822 million in 1997. Net income during the same time grew 22 percent to $147 million, as the franchise expanded beyond the United States and Canada to Mexico, the United Kingdom, Germany, and Australia.

"The hallmarks of a successful finance company go well beyond the measures of portfolio growth and financial returns," says John Volkert, president of John Deere Credit. "Equally important to our heritage is our commitment to our customers and employees, a continued investment in technology and information systems, and the vision of continual process and quality improvement. At John Deere Credit, we continue to invest in all of these important areas and look forward to the benefits they will provide for the entire John Deere organization and our customers in the future."

A BRIGHT FUTURE

In the spring of 1998, Barry Schaffter became general manager of the John Deere Des Moines Works, and is enthused about its future. All of the John Deere Des Moines operations—like the parent Deere & Company—are committed to providing genuine value to the company's stakeholders, including its customers, dealers, shareholders, employees, and communities.

The John Deere Des Moines Works continues to emphasize its purpose of being a world-class manufacturer. Its mission is to better serve its customers by engineering, manufacturing, and marketing the highest-quality products with value-added features, and to provide superior customer service.

BY 1989, JOHN DEERE DES MOINES WORKS HAD DESIGNED AND PRODUCED A STATE-OF-THE-ART, SELF-PROPELLED COTTON PICKER, AS WELL AS GRAIN DRILLS, GRINDER MIXERS, ROTARY HOES, SEEDERS, FIELD CULTIVATORS, DISKS, PLOWS, AND OTHER FARM EQUIPMENT. TODAY, THE FACTORY MANUFACTURES ALL OF DEERE'S TILLAGE IMPLEMENTS AND COTTON HARVESTING EQUIPMENT, AS WELL AS A LINE OF SELF-PROPELLED SPRAYERS.

GEOGRAPHICALLY SPEAKING, DIAMOND ANIMAL HEALTH, INC. IS tucked deep in the heart of Des Moines' industrial area on the east side of town. Within its field, however, the company is located on the cutting edge of biotechnological research. A subsidiary of Heska Corp., Diamond specializes in the contract

manufacturing of animal vaccines for farm and domestic animals. The company also provides a full line of services, from research and development to manufacturing, testing, and distribution of veterinary pharmaceuticals and biological drugs. In addition to its myriad treatments for animals, Diamond is set to branch out into the production of health and personal care products for the consumer market.

The company's winding history began in 1952 under the name of Diamond Labs, L.P., with a handful of veterinarians working on a vaccine for hog cholera. As the research team grew, Diamond expanded to offer a complete line of medicines to meet the health care needs of animals. In 1972, the company was sold to Syntex Corp., which added a pharmaceutical branch to the business. The firm was sold again in 1985, this time to Agrion, which renamed its new subsidiary Diamond Sci-

entific. Four years later, it joined Miles, Inc., until the company decided to consolidate its operations and sell the animal vaccine manufacturer. With the financial assistance of the City of Des Moines and the State of Iowa, an employee-led team bought the company in 1994 and rechristened it Diamond Animal Health, Inc.

In 1996, Diamond merged with Heska Corp., an animal products conglomerate based in Fort Collins. The partnership now enables Diamond to produce vaccines for a number of companies instead of one parent corporation. Between 20 and 25 companies market Diamond's animal medicines in the United States and Canada, and soon its products will be made available to veterinarians in Europe and South America.

Despite the years of changing hands, Diamond Animal Health has continued to evolve and grow, more than doubling its number of employees between 1994 and

1998. Its financial success is equally impressive, with annual revenues of $11 million in 1997 and expected revenues of $14.5 million in 1998. By the end of 1999, the company is anticipating an increase to $20 million. And it won't stop there. Diamond is expected to shine financially through the millennium, with revenues rising $5 million a year. The business is planning to invest millions in facility and capital improvements to keep up with the demand for its products. The firm currently operates with 176,000 square feet in Des Moines and a 180-acre animal research farm near Carlisle.

EXPANDING PRODUCT LINES

As Diamond Animal Health continues to grow, the firm is augmenting its traditional line of biological products by branching into the contract manufacturing of consumer products. The company's full line of manufactured products includes pharmaceuticals;

AS DIAMOND ANIMAL HEALTH, INC. CONTINUES TO GROW, THE FIRM IS AUGMENTING ITS TRADITIONAL LINE OF BIOLOGICAL PRODUCTS BY BRANCHING INTO THE CONTRACT MANUFACTURING OF CONSUMER PRODUCTS.

A HIGHLY TRAINED, WELL-EDUCATED STAFF—INCLUDING A HOST OF BACTERI-OLOGISTS, MICROBIOLOGISTS, CHEMISTS, AND VIROLOGISTS—USES INGENUITY AND INNOVATION TO CREATE NEW, EXCITING MEDICINES TO RELIEVE ILL-NESSES AND PREVENT SICKNESS IN FARM ANIMALS AND DOMESTIC PETS.

over-the-counter soaps or medicines that do not require licensing; general human appearance products; topicals such as creams for animals; dermatological products for animal allergies; and biological products such as vaccines. The firm also engages in animal research to test and prove that products work.

Diamond's expansion into this new territory is led by a four-member executive group that combines manufacturing and research experience for both farm animals and household pets. Lou Van Daele, president and chief executive, leads the team with three vice presidents: Connie Phillips, vice president of operational and strategic planning; Dr. Bill Aitchison, vice president of operations; and Gary Neal, vice president of finance and administration.

In addition to the management team, a highly trained, well-educated staff—including a host of bacteri-ologists, microbiologists, chemists, and virologists—uses ingenuity and innovation to create new, exciting medicines to relieve illnesses

and prevent sickness in farm animals and domestic pets. Diamond has created an entrepreneurial culture that helps the company reach a superior return for shareholders, and build the challenging, exciting, creative environment necessary to create high-quality products today and to develop the medicines of tomorrow.

Contributing to the Community

Diamond Animal Health is a vital component of the Des Moines community for more than its provision of high-skilled jobs. The company donates to charitable groups concerned with the welfare of animals, including the Animal Rescue League of Iowa and Blank Park Zoo in Des Moines. It is a contributing member of the Greater Des Moines Chamber of Commerce and the Iowa Association of Business and Industry. Staff members are also active in community activities such as the annual holiday Toys for Tots campaign, the Better Business Bureau, and a variety of local and

national organizations that support business and the manufacture of animal vaccines.

Always a bold, innovative company, Diamond Animal Health is also a trailblazing presence in biotechnical research, as well as a critical part of Des Moines' economic and social fabric.

LARGE-CAPACITY TANKS ARE AVAILABLE FOR LIQUID PRODUCT MANUFACTURING.

I N 1953, HELEN LYNCH, A NATIVE OF CRAIG, NEBRASKA, ARRIVED IN Des Moines to open a new franchise for a young company that was trying to spread its wings. But being a newcomer to Des Moines didn't stop Lynch from building a successful Manpower franchise, which today is one of the city's largest and most valuable employers.

It began when Lynch was referred by a friend to Manpower International in Milwaukee as a potential franchisee. Impressed with what she heard from the company, she decided to start her own branches of the temporary employment agency. Lynch founded Manpower Inc., of Des Moines, and set the standard of quality for temporary help and staffing in central Iowa.

GROWTH OF AN INDUSTRY

Lynch, president and owner of Manpower, has witnessed her company grow as it has adapted to the needs of its customers. The company started by offering secretarial services, and soon after began matching applicants and employers in the light industrial area. The business expanded to include a technical and professional services division in the mid-1970s, and a training services division in the early 1980s. Today, Manpower provides staffing solutions from traditional needs to on-site management for employers in office, industrial, technical, and training atmospheres. Manpower helps large, medium, and small companies across all industries, from insurance to manufacturing.

As the company has helped its corporate customers to grow, Manpower has also grown. Early on, the firm expanded to meet the needs of central Iowa by opening offices in the surrounding communities of West Des Moines, Ankeny, Ames, and Fort Dodge, and also maintains on-site offices at some client companies. Sales doubled in the two-year period preceding 1998. Lynch's eldest son, Michael, also joined the company in 1981 and has since become vice president. Helen's younger son, Doug, has been with Manpower since 1988 and has been very instrumental in developing the company's technical division. Other key members of the team who have helped guide the company's growth include Eric Zingler, executive vice president, with Manpower since 1975, and Gini Wolf, on-site manager, with Manpower since 1977. Dedicated staff in all facets of the business ensure that Helen Lynch's vision will be carried on for decades.

Manpower uses cutting-edge technology to keep itself, as well as its professional employees, ahead of the competition. The Des Moines franchise was one of the first Manpower offices to heavily invest in computer technology, sharing its employee database with all central Iowa offices. The company also offers Internet recruiting, an increasingly important job-search tool. Plus, Manpower employees have access to the resources of the world's largest—and leading—staffing firm and all the perks that are associated with being a franchise of Manpower International.

FINDING THE BEST MATCH

A variety of people seek employment with Manpower. They include those who are reentering the workforce, those who are making the transition from one field of work to another, students, people who are new to town or new to the workforce, and those seeking to upgrade their skills. Manpower

MANPOWER INC., OF DES MOINES PROVIDES QUALITY TRAINING TO ITS EMPLOYEES TO EQUIP THEM WITH THE SKILLS NEEDED TO DELIVER EXCEPTIONAL SERVICE.

PAUL GATES

▲ PAUL GATES

meets the needs of its applicants with temporary help positions, temporary-to-hire positions, and permanent placement. An equal opportunity employer, the company annually provides jobs to more than 3,000 men and women over the age of 18.

Manpower utilizes a comprehensive skill assessment process to learn not only an applicant's job-related skills, but also that person's likes, dislikes, hobbies, and recreational activities. This helps to ensure a good match between the prospective employer and the Manpower employee. Manpower treats each placement as an opportunity not only to satisfy a client needing an employee, but also as a chance to enrich the life of the Manpower applicant.

Manpower extends its placement capabilities by providing specialized training to its applicants free of charge. Training can be obtained in areas such as computer software, quality control, customer service, computer programming, and other fields. The help and training available through Manpower often

enable applicants to move into permanent employment.

STRIVING TOWARD EXCELLENCE
Since its beginnings, Manpower has adhered to its original goal of setting the standard of quality for temporary help and staffing with its professionally trained and knowledgeable staff in central Iowa. Still locally owned and operated, the firm takes its philosophy seriously, attaining internationally recognized standards of excellence, such as ISO 9002 certification, and using the Predictable Performance System to ensure that Manpower matches the most qualified person to the position and that the person is successful in his or her new position once placed. "This is an extremely rewarding business because we have an opportunity to positively impact everyone whose lives we touch," says Michael Lynch.

Manpower has an ongoing commitment to the community through its work with United Way and its efforts to educate

members of the community on how to find employment. Manpower personnel donate time and resources to high school school-to-work programs, community colleges, and social programs designed to help people become work ready, such as the YWCA Des Moines Register Learning Center. The company came to the community's aid in a different way during an especially crucial time of need: after the devastating 1993 flood, Manpower found hundreds of men and women to help repair the damage left behind.

The high quality and professionalism of Manpower employees have won the company repeated recognition by local and national media, which label the firm the city's largest and most admired staffing firm. The weekly *Des Moines Business Record*'s readers voted the firm Best of Des Moines Business for three consecutive years. The community is well served by Manpower, a company that touches the lives of Des Moines' citizens every day.

STATISTICALLY VALIDATED TESTING ENSURES THAT EACH MANPOWER APPLICANT IS EVALUATED FAIRLY AND ACCURATELY (LEFT).

MANPOWER VICE PRESIDENT MICHAEL LYNCH AND MARKETING COORDINATOR CARRIE DINGLE COLLABORATE ON A PROJECT (RIGHT).

IN THE LATE 1930S, DR. DOUGLAS N. GIBSON BECAME THE FIRST orthopedist to establish a practice in Des Moines. One of his early patients was a 12-year-old boy with a broken arm, and Gibson asked the young man what he wanted to be when he grew up. When he replied, "A doctor," Gibson suggested he study orthopedics and

join him in practice someday. In 1955, John H. Kelley, M.D., did just that, and the Des Moines Orthopaedic Surgeons (DMOS) group was founded.

The two were subsequently joined by Ronald K. Bunten, M.D., and Richard C. Johnston, M.D. While those doctors are now retired, the group has grown to include 20 surgeons, all board certified or approved as board eligible by the American Board of Orthopaedic Surgery. These surgeons include Arnis B. Grundberg, M.D.; Joe F. Fellows, M.D.; Douglas S. Reagan, M.D.; Stephen G. Taylor, M.D.; Patrick M. Sullivan, M.D.; Delwin E. Quenzer, M.D.; Daniel J. McGuire, M.D.; Devon D. Goetz, M.D.; Lynn M. Nelson, M.D.; Jeffrey P. Davick, M.D.; Kary R. Schulte, M.D.; Robert F. Breedlove, M.D.; Jeffrey A. Rodgers, M.D.; Matthew J. Weresh, M.D.; Ian Lin,

SINCE MOVING INTO ITS 65,000-SQUARE-FOOT ORTHOPAEDIC CENTER NEAR THE JUNCTION OF INTERSTATES 80 AND 35 IN WEST DES MOINES IN 1994, DMOS HAS BEEN ABLE TO PROVIDE CLINICAL EVALUATION, SURGERY, PHYSICAL THERAPY, AND REHABILITATION IN ONE CONVENIENT LOCATION. THE CENTER INCLUDES 32 EXAM ROOMS, EIGHT CONFERENCE ROOMS, FOUR X-RAY ROOMS, AND AN MRI SUITE WITH THE LATEST TECHNOLOGY IN MRI SCANNERS.

M.D.; David L. Groen, D.P.M.; Julie K. Albrecht, D.P.M.; and K. Linda Bratkiewicz, D.P.M. DMOS physicians have completed residency or specialty training in the field of orthopedic surgery, and

are qualified to handle the full range of orthopedic conditions. They also have completed additional, concentrated training in areas of special interest, including total joint replacement, knee and shoulder surgery, spine surgery, hand and microvascular surgery, fracture and reconstruction surgery, and foot and ankle surgery.

Since moving into its 65,000-square-foot Orthopaedic Center near the junction of Interstates 80 and 35 in West Des Moines in 1994, DMOS has been able to provide clinical evaluation, surgery, physical therapy, and rehabilitation in one convenient location. The center includes 32 exam rooms, eight conference rooms, four X-ray rooms, and an MRI suite with the latest technology in MRI scanners—all located on the first floor for the convenience of patients.

Providing the highest-quality care possible is the primary commitment of all DMOS physicians. Open and spacious, the Orthopaedic Center was designed to be as comfortable and soothing for patients as possible. A focal point

◀ JAMES R. COBB PHOTOGRAPHY

◀ JAMES R. COBB PHOTOGRAPHY

of the facility's reception area is a giant aquarium, which is home to an assortment of vibrantly colored tropical fish.

DMOS physicians provide services at the Orthopaedic Center and at Penn Medical Plaza, along with 20 satellite offices in an 80-mile area surrounding Des Moines. The physicians are on staff at Iowa Methodist Medical Center, Iowa Lutheran Hospital, and Mercy Medical Center.

WORKERS' COMPENSATION SPECIALISTS

D MOS is known for its innovative methods in controlling workers' compensation costs. The group guarantees that urgent medical services will be provided to workers' compensation patients the same day as requested, and that nonemergency services will be scheduled within two to four business days of the initial request.

In addition, a completed patient status report form, outlining return-to-work restrictions, physical therapy instructions, and a treatment plan, is prepared by the surgeon at the conclusion of the office visit. Records are completed within four days of the office visit, and impairment ratings are available 10 to 12 business days from the receipt of the request.

DMOS conducts seminars to educate employers on treatment of workers' compensation patients. The physicians also suggest modified duties for injured workers, in order to reduce time off for patients during their recovery. In some cases, physicians make on-site visits to workplaces to help determine why multiple employees develop similar injuries.

SURGERY, MRI, AND PHYSICAL THERAPY

D MOS physicians conduct about 80 percent of their surgical procedures in three operating rooms at their same-day surgery center, located on the second floor of the Orthopaedic Center. The surgery center

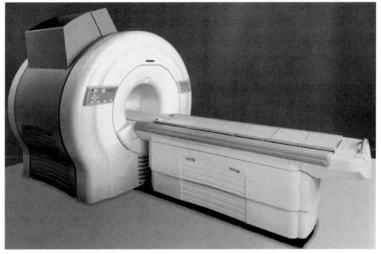

is leased to Iowa Health System, which includes Iowa Methodist Medical Center and Iowa Lutheran Hospital.

Outpatient surgical procedures are more convenient and comfortable for patients and families, and help to contain medical costs. Like the DMOS physicians, the staff of the surgery center specializes in the surgical care of orthopedic patients only.

Recognizing the need for high-quality, convenient MRI scans, DMOS offers a state-of-the-art MRI suite designed with patient comfort, convenience, and image quality in mind. It has always been a high priority of DMOS physicians to provide as many services as possible at the Orthopaedic Center, where they can monitor and improve upon service and quality. The DMOS MRI Center offers a cost-effective, service-oriented option for patients.

Iowa Health System also leases space in the building for physical therapy and hand therapy. The Orthopaedic Therapy Center includes treatment rooms, a well-equipped strengthening and conditioning area, work hardening and assessment equipment, and a classroom. The center's complete rehabilitation program often decreases the time required for resolution of an injury, thus reducing time lost from physical activity and work.

In recent years, DMOS has focused on attracting and retaining

orthopedic surgeons who have subspecialty interests requiring additional fellowship training of one or more years.

The Des Moines Orthopaedic Surgeons Speakers Bureau routinely presents programs on orthopedic and work-related topics to organizations or individual groups concerned about wellness. At its annual KidsFest booth in downtown Des Moines, doctors introduce youngsters to skeletons, X rays, and today's brightly colored choices for casts and tapes.

DMOS serves as team physician to the Iowa Barnstormers arena football team and the Des Moines Buccaneers hockey team. DMOS also is a sponsor of the annual Sports Medicine Symposium, a one-day event addressing sports medicine issues relevant to family practice physicians, residents, coaches, and athletic directors. The program provides guidance for keeping athletes motivated, reducing sports-related injuries, and administering treatment for common sports injuries.

For more than 40 years, Des Moines Orthopaedic Surgeons has maintained a singular mission to provide patients with the highest-quality care possible. As a result of its commitment, DMOS has continued to grow and has earned the respect of patients, insurance companies, employers, and the Des Moines medical community.

HY-VEE, INC. IS AN EMPLOYEE-OWNED RETAIL CORPORATION dedicated to providing shoppers with quality products, low prices, and superior customer service. Since its inception in 1930, the business has focused on a special brand of home-town friendliness—a philosophy that was articulated in 1964

CLOCKWISE FROM TOP RIGHT: CURRENTLY, HY-VEE IS FOCUSING ON BUILDING MODERN STORES OF THE FUTURE, WHERE FRESHNESS, VARIETY, AND ONE-STOP-SHOPPING CONVENIENCE ARE EMPHASIZED.

SINCE ITS INCEPTION IN 1930, THE BUSINESS HAS FOCUSED ON A SPECIAL BRAND OF HOMETOWN FRIENDLINESS— A PHILOSOPHY THAT WAS ARTICULATED IN 1964 WITH THE POPULAR SLOGAN A HELPFUL SMILE IN EVERY AISLE.

TOGETHER WITH THE WEITZ COMPANY, HY-VEE HAS FORMED HY-VEE/WEITZ CONSTRUCTION, A FIRM THAT HANDLES GENERAL CONTRACTING FOR HY-VEE CONSTRUCTION PROJECTS. HY-VEE CHAIRMAN, PRESIDENT, AND CEO RON PEARSON (LEFT) CONFERS WITH CONTRACTORS AT A JOB SITE.

with the popular slogan A Helpful Smile in Every Aisle.

Hy-Vee started out as a partnership between Charles Hyde and David Vredenburg, who operated a general store in Beaconsfield, Iowa. In 1938, the company incorporated as Hyde and Vredenburg, Inc., with 15 stores and 16 employee stockholders. The company's first modern-era supermarket opened in 1949 in Centerville, Iowa, and the name Hy-Vee—a contraction of the founders' names—was selected through an employee contest in 1952.

MORE IN STORE
THAN JUST GROCERIES

Today, Hy-Vee operates 247 retail outlets in Iowa, Illinois, Missouri, Kansas, Nebraska, South Dakota, and Minnesota. With annual sales of nearly $3 billion, Hy-Vee ranks among the top 20 grocery chains in the nation and is listed among the 40 largest private companies in the world. In 1997, readers of *Consumer Reports* magazine rated Hy-Vee among the top five supermarket chains in the country.

Hy-Vee's retail operations include 179 supermarkets, 26 Drug Town stores, and 42 Heartland Pantry convenience stores. The company's corporate offices are located in West Des Moines, with distribution centers in Chariton and Cherokee, Iowa. Together, the two distribution complexes total more than 2 million square feet.

Currently, Hy-Vee is focusing on building modern stores of the future, where freshness, variety, and one-stop-shopping convenience are emphasized. Not only can customers at these stores buy groceries, but also they can fill prescriptions, order flowers, make bank deposits, drop off dry cleaning, and rent videos, as well as purchase housewares, gifts, clothing, cosmetics, pet care products, and lawn and garden supplies.

To support its retail operations, Hy-Vee established a distribution system to deliver the highest-

quality merchandise efficiently to its customers. It also operates subsidiary companies to maintain a more cost-efficient supply of goods to its stores.

Other Hy-Vee holdings include the Midwest Heritage Bank of Chariton; Perishable Distributors of Iowa, a distribution facility for meat, seafood, and ice cream; Lomar Distributing, Inc., which handles specialty foods; D&D Salads, a manufacturing plant; Florist Distributing, Inc.; Meyocks & Priebe Advertising; and Iowa Beverage Manufacturers. Together with the Weitz Company, Hy-Vee has formed Hy-Vee/Weitz Construction, a firm that handles general contracting for Hy-Vee construction projects.

PROUD TO BE
EMPLOYEE OWNED

As Iowa's largest employer, Hy-Vee provides career opportunities for more than 40,000 men and women. Profits are shared with employees through the Hy-Vee Employees Trust Fund and through a bonus and commission system. Bonuses at the retail level are based upon individual store profits.

Every employee contributes to the success of the company. Hy-Vee's outstanding employees have been the force that has transformed it from a single, small-town grocery store to one of the nation's leading supermarket chains.

To absorb future growth and meet increasing challenges from competitors, Hy-Vee will continue to rely on the fundamentals that have made the company a success over seven decades: adhering to the values upon which the company was founded, and meeting the demands of changing consumer lifestyles.

SINCE FOUNDING HIS FIRST BUSINESS NEARLY FOUR DECADES AGO, Marvin A. Pomerantz has maintained the entrepreneurial premise that the products and services offered by his organization should be of the highest quality in any specific field in which the company operates. ■ That philosophy has been the basis for the

evolution of the multifaceted Mid-America Group, now recognized as a premier corporate resource for planning, construction, and management of real estate needs.

The company originated in 1961 as the Great Plains Bag Corp.—a manufacturer of paper and polyethylene bags. Owner Pomerantz built a warehouse for Great Plains' expanding needs, then leased it to a long-term tenant and built a different warehouse. His theory—to construct buildings for a variety of uses, lease them, and build again—led to the formation of Mid-America Development Company in 1972.

Today, The Mid-America Group is an investment holding company focusing on land development; the development, construction, and leasing of prime office buildings and industrial buildings; property management services; corporate relocation and real estate consulting; and residential and commercial real estate brokerage services through Coldwell Banker Mid-America Group, REALTORS®.

COMMERCIAL AND RESIDENTIAL IMPACT

Mid-America owns, operates, or manages more than 1 mil-

lion square feet of industrial space and more than 900,000 square feet of office space. The firm's build-to-suit projects span from Greater Des Moines to Naperville, Illinois, and Jacksonville, Arkansas.

In a joint venture, Mid-America developed Westridge Office Park in West Des Moines, and with Des Moines Northwestern Bell Telephone Company, it built Piekenbrock Work Center. The firm also is the developer of the 44-acre Regency West complex in West Des Moines, Mid-America Business Park in southwest Des Moines, and NorthPark Business Centre in Urbandale.

Subsidiaries concentrate on commercial and residential land development, with covenants dictating land usage and construction accompanying lots for single-family homes in attractive neighborhoods such as The Woodlands, a 155-acre development of tree-lined streets and executive-style, single-family homes in Clive.

CONTAINER INDUSTRY PROMINENCE

Pomerantz and other investors acquired the Arkansas firm of Mid-America Packaging,

Inc. in 1985, and Gaylord Container Limited of Deerfield, Illinois, in 1986. Following a merger of the two in 1988, the new Gaylord Container Corporation became a public company, listed on the American Stock Exchange, with total assets of approximately $800 million.

Pomerantz serves as chairman and CEO of Gaylord Container Corporation, which includes three containerboard and paper mills, 17 corrugated container and sheet plants, two multiwall bag plants, a specialty chemicals facility, and a cogeneration facility. Gaylord employs more than 4,150 people and ranks among the top 10 producers of domestic linerboard and craft paper. It is the 10th largest domestic converter of corrugated containers.

The Mid-America Group owes its success to its dedicated officers and employees. The management team includes Pomerantz, chairman, president, and CEO; David B. Hawkins, vice chairman; Joseph E. Pierce, executive vice president and treasurer; Eric W. Burmeister, vice president and secretary of the board; Michael R. Oliver, telecommunications manager; Dennis J. Tinker, controller; Steven W. Churchill, marketing manager; and Steven M. Coleman, property manager.

SINCE FOUNDING HIS FIRST BUSINESS NEARLY FOUR DECADES AGO, MARVIN A. POMERANTZ HAS MAINTAINED THE ENTREPRENEURIAL PREMISE THAT THE PRODUCTS AND SERVICES OFFERED BY HIS ORGANIZATION SHOULD BE OF THE HIGHEST QUALITY IN ANY SPECIFIC FIELD IN WHICH THE COMPANY OPERATES.

THE MID-AMERICA GROUP IS THE DEVELOPER OF THE 44-ACRE REGENCY WEST COMPLEX IN WEST DES MOINES.

EVERYONE HAS SEEN THE ARCHITECTURAL BEAUTY OF MASONRY IN use everywhere—on homes, buildings, patios, sound walls, and fireplaces—but most people wouldn't even consider attempting such a hard, labor-intensive trade. However, to Dick Felice, it has proved to be a gratifying form of art. To Felice, masonry

is a craft that allows working with one's hands, using various masonry materials, to combine a multitude of small pieces together to create a masterpiece. Felice first experienced masonry while in school, felt compelled to pursue his journeyman's card after graduation, and then, along with his friend Dale Forrest, proceeded to start his own firm in 1960. Together, they built Forrest & Associate into a company that has grown over the years into one of Des Moines' most experienced and knowledgeable masonry contracting firms, capable of providing quality crafts-

manship and superior expertise throughout the state of Iowa.

Forrest and Felice started with 10 employees, building commercial, industrial, educational, and residential buildings using various masonry materials, such as block, brick, stone, granite, marble, tile, and terra-cotta. This company played a significant role in aiding the beautification and growth programs of cities across the state. Felice purchased Forrest's stock in 1993 and the company has continued to flourish. Today, with more than 100 employees, Forrest & Associate strives to pro-

vide the highest standard of total quality masonry construction and service to its clients.

MEETING CUSTOMER EXPECTATIONS

Forrest & Associate is committed to consistently meeting customer expectations by employing craftsmen with the highest degree of skill and professionalism, and ensuring that top-quality standards are met by keeping the lines of communication open with design teams. The company is also dedicated to providing the most comprehensive program of continuing training available to its employees. Following these practices through the years has allowed Forrest & Associate to evolve into a premier masonry contracting firm.

Felice has adapted to changes in the construction industry and, wanting to ensure that masonry is a major part of building design, has become part of those changes by consistently being active in the industry's organizations. While running a business on a full-time basis, Felice still finds time to serve on the board of directors of the Masonry Institute of Iowa and the Des Moines Construction Council. He also serves on various committees for organizations such as Master Builders, Council for Masonry Research, Building Stone Institute, National Masonry Standards, Associated American Society of Testing Materials C15, and the Mason Contractor's Association of America, of which he served as president two consecutive years.

MAKING ITS MARK

Forrest & Associate averages 200 projects annually, mostly within the state of Iowa. The more notable projects are the

FORREST & ASSOCIATE AVERAGES 200 PROJECTS ANNUALLY, MOSTLY WITHIN THE STATE OF IOWA. PAST PROJECTS INCLUDE THE WESLEY ACRES RETIREMENT HOME.

FORREST & ASSOCIATE HAS GROWN OVER
THE YEARS INTO ONE OF DES MOINES'
MOST EXPERIENCED AND KNOWLEDGE-
ABLE MASONRY CONTRACTING FIRMS,
CAPABLE OF PROVIDING QUALITY CRAFTS-
MANSHIP AND SUPERIOR EXPERTISE
THROUGHOUT THE STATE OF IOWA.
FROM THE FARMLAND INSURANCE
COMPANY BUILDING (TOP) TO THE
DRAKE LAW LIBRARY (BOTTOM), THE
FIRM PROVIDES THE HIGHEST STANDARD
OF TOTAL QUALITY MASONRY CONSTRUC-
TION AND SERVICE TO ITS CUSTOMERS.

Iowa State Historical Building, Living History Farms Visitor's Center, restoration of the Old Historical Building in Des Moines, and the Mark of the Quad Cities in Rock Island, Illinois. In 1997, the Masonry Institute of Iowa presented the Golden Trowel Award to Forrest & Associate for its work on the Oskaloosa Library, and in 1998, the Coveted Golden Trowel Award was again awarded to Forrest & Associate for its work on the Third Reformed Church in Pella. The company has also been awarded the National Excellence in Masonry Award for the Kirke-Van Orsdale Headquarters in West Des Moines and for St. Francis of Assisi Church in Des Moines, which also was awarded first place by the Nebraska Masonry Institute.

While Forrest & Associate is proud of the numerous projects it has completed over the years, Felice says that one of the company's most prestigious projects is the Iowa State Capitol renovation. Since 1985 workers have perched on scaffolding at the sides of the capitol replacing deteriorated stones piece by piece. For its painstaking efforts and quality craftsman-

ship on the capitol's restoration, Forrest & Associate received two craftsman awards, one in 1997 and one in 1998 from the Construction Specification Institute. This masonry contractor's excellence has also been recognized on a national level with the 1997 Tucker Award, which is given by Building Stone Institute in New York City.

Not only has Forrest & Associate helped communities grow, but it has also made personal contributions to the community by donating to such projects as Lincoln High School, Salisbury House, St. Anthony's Church, and Living History Farms.

MISSION STATEMENT

It is the mission of Forrest & Associate to provide the highest standard of total quality masonry construction and service to its customers, and to meet its customers' expectations 100 percent of the time by employing the highest degree of quality, skilled, and professional people. Forrest & Associate will accept no less than a total quality commitment to its customers, enabling Forrest & Associate to remain the premier mason contracting firm in Iowa.

ESTABLISHED IN 1962, THE ATLAS COMPANIES SERVES AS THE parent entity to Basic Coatings, Inc.; Matrix Coatings, Inc.; and TW Graphics Group, three successful firms in the wood coatings and ink industries. Headquarters for The Atlas Companies is based in Des Moines, a location that

enhances Atlas' ability to serve its customers globally and attracts highly motivated professionals to its family-oriented work environment.

Atlas Products, Inc. serves as the manufacturing entity for The Atlas Companies, and is recognized as an industry leader in national and international markets, thanks to the firm's 125 dedicated employees who manufacture and distribute its products.

The Atlas Companies is founded on a commitment to its employees and to the excellence of its products. Atlas' water-based technologies serve thousands of customers and are used in diverse applications in the hardwood flooring, credit card, fine art, graphics, and screen-printing industries.

Through innovative technology and the continued empowerment of its employees, The Atlas Companies stands confident to meet future challenges.

Over the years, Atlas Products has evolved through its experience in a variety of industries—including bowling sport coatings, managed care, and hardwood floor coatings—to meet the needs of its employees and its customer base.

CLOCKWISE FROM TOP:
THE ATLAS COMPANIES IS FOUNDED ON A COMMITMENT TO ITS EMPLOYEES AND TO THE EXCELLENCE OF ITS PRODUCTS.

THROUGH INNOVATIVE TECHNOLOGY AND THE CONTINUED EMPOWERMENT OF ITS EMPLOYEES, THE ATLAS COMPANIES STANDS CONFIDENT TO MEET FUTURE CHALLENGES.

ATLAS PRODUCTS, INC. SERVES AS THE MANUFACTURING ENTITY FOR THE ATLAS COMPANIES, AND IS RECOGNIZED AS AN INDUSTRY LEADER IN NATIONAL AND INTERNATIONAL MARKETS, THANKS TO THE FIRM'S 125 DEDICATED EMPLOYEES WHO MANUFACTURE AND DISTRIBUTE ITS PRODUCTS.

FLAGSHIP COMPANIES

Basic Coatings, Inc. is currently a major manufacturer of coatings and maintenance products designed specifically for hardwood floors. Basic Coatings, Inc. distributes its products globally through its sales force and an international distributor network of more than 450 outlets.

With Basic Coatings, Inc., The Atlas Companies has solidified its position in the wood flooring industry and has branded its formulas to target specific areas of the industry. As a result, Matrix Coatings, Inc. was established in 1993 to manufacture industrial coatings for wood and wood products such as cabinetry, ready-to-assemble furniture, and musical instruments.

In 1994, in an effort to extend its product lines into other areas of the coatings industry, The Atlas Companies acquired J&S Ink Company, headquartered in Longwood, Florida, a company recognized as an international manufacturer and distributor of textile screen-printing inks. TW Graphics Group, a manufacturer

of specialty and graphic inks was acquired in 1996, and in 1998, J&S Ink Company merged with TW Graphics Group to provide both textile and graphic printers with a complete line of inks and supplies.

The Atlas Companies has achieved success by recognizing profitable business opportunities and seeking to fulfill them through quality and excellence in its products and services. The Atlas Companies' success is directly related to its relationship with its employees, a solid customer base, and its knowledge of the marketplace.

THERE IS A COMPANY IN DES MOINES THAT WAS BUILT ON THE idea of making customer service its paramount concern. This was a forward-thinking philosophy in 1971 for the envelope-supply industry, but it has served The Straub Corporation well. Through the years, the company has forged a tight-knit

relationship with its customers, its suppliers, and the Des Moines community.

The company was formed after Mel Straub found a niche in the envelope market when he concluded that the key to success was in satisfying his clients, not just selling them a product. Starting with only two employees, The Straub Corporation was aggressive in obtaining envelope sources that were diverse in their product capabilities and willing to commit to excellence in service. The company tailored its operations to accommodate each customer's specific needs. Every order, every delivery, every invoice supports this unique service philosophy.

Within two years of starting his company, Straub built a 6,120-square-foot facility on Sunset Road near downtown Des Moines. The central location made it easy to reach clients within a short period of time. By 1976, The Straub Corporation had diversified to become a full-service distributor by adding business forms. This opened an opportunity for customers to one-stop shop for their envelope and business form needs. As the firm grew, it also added state-of-the-art printing equipment, thus expanding its services even further.

In the summer of 1993, The Straub Corporation's thriving business suffered devastating losses in a flood that engulfed portions of Des Moines. The dedicated staff, however, refused to be set back by disaster. They retrieved computers and orders by boat, while The Straub Corporation's suppliers helped replenish the company's inventory. The company was temporarily relocated at Straub's home and, later, at the Des Moines Area Community College. As it turned out, the flood was a turning

point. In the face of adversity, the bond was further strengthened among The Straub Corporation's employees and the firm's suppliers and customers. It was during this difficult time that the company hit record-breaking sales.

After the flood, the company returned to its home in Des Moines. In 1996, construction began on a new, 20,000-square-foot facility on Sunset Road. From this new facility, The Straub Corporation controls the production, storage, inventory management, and distribution needs of its clients.

Beyond its close relationship with its clients, The Straub Corporation works within the city in fulfilling partnerships that support the community. Straub is the founder of the annual John Ruan MS Charity Golf Exhibition, which raises funds for multiple sclerosis research. Fulfilling a promise made years ago, Straub has dedicated 25 percent of his time to charitable boards and fund-raising drives. His wife, Jan Miller Straub, president of The Straub Corporation, is chair of the board of directors of the Riverfront YMCA. In addition, she is an appointee to the Terrace Hill Commission (the group responsible for the care

and management of Terrace Hill) and is chair-elect of Executive Women's Golf (an organization that helps to positively position career-oriented women golfers in the world of business). The Straubs' eagerness to be active participants in the Des Moines area is shared by their employees, who support various causes and assist in the charity work the firm's customers take on.

"We're not just residents here," explains Miller Straub of the company's dedication to Des Moines. "We're citizens."

UNDER THE LEADERSHIP OF MEL STRAUB AND HIS WIFE, JAN MILLER STRAUB, THE STRAUB CORPORATION HAS FORGED A TIGHT-KNIT RELATIONSHIP WITH ITS CUSTOMERS, ITS SUPPLIERS, AND THE DES MOINES COMMUNITY (TOP).

STATE-OF-THE-ART PRINTING EQUIPMENT ALLOWS THE STRAUB CORPORATION TO PROVIDE UNEQUALED LEVELS OF SERVICE IN THE PRODUCTION AND DISTRIBUTION OF ENVELOPES AND BUSINESS FORMS. (BOTTOM).

SINCE ITS FOUNDING AS A ONE-PHYSICIAN PRACTICE IN DES MOINES in 1970, Iowa Heart Center's focus has remained the same: to provide quality, leading-edge, compassionate care to its patients and their families. That dedication to being the best has helped Iowa Heart Center grow to be one of the premier

cardiology and cardiovascular surgery practices in the nation, as well as one of the 10 largest private cardiology practices in the United States.

David Gordon, M.D., came to Des Moines as central Iowa's first board-certified cardiologist and founded what is now known as Iowa Heart Center in 1970. As technology exploded and more options for treating heart disease became available, Iowa Heart Center responded by growing and offering more services to Iowans.

MAKING HISTORY

Iowa Heart Center made history on November 29, 1979, when Dr. L.A. Iannone performed the state's first balloon angioplasty procedure to clear a patient's clogged coronary artery, known today as percutaneous trans-luminal coronary angioplasty

(PTCA). Gordon scored a first for Iowa Heart Center in January 1980 by being the first cardiologist to administer the drug streptokinase to a patient who had suffered a heart attack. The drug dissolved a life-threatening clot, allowing the patient to go home without surgery.

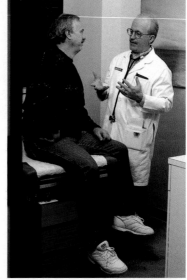

In the next decade, the number of Iowa Heart Center physicians quadrupled, with each new physi-cian bringing special interest and expertise to the practice. Iannone continued to make Iowa medical history when, in 1990, he became the first cardiologist to perform a directional coronary arthrectomy. This procedure uses a catheter equipped with a small, rotary cut-ting tool to shave through a blocked artery, removing the clogging plaque.

Today, Iowa Heart Center has grown to more than 40 cardiolo-gists and surgeons who specialize in the care of the heart. Iowa Heart Center physicians perform more than 10,000 cardiac inter-ventions annually, and are respected for their aggressive treatment and prevention of heart and vascular problems.

The experience of the physi-cians, coupled with their wide array of knowledge, gives Iowa Heart Center patients the comfort of knowing they are receiving the best care that is currently available. In fact, research has shown that in complex heart disease cases, the more experience a doctor has, the better the outcomes.

A GROWING PRESENCE

Cardiovascular disease remains the leading cause of death in the United States, killing nearly 1 million men and women yearly and affecting 68 million Americans. Iowa is no different, with more Iowans dying annually of heart disease than any other illness.

Iowa Heart Center has a team of more than 300 excellent staff members to better serve its pa-tients. Iowa Heart Center has offices and clinics throughout central, northern, and southern Iowa. In Des Moines, Iowa Heart

PREVENTION IS A FOCUS OF IOWA HEART CENTER. CARDIOLOGIST WILLIAM WICKEMEYER, M.D., ENCOURAGES A PATIENT TO MAKE LIFESTYLE CHANGES (TOP).

IOWA HEART CENTER PHYSICIANS PER-FORM MORE THAN 10,000 CARDIAC IN-TERVENTIONS EVERY YEAR. MARK TANNEBAUM, M.D., LEADS THE CARDIAC CATHETERIZATION TEAM THROUGH A PROCEDURE (BOTTOM).

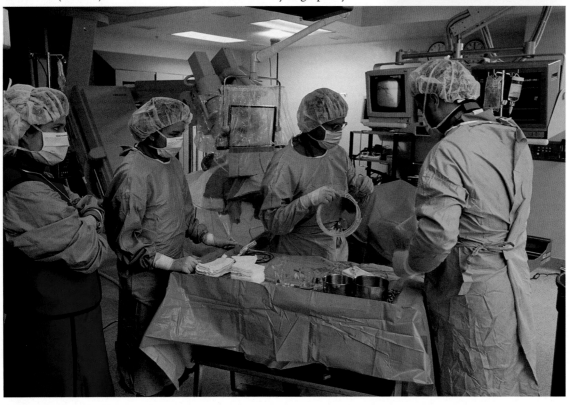

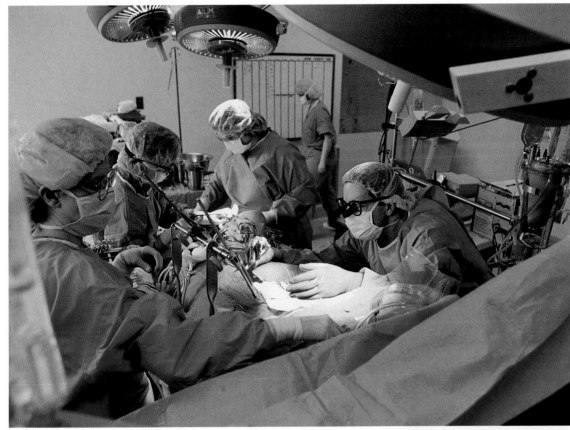

CARDIOTHORACIC SURGEON DAVID HOCKMUTH, M.D., CONCENTRATES WHILE PERFORMING TRANSPLANT SURGERY (TOP).

EDUCATING PATIENTS ABOUT HEART DISEASE IS A FOCUS OF IOWA HEART CENTER PHYSICIANS. RANDOLPH ROUGH, M.D., EXPLAINS A DIAGNOSIS TO A PATIENT (BOTTOM).

Center has offices at Mercy Hospital Medical Center, Iowa Methodist Medical Center, and Iowa Lutheran Hospital, as well as the Mercy West Office Building in the western suburbs, to give patients a choice of where they want to be treated.

In addition, Iowa Heart Center operates offices in Ames, Fort Dodge, and Carroll, and holds clinics in 28 communities on a regular basis. These outreach efforts give patients the ability to receive the best cardiology care available without having to travel far from home. To make it easier for patients to learn about the Iowa Heart Center's services, the group has established a Web site on the Internet at www.iowaheart.com.

RESEARCH LEADS THE WAY

Iowa Heart Center helps pave the way in finding new, better, and more cost-effective ways to deliver heart care by being active in research. Currently, Iowa Heart Center physicians are participating in more than 50 clinical research studies. These studies involve trying new devices such as pacemakers and stents, testing new drugs, and looking at new and different ways to treat and prevent heart disease. Often, drug companies and equipment manufacturers seek out advice from Iowa Heart Center physicians when developing improvements in treating heart disease.

In addition, Iowa Heart Center physicians have received patents on several devices that improve how heart disease is treated. By being at the forefront of research, Iowa Heart Center patients can receive the latest care available—often resulting in better outcomes and quicker recoveries.

As health care continues to grow and change, Iowa Heart Center is proud to be a leader in how cardiovascular disease is treated throughout the state of Iowa. From creating various programs that help prevent heart disease to being the first in the state to try new procedures, Iowa Heart Center physicians and staff remain dedicated to providing quality, leading-edge, and compassionate care to patients and their families.

G RATIAS CONSTRUCTION INC. WAS ESTABLISHED IN 1972, AND its founder, a small-town boy from Nora Springs, Iowa, has earned a giant name among home builders across the country. Tom Gratias was studying for his degree in business administration and finance at Drake University when he took a part-time job with a local builder. Only a few years thereafter, Gratias Construction Inc. opened its doors, starting out as a small custom builder.

It is not surprising when you look at Gratias' credentials and involvement in the building industry that he has become one of the Des Moines area's largest and most prestigious home builders. In addition to being president of his own company, Tom Gratias has served as president of the local and state Home Builders Association (HBA), and has served as an area vice president and chaired numerous committees for the National Association of Home Builders (NAHB). Still further, he has been named the Greater Des Moines Builder of the Year three times and is one of fewer than 25 people in Iowa certified by the NAHB as Master Builder.

MORE THAN BRICKS AND MORTAR

A lthough Gratias Construction develops land, creates housing designs, and builds quality town houses and custom homes, Gratias describes himself as being in the people business. "The measuring stick for our success," he maintains, "is more than houses; it's people's lives. It's as much about people as it is bricks and mortar."

The motto of Gratias Construction is We Build Dreams, and this is a process that takes place in every Gratias-built home. Whether the preference is traditional or contemporary, ranch or two-story, big or small, Gratias incorporates specialized features to make the design the personal dream home of each buyer.

Gratias' "people business" also involves the construction teams who work on each home. Daily quality controls include not only constructive criticism but also praise for work well done. "I believe by paying attention to the workmen and treating them with dignity, you truly get a better product," Gratias says. Still further, the Gratias family plays a big part in the company's success. Tom's wife, LaDonna Gratias, is vice president and personally is involved in the closing and walk-through of every Gratias Construction home; his son, Craig, is a job superintendent and manages the Ankeny projects;

FAMILY INVOLVEMENT IS WHAT SEPARATES GRATIAS CONSTRUCTION INC. FROM MANY OF ITS COMPETITORS. (CLOCKWISE FROM TOP) TOM GRATIAS, HIS WIFE LADONNA, THEIR SON CRAIG, AND DAUGHTER JENNIFER GRATIAS-WILLE ALL PLAY A BIG PART IN THE COMPANY'S SUCCESS.

▲ DAVID PENNEY PHOTOGRAPHY

▲ DAVID PENNEY PHOTOGRAPHY

and his daughter, Jennifer Gratias-Wille, helps manage real estate marketing at all locations. This family involvement is what separates Gratias Construction Inc. from many of its competitors.

DIFFERENT DREAMS FOR DIFFERENT DREAMERS

While Gratias Construction finds nothing more satisfying than building people their dream homes, it also recognizes the many levels of affordability of its clients. Although his company specializes in luxurious homes and town houses from $200,000 and up, Tom Gratias has not overlooked clients seeking quality, lower-priced dream homes either.

With fellow Master Builder Darrel Avitt, Gratias formed Country Classic Homes L.C. to specialize in homes and town houses ranging in price from $120,000 to approximately $150,000 that are geared toward professional singles, young couples looking for their first homes, and empty nesters. Gratias has also formed Village Classic Homes L.C. with his son-in-law, Al Wille, and together, they produce homes for move-up buyers ranging in price from $160,000 to $210,000.

Regardless of whether the project is a starter home or town house, move-up house, or luxury home or town house, Gratias Construction Inc., along with its affiliated companies, puts an emphasis on quality, time, and cost. Known for its woodworking, Gratias will include such extras as plyth blocks at the corners of doors and windows or special built-ins, such as computer desks or bookcases. The company also emphasizes the importance of keeping current on the latest building materials and advises clients about products that are the best choices for quality, availability, and price.

Gratias Construction Inc. builds dreams, but dreams often change through the years. When his clients want something new, they often come back to Gratias. It is not uncommon for the com-

pany to build for a customer two or even three times.

STRONG AND SOUND

Gratias founded his construction company with only a few thousand dollars and a chest of tools—in what he now realizes was a different economic era. The home-building business was flourishing, and with his degree in business and finance, he was fortunate to make what he calls some right decisions.

But the early 1980s brought an era of trouble to local builders with high interest rates and a slow housing market, and in 1983, Gratias Construction built only four homes. Still, the company weathered this rough period. "That's part of it," Gratias says, "to be able to manage the risk you've taken." Since those low times of the early 1980s, the company has enjoyed a continual growth where it is not unusual for 80 to 100 homes to be built in any given year.

In the late 1980s, Gratias began developing land, some of which had been purchased a decade earlier— carefully preserving and enhancing the natural beauty of the land; incorporating curved streets, trees,

creeks, and ponds; and landscaping walk-out lots in the style for which the company has become known.

Gratias Construction has land— for its current and future projects— in Ankeny, Des Moines, Urbandale, West Des Moines, and Clive, where Gratias Construction's offices are located on Northwest 138th, just north of the West End Diner.

Gratias Construction understands that few purchases are more valuable or precious than a home. With that in mind, the company plans to continue delivering quality workmanship to make home owners' dreams come true. "I'm one of those lucky people," says Gratias. "I love what I do for a living."

GRATIAS CONSTRUCTION STRIVES TO PRESERVE NATURAL BEAUTY IN ALL ITS PROJECTS.

REGARDLESS OF WHETHER THE PROJECT IS A STARTER HOME OR LUXURY HOME, GRATIAS CONSTRUCTION INC., ALONG WITH ITS AFFILIATED COMPANIES, PUTS AN EMPHASIS ON QUALITY, TIME, AND COST.

SINCE ITS FOUNDING IN 1973, TRIPLETT COMPANIES HAS GROWN TO occupy a 36,000-square-foot showcase location for its office furniture, supplies, printing, and customer inventory management businesses. ■ As the volume of the firm's business grew, it became necessary for specialized management expertise to operate the

office furniture and marketing functions. Tom and Tim Triplett, sons of founders Dick and Sue, earned their own responsibilities through formal education and on-the-job training: Tim as marketing director and Tom as furniture sales manager.

A FULL-SERVICE COMPANY

Triplett Companies services its customers through three divisions. Triplett Office Essentials, the office supply division, is known for keeping high-volume office supplies at inventory levels consistent with customer demand, and at competitive prices made possible by a history of excellent supplier discounts and vendor relationships.

The customer can order from Office Essentials and either utilize the standard ordering system or develop a custom ordering system. With full electronic data integration, issuing purchase orders, checking inventory, and paying invoices are state of the art, resulting in fewer errors and lower processing costs.

Triplett Corporate Interiors offers complete office furnishings, seating systems, floor and wall coverings, and computer-aided design (CAD) services to meet the challenge of efficient space planning. By giving complete, full service to customers, Triplett saves them money and the extra time it takes when working with more than one vendor. A team of well-trained professionals helps customers craft the look they want with the versatility that multifunctional offices need. Triplett conducts interviews, gathers information from on-site visits, and uses blueprints to make an educated cost estimate for furniture and finishing options for its clients.

Triplett Corporate Interiors offers premium brand names in office furnishings. The firm holds the city's only preferred dealer status for Haworth, and also carries Gunlocke, Lacasse/Avenue, Hon, Chromcraft, Grahl, KI, Falcon, Paoli, Design Options, and Egan furnishings.

Triplett Printing Services, the third division of the company, produces custom-designed stationery, business cards, letterhead, brochures, fliers, envelopes, and other printed materials with speed and efficiency. Triplett provides

THE TRIPLETT COMPANIES' SHOWROOM SHOWCASES A WIDE SELECTION OF OFFICE FURNITURE (TOP).

SINCE ITS FOUNDING IN 1973, TRIPLETT COMPANIES HAS GROWN TO OCCUPY A 36,000-SQUARE-FOOT SHOWCASE LOCATION FOR ITS OFFICE FURNITURE, SUPPLIES, PRINTING, AND CUSTOMER INVENTORY MANAGEMENT BUSINESSES (BOTTOM).

creative and innovative capabilities to enhance the printed media of its customers.

Triplett Companies has added customer value through its acquisition of a Des Moines branch of Office Furniture USA at its 5,000-square-foot retail showroom in Urbandale. This facility is fully supported with the expertise of 26 manufacturers. Office furniture with discounts as high as 50 percent off manufacturer's list price is available daily, with most items available for pickup or delivery within 15 business days.

Triplett Companies publishes two catalogs: one for the products offered through Office Furniture USA, and a second, with more than 1,000 pages, that lists details of Triplett products. Another means of accessing the company and its products is through the World Wide Web. Office Furniture USA can be found at www.officefurniture-usa.com, and Triplett Companies can be found at www.tripletts.com.

A Des Moines Fixture

Triplett has become a part of the community not only through its service to customers, but also through the time and energy the company devotes annually to the Foundation for Children and Families of Iowa. Since 1993, the firm has sponsored the Triplett Holiday Golf Classic, an annual December golf outing at the Terrace Hills Golf Club in nearby Altoona. Hundreds of brave golfers who thrive on the challenge of hitting golf balls—or tennis balls if it snows—in the dead of winter have raised thousands of dollars for the family service agency. The event is Triplett's innovative way of giving back to the community that has been good to the company.

Triplett Companies and its 50 employees have been recognized by the business community as among the best in their class. The weekly *Business Record*'s readers voted Triplett a Best of Des Moines Business for 1997 and 1998 in office supplies and furniture. Since the beginning, when Dick and Sue Triplett had to make many personal sacrifices to get supplies to clients as quickly as possible, customer service, quality, and competitive pricing—the three elements of value—have built an enduring customer base and long-term business relationships.

TRIPLETT'S OFFICE FURNITURE USA STORE HAS MORE THAN 5,000 SQUARE FEET OF FURNITURE ON DISPLAY FROM 26 DIFFERENT MANUFACTURERS.

TRIPLETT'S HUGE INVENTORY ALLOWS FOR QUICK DELIVERY.

THE MOTORIST'S GAS TANK IS EMPTY, AND SO IS HIS OR HER wallet. But if the motorist is a holder of an Amoco or Clark Refining & Marketing credit card, he or she need not worry about being stranded. A swipe of a handy plastic card pays for the fuel, gets the motorist back on the road, keeps the

retail world humming—and puts The Associates Credit Card Center (ACCC) in West Des Moines to work processing the transaction.

Through its nearly 600 employees, the processing center functions as a payment processing center, customer service facility, collections location, and marketing agent for Amoco Oil Company and Clark Refining & Marketing credit card products. The facility handles in excess of 100 million transactions annually for its partners and parent company, Associates First Capital Corporation (The Associates) of Dallas.

The West Des Moines facility was opened in September 1974, under the auspices of the Amoco Oil Company. It functioned for 20 years as the Amoco Customer Service Center, until the gasoline company decided to concentrate on its core business of petroleum products and to outsource its credit card operations to a company familiar with the credit card industry. The Amoco credit card portfolio, the Amoco Customer Service Center operation, and the building in West Des Moines were purchased by Dallas-based Associates First Capital Corporation, and The Associates Credit Card Center was created.

THE ASSOCIATES

The Associates is a leading diversified finance company that provides consumer and commercial finance, leasing, and related services through more than 2,200 offices in the United States, Japan, the United Kingdom, Canada, Puerto Rico, Mexico, Taiwan, and Costa Rica. Founded in 1918, it is the largest publicly traded finance company in the United States, with managed assets of more than $60 billion. The Associates has achieved record earnings growth yearly since 1974.

Gulf & Western Industries Inc. acquired The Associates in 1968, and the company went on to become a majority-owned subsidiary of Ford Motor Company in 1989. In April 1998, Ford completed a spin-off of its Associates First Capital stock to Ford shareholders, and the company became fully independent for the first time in 30 years.

Today, The Associates is one of the leading issuers of Visa and MasterCard, as well as private label credit cards, serving approximately 11 million active customers in the United States. The company issues private label credit cards for Amoco, Texaco, and Clark Refining & Marketing, and is a provider of automobile club services for major companies.

IMPROVEMENT THROUGH DETERMINATION

The passion for constant improvement is a key force at ACCC. As the result of a strong attentiveness to customer needs, performance measurements, and continued superior standards, customer satisfaction is at an all-time high. The company takes pride in its work, and conducts business with integrity and trust, responding quickly to customer inquiries and requests.

The Associates believe that continued growth and acceleration of products and services can be achieved through providing the highest levels of service quality in the industry. At the Associates Credit Card Center, the satisfaction of customers is achieved in part by the recognition and rewarding of employees. Believing that customer loyalty is the result

THE AMOCO CREDIT CARD PORTFOLIO, THE AMOCO CUSTOMER SERVICE CENTER OPERATION, AND THE BUILDING IN WEST DES MOINES WERE PURCHASED BY DALLAS-BASED ASSOCIATES FIRST CAPITAL CORPORATION, AND THE ASSOCIATES CREDIT CARD CENTER (ACCC) WAS CREATED.

◀ JAMES R. COBB PHOTOGRAPHY

of being treated well by a satisfied employee, the company focuses on building a loyal customer and employee base that will earn the customer's repeat business.

ACCC employees are rewarded for reaching program incentive goals, as well as for achieving individual goals. An on-site fitness center, open to employees and their spouses, was added to the facility in February 1998. The fitness facility contains cardiovascular machines, weight machines, free weights, an aerobics room, and shower facilities, and offers a staff of trained professionals to assist members in meeting their health and fitness goals. The company also has an on-site, subsidized cafeteria that serves a complete breakfast and lunch menu.

The efforts of the West Des Moines operation to meet and exceed both customer and employee expectations have not gone unnoticed by its parent company. ACCC was an inaugural winner of the Chairman's Excellence Award, an honor competed for by all divisions of The Associates.

A Good Corporate Neighbor

The Associates is a major annual contributor to United Way, and ACCC is an active participant in that effort in central Iowa. In addition to corporate contributions, nearly 100 percent of employees donate annually to United Way programs. Employees also participated in the United Way Key Accounts Group and the United Way Executive Cabinet Committee, and provide a loaned executive annually to assist with the organization's campaign. In addition, many employees volunteer their time and energies to charitable causes. Some of these include the United Way Day of Caring, the Holiday Angel Tree Programs, Junior Achievement, and other worthwhile causes.

ACCC values diversity in its workplace and in its community. It believes in respecting others and recognizing their excellent performances, but it also believes that intensity and competition fuel success. In West Des Moines

and in sister facilities around the country, the company believes that quality growth and increasing profit are the result of working hard to exceed the expectations of both its employees and its customers.

Customers of The Associates Credit Card Center can rest assured that no matter when or where they travel, there are hardworking individuals available to assist their credit card needs, waiting and wanting to serve and exceed their expectations.

ACCC ISSUES PRIVATE LABEL CREDIT CARDS FOR AMOCO AND CLARK REFINING & MARKETING.

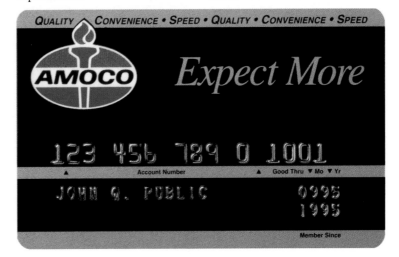

QuikTrip Corporation, a Tulsa-based organization, arrived in Des Moines in 1974, and its distinctive QT logo quickly created name recognition for the fast-growing company. But QuikTrip employees know the logo initials could also stand for "quality throughout." In an industry where

competition is fierce, QuikTrip is dedicated to a philosophy of maintaining quality in its facilities, merchandise, employees, management, security standards, and community support.

When Chester Cadieux and Burt Holmes of Tulsa pooled their borrowed money to found QuikTrip in 1958, there were only 500 small, drive-up grocery stores—called bantam stores—in the country. The men knew little about the grocery business, and struggled for an identity. Through trial and error, they established standards that remain in force in their more than 300 locations today: keep stores quick, courteous, and neat; guarantee all merchandise; train employees well; and offer variety, fairness, and service.

DES MOINES MARKET

QuikTrip has more than 25 stores in Des Moines today, which is also home to the administrative headquarters for the company's Des Moines Division. The Des Moines Division handles supervision, buying, and hiring for stores in Des Moines, Cedar Rapids, Iowa City, and Omaha.

QT locations in Des Moines employ approximately 170 full-time and 150 part-time staff. The company requires intensive training for all its employees, providing consistently efficient and courteous service to each customer.

The stores' clientele, according to Des Moines Division Personnel Manager Mike Webber, is "everybody," with the average customer stopping twice a day to buy mainly gasoline, soft drinks—including fountain drinks—coffee, cappuccino, beer, cigarettes, and candy.

QuikTrip guarantees everything it does or sells. If a customer is not completely satisfied, QT will refund his or her money. QT spends more than $20,000 a year per location on landscaping, remodeling, and maintenance to retain a quality appearance that is pleasant for customers and an asset to its neighborhood. To ensure top-quality customer and employee security, stores are well-lit inside and out, with video cameras and raised checkout stands for better visibility. Sophisticated alarm systems and monitoring devices, specially designed drop safes, and comprehensive safety

training for employees all exceed the standards for the convenience store industry.

A GOOD NEIGHBOR

QuikTrip's Des Moines Division has been a consistent leader in per-store and per-employee contributions to the United Way, with 1997 donations totaling $125,000. QT also supports local neighborhoods through donations of food items or supplies to schools, picnics, and community events.

QuikTrip strives for a family-oriented atmosphere that is consistent from store to store. It provides a safe place for teenagers and others to shop, and sells no adult magazines or items that could be used as drug paraphernalia. Its company-wide policies on alcohol and tobacco sales are strict—employees consistently check the identification of customers buying these items, and sell no alcohol to any customer who appears to be intoxicated.

Store location makes shopping convenient for QT customers. But Webber says the main philosophy behind QT's success is stressed in all Des Moines stores and throughout the QuikTrip Corporation: "The customer wants to get in and out quickly, and to be treated with respect." Added to QuikTrip's mission of quality throughout, this philosophy will ensure the company's success for many years to come.

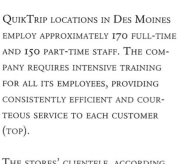

QUIKTRIP LOCATIONS IN DES MOINES EMPLOY APPROXIMATELY 170 FULL-TIME AND 150 PART-TIME STAFF. THE COMPANY REQUIRES INTENSIVE TRAINING FOR ALL ITS EMPLOYEES, PROVIDING CONSISTENTLY EFFICIENT AND COURTEOUS SERVICE TO EACH CUSTOMER (TOP).

THE STORES' CLIENTELE, ACCORDING TO DES MOINES DIVISION PERSONNEL MANAGER MIKE WEBBER, IS "EVERYBODY," WITH THE AVERAGE CUSTOMER STOPPING TWICE A DAY TO BUY MAINLY GASOLINE, SOFT DRINKS—INCLUDING FOUNTAIN DRINKS—COFFEE, CAPPUCCINO, BEER, CIGARETTES, AND CANDY (BOTTOM).

AROUND DES MOINES, THIRSTY YOUNGSTERS GROW UP WITH A simple understanding of the retail beverage business. They know that grocers' milk comes from cows on the farm; orange juice comes from citrus groves in Florida; and Coca-Cola comes from the building on Hickman Road near Waukee.

The "Coke building" is a distribution center for Atlantic Coca-Cola Bottling Company, a family-owned business headquartered approximately 75 miles west of Des Moines in Atlantic. The company's territory includes portions of central and southwest Iowa—serving approximately 625,000 people. The Atlantic plant and the Waukee distribution center each employ 65 people, with 11 more assigned to a Creston distribution center.

A LUCKY DISCOVERY

In 1909, brothers Harry and Henry Tyler became partners in an ice-cream and dairy business in their hometown of Villisca. Three years later, they bought a creamery in nearby Clarinda, and while sorting through papers found in the creamery's warehouse safe, discovered a document granting a Coca-Cola franchise to the business.

The brothers concocted some of the bubbly beverage and bottled it to sell alongside their flavored soda waters. By 1930, they were producing soft drinks full-time, with plants in several towns.

When an estate planner recommended that the brothers divide the business, a draw of straws gave Harry the plants in Atlantic and Creston. Harry's son, Jim, joined the business as a bottle washer and eventually became president of the company that, on April 1, 1975, also took over the huge Des Moines Coca-Cola franchise.

THE QUEST TO QUENCH IOWA'S THIRST

Today, the Atlantic Coca-Cola Bottling Company is one of 100 entities authorized to sell Coca-Cola products in the United States—and one of only a few not headquartered in a major metropolitan area. Producing nearly 24,000 cases of canned and bottled soft drinks each day, the company lists Coca-Cola Classic as its top seller, followed by Diet Coke and Sprite. Until 1997, the company also bottled 7-Up products.

Cans account for nearly 68 percent of the Atlantic Coca-Cola Bottling Company's business, with the most popular package being 12-packs. Two-liter bottles are the second-largest seller, followed by 20-ounce bottles.

A FAMILY BUSINESS

Jim Tyler's son, Kirk, grew up in the bottling business, sweeping floors and sorting bottles. A self-proclaimed SOB (son of a bottler), he drove a Coke truck after college, then took a year's training at the Coca-Cola headquarters in Atlanta. Kirk became president of the company in 1991. Jim, who remains as chairman of the board, has served on the National Soft Drink Association Board, the Iowa Board of Regents, and the Coca-Cola Bottlers' Association Board of Governors.

Proud of its successful past, the Atlantic Coca-Cola Bottling Company looks forward to tremendous future growth, particularly with its concentrated effort to expand its vending and fountain sales.

Meanwhile, the Tyler family business has worked to take care of its company family. In 1983, the Atlantic Coca-Cola Bottling Company established an employee profit-sharing plan that has now grown to more than $4 million. "We tell our people every year, 'The more we make, the more we share,' " Kirk says. "And they help us do that."

TODAY, THE ATLANTIC COCA-COLA BOTTLING COMPANY IS ONE OF 100 ENTITIES AUTHORIZED TO SELL COCA-COLA PRODUCTS IN THE UNITED STATES—AND ONE OF ONLY A FEW NOT HEADQUARTERED IN A MAJOR METROPOLITAN AREA. PICTURED HERE ARE JIM TYLER, CHAIRMAN OF THE BOARD (LEFT), AND KIRK TYLER, PRESIDENT AND CEO.

ALEXANDER'S COMMERCIAL PHOTOGRAPHY

BEFORE 1975, THERE WAS LITTLE MORE THAN CORN SEEDED west of Des Moines along Interstate 235. But Frederick M. Watson—who then was owner of a Minneapolis-based construction company—saw much more than golden kernels springing from the rich soil. He foresaw growth of a different

kind—a growth that would bring people into new communities around Des Moines. Planted in Watson's mind was the idea that a shopping facility should be built in the West Des Moines area. Today, more than 1 million people—city and farm dwellers alike—set foot inside Watson's dream each month, choosing Valley West Mall as their shopping destination.

The shopping center opened in August 1975 with two well-known anchors: Brandeis (which later became Younkers) and JCPenney Company. A third department store, Petersen Harned Von Maur, known today as Von Maur, opened in 1976. Located between the anchor stores, today as in 1975, are exclusive specialty shops that can't be found anywhere else in the Des Moines area. Such nationally known companies as Eddie Bauer, Gap Kids, and Natural Wonders call Valley West Mall home.

A BUSTLING MARKETPLACE

From the time stores open their doors to the time they close for the night, the center is humming with activity. The latest research from 1997 shows about 13 million visitors enter the mall annually, or more than 200,000 per week. At the height of the holiday shopping season in December 1997, nearly 1.3 million people walked the mall's expansive corridors.

Valley West Mall is constantly changing to offer the most up-to-date fashions and a pleasurable shopping experience for all who enter its doors. Younkers added 40,000 square feet in 1995, and a new food court with nine restaurant bays opened in August 1998.

TIES TO THE LOCAL COMMUNITY

As a member of the community, Valley West Mall contributes to local charitable organizations. The center donates 10 percent, up to $1,000 each, of what shoppers contribute to five children's charities during the winter holiday season. The mall also makes a donation to the top 10 area schools in the fall based on purchases that parents and students from those schools make at the mall.

Valley West Mall has been recognized and awarded for its advertising achievements, recycling efforts, and community contributions.

Valley West Mall plans to continue offering the best shopping selection and exclusive stores while remaining a vital and active member of the community.

WITH THREE ANCHOR STORES AND NUMEROUS EXCLUSIVE SPECIALTY SHOPS, VALLEY WEST MALL HOUSES A VARIETY OF MERCHANDISE.

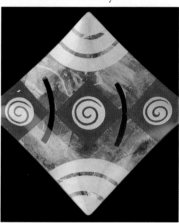

HOW DO YOU BUILD A PUBLISHING EMPIRE COMPRISED OF more than 10 different publications—including two weekly newspapers—from a modest, four-page court- and legal-reporting tabloid? Ask Connie Wimer, owner, CEO, and publisher of Business Publications Corporation (BPC).

In 1981, Wimer, owner and president of Iowa Title Company, purchased the *Des Moines Daily Record*, Polk County's official legal newspaper. What she thought would be a tranquil continuation of the *Des Moines Daily Record*'s business soon turned into an entrepreneur's nightmare. The district judges decided that the legal proceedings published in the *Daily Record* were no longer needed. Literally from one day to the next, the little court paper purchased with a 20-year loan had no content and no revenue.

PAUL GATES, BPC

STARTING FROM SCRATCH

Wimer assessed the local publishing scene and decided Des Moines' vibrant business community needed a hard-hitting, factual, topical, community-oriented business paper. Thus was born the *Des Moines Business Record*. The first issue hit the streets in October 1983. Today, circulation has swelled from 700 to more than 35,000 weekly readers. In 1998, the *Des Moines Business Record* received 12 Iowa Newspaper Association prizes, an outstanding accomplishment for a publication not even 15 years old.

Following on the heels of the *Des Moines Business Record*'s success, the company gambled on a new publishing trend—alternative newspapers. Purchasing the *Skywalker* in 1983, BPC converted a sleepy, conservative entertainment and lifestyle paper into the witty, controversial, and immensely popular *Cityview*. The weekly, free-of-charge newspaper is distributed to more than 800 newstands, institutions, and retail outlets in a four-county area surrounding Des Moines. Readership has grown from the original *Skywalker* total of 12,000 to an astounding 108,000.

FILLING IMPORTANT NICHES

Supported by two successful papers, Business Publications Corporation began to seek out other niches that begged to be filled but were so small as to be ignored by its giant publishing competitors. In short order, a grand coalition of informational books, pamphlets, and magazines followed: *Intro* in 1987; *Metropolitan Des Moines* in 1988; *The Book of Lists* in 1990; *Midday Record* in 1994; *Iowa Small Business Resource Guide* in 1996; and *Happenings Calendar* in 1996.

Midday Record is a just-before-noon, one-page fax transmission to a who's who of Des Moines' business community. It offers late-breaking news, stock market updates, and other timely but quickly digestible bits of information to busy executives. It frequently "scoops" the daily newspaper on big stories. The format has been copied by other business papers in approximately 35 metropolitan markets.

BPC's headquarters is The Depot at Fourth, the well-remembered Rock Island passenger station. The ruins of the once-proud depot were restored to their former grandeur and significance in downtown Des Moines. Preserving the

historic brick exterior, the interior was converted to a modern, state-of-the-art office facility housing BPC's 50 employees on the ground floor, as well as the 75-person staff of Iowa Title Company on the second floor.

From humble beginnings, BPC has grown to become a vibrant and spirited force for change and development in a fast-growing and ever evolving central Iowa business community. Through it all, Business Publications Corporation has kept its eyes on the far horizon, constantly seeking out new opportunities.

BUSINESS PUBLICATIONS CORPORATION'S HEADQUARTERS IS THE DEPOT AT FOURTH, THE WELL-REMEMBERED ROCK ISLAND PASSENGER STATION. THE RUINS OF THE ONCE-PROUD DEPOT WERE RESTORED TO THEIR FORMER GRANDEUR AND SIGNIFICANCE IN DOWNTOWN DES MOINES (TOP).

FROM HUMBLE BEGINNINGS, BPC HAS GROWN TO BECOME A VIBRANT AND SPIRITED FORCE FOR CHANGE AND DEVELOPMENT IN A FAST-GROWING AND EVER EVOLVING CENTRAL IOWA BUSINESS COMMUNITY (BOTTOM).

PAUL GATES, BPC

A TABLE SAW, HIS LIFE SAVINGS, A LITTLE FRUSTRATION, AND a dream. That's what it took for Donald Peschke to publish the first issue of *Woodsmith* magazine in 1979. Within 10 years, his entrepreneurial efforts paid off, as the publishing company he founded landed twice

on *Inc.* magazine's list of the 500 fastest-growing privately owned companies in America.

Today, August Home Publishing Company publishes five national, award-winning magazines: *Woodsmith, ShopNotes, Garden Gate, Cuisine,* and *Workbench*. In addition, the company has expanded to meet its mission of "surrounding our customers with service."

August Home also publishes woodworking books; operates the Woodsmith Store in Des Moines (a dream store for woodworkers); has a mail-order business that supplies woodworking and gardening products; provides home centers and woodworking stores around the country with Woodsmith tools, plans, and hardware kits through its wholesale division; and has a new media group devoted to producing an active commerce and information site on the World Wide Web (www.augusthome.com).

BORN OF FRUSTRATION

In 1978, Peschke was 30 years old—and a frustrated, beginning woodworker. He wanted plans and instructions to help him build furniture, but all he

could find in magazines at the time were articles showing a picture of the project, one large drawing, and a few details about building it. What he wanted was a magazine that showed how to build projects step-by-step, down to the last detail, in down-to-earth language. That magazine didn't exist. So he quit his job and set out to produce it on his own.

The first issue of *Woodsmith* magazine contained only eight pages, with no advertising. Peschke designed and built the projects in his basement shop, wrote the copy on a small desk in a spare

bedroom, and learned how to draw the illustrations. Then he spent his life savings of $7,000 to print and promote the first issue.

His dream worked. There were thousands of frustrated woodworkers, like him, around the country. That was all it took for Woodsmith Publishing Company (as it was known then) to be born.

What started as a single magazine with only 300 subscribers has grown to five titles with more than a million subscribers. More than 100 professionals work for the company at five facilities in Des Moines.

GROWTH AND ACQUISITION

For the first 14 years, the company concentrated on woodworking. After launching *Woodsmith* in 1978, it opened the Woodsmith Store in 1985, and also began a tool and hardware mail-order business for its readers. *Woodsmith*'s popularity led to a second magazine, *ShopNotes*, launched in 1992, and expanded the company's interest in publishing.

In 1995, *Garden Gate*, a magazine for home gardeners, was launched. This was followed in 1996 with the purchase of *Work-*

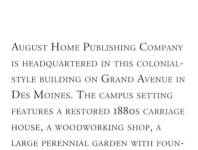

AUGUST HOME PUBLISHING COMPANY IS HEADQUARTERED IN THIS COLONIAL-STYLE BUILDING ON GRAND AVENUE IN DES MOINES. THE CAMPUS SETTING FEATURES A RESTORED 1880S CARRIAGE HOUSE, A WOODWORKING SHOP, A LARGE PERENNIAL GARDEN WITH FOUNTAINS, AND A SECOND OFFICE BUILDING.

THE COMPANY PUBLISHES FIVE NATIONAL, BIMONTHLY PUBLICATIONS FOR HOME ENTHUSIASTS: *WOODSMITH, SHOPNOTES,* AND *WORKBENCH* FOR WOODWORKERS AND THOSE INTERESTED IN HOME IMPROVEMENT, *GARDEN GATE* FOR GARDENERS, AND *CUISINE* FOR COOKS.

bench, a 40-year-old home improvement and woodworking magazine, and in the same year, the launch of *Cuisine*, a magazine for those who love to cook.

As the company branched out to these other interests, Peschke renamed it August Home Publishing. This reflected its mission to publish guidance and inspiration in four core areas: woodworking, gardening, cooking, and home improvement.

Unlike traditional publishing companies, August Home relies almost entirely on revenue from subscriptions rather than advertising. In fact, with the exception of *Workbench*, none of the magazines accepts advertising. Instead, they concentrate on producing top-quality, compelling magazines to which a very high percentage of readers will renew their subscriptions each year.

The publications also incorporate a friendly, first-person writing style, intended to make the reader feel as though he or she is actually in the workshop, garden, or kitchen, exchanging ideas with a fellow enthusiast.

FROM HUMBLE BEGINNINGS

The headquarters for August Home is a handsome, brick, colonial-style building on Grand Avenue that reflects the company's personality by resembling a home more than an office. The pleasant campus also includes another office building next door, a restored 1880s brick carriage house, and a large perennial garden.

In keeping with the hands-on nature of the magazines, the office houses a full-fledged workshop, where all woodworking projects are built. Close by is a seven-acre site with the test kitchen for *Cuisine*, a working test garden for *Garden Gate*, and a large photo studio.

The Woodsmith Store, in Des Moines' Beaverdale neighborhood, is a one-stop shopping center for woodworkers, providing power tools, hand tools, hardwood lumber, and a myriad of supplies. The wholesale and mail-order products

division warehouse is based on Bell Avenue. Each day, hundreds of orders for tools, hardware kits, and back issues of the company's publications are shipped all over the world.

FROM ENTREPRENEURSHIP TO CORPORATION

Like most entrepreneurs, Peschke was originally very active in every decision. To foster growth and creativity, the organization has evolved so that today, group managers are responsible for the day-to-day operations of the company, as well as for its future. Each manager works with her or his group of professionals (everyone has the title "professional"

AUGUST HOME'S PROFESSIONALS WORK TOGETHER IN GROUPS AND TEAMS TO COME UP WITH CREATIVE PRODUCTS, PUBLICATIONS, AND THE BEST CUSTOMER SERVICE AVAILABLE (TOP).

THE WOODSMITH STORE, IN THE BEAVERDALE NEIGHBORHOOD OF DES MOINES, IS A WOODWORKER'S DREAM SHOP. IT PROVIDES POWER AND HAND TOOLS, HARDWOOD LUMBER, A WIDE VARIETY OF SUPPLIES, AND EXCELLENT CUSTOMER SERVICE FOR BOTH THE PROFESSIONAL AND HOME WOODWORKER (LEFT).

at August Home). The groups have the freedom of an independent business, while still receiving the support of the larger company. "The role of a manager is not to supervise other people," Peschke says. "It's to help other people, including our customers, be successful."

August Home is in a strategic position to move into the future as the world progresses into the information age. Whether it be through printed magazines, the Internet, or multimedia delivery, the company is committed to publishing the highest-quality information and services to customers who enjoy creative endeavors around their homes.

DES MOINES BUSINESSMAN CARL MOYER IS FREQUENTLY asked why the logo of his Chevrolet dealership, Karl Chevrolet, is a large, red, backward letter *K*. An amateur cartoonist since childhood, Moyer devised the eye-catching logo while awaiting the initial approval for his

dealership from the Chevrolet Motor Division in Detroit.

Today, the logo is a familiar sight on the dealership's letterhead, invoices, sales receipts, and key chains. It is also prominent on racing events sponsored by the dealership and televised across the country. While customers don't always understand the origin of the big red *K*, they do recognize the excellence of the dealership it symbolizes.

KARL CHEVROLET HAS A FULLY STOCKED GENERAL MOTORS (GM) PARTS DEPARTMENT, AS WELL AS A REPAIR SHOP WITH STATE-OF-THE-ART EQUIPMENT AND FULLY TRAINED TECHNICIANS.

SOLID GROWTH

When Moyer first bought his dealership, he had no employees and no cars to sell. The young man persuaded Norwest Bank to risk financing his venture, and Karl Chevrolet opened its doors as a full-service Chevrolet dealership with an inventory of approximately 20 new cars and trucks.

Since its founding in 1978, Moyer's dealership has grown from 15 to 118 employees. In its first year, sales totaled $6 million, and by 1997, sales had jumped to more than $70 million. Recognizing the value of competition, the firm adheres to its popular slogan: Working to be Number One. "I'd rather be nipping at competitors' heels than having them trying to

knock us out of the top spot," Moyer says.

Karl Chevrolet moved to its present location in 1983, and in 1996, expanded from 32,000 square feet to 60,000 square feet. Each of its five departments—new car sales, used car sales, body shop, service, and parts—has a separate customer entrance. The company has the specialized technicians and accommodations to service motor homes and medium-duty trucks. It is also an authorized dealer of medium-duty Kodiak trucks. Keeping the business in the family, Carl Moyer's son Bret manages used car sales, and his son Brad and son-in-law Joe Fontana are used car sales associates.

Karl Chevrolet was the first business to locate in the Metro

North business park on the outskirts of Ankeny. Its move paved the way for developing the area, and set the standard for the many businesses now established there.

CHEVROLET PRODUCTS

Karl Chevrolet offers a wide selection of every Chevrolet product, including Corvettes, and a used-car inventory of late-model, top-of-the-line vehicles. It has a fully stocked General Motors (GM) Parts department, as well as a repair shop with state-of-the-art equipment and fully trained technicians, many of whom are GM Master Mechanics. Its body shop is a completely new facility with the latest technology, including new paint booths and frame machines.

THE DEALERSHIP IS UNIQUE IN ITS INSISTENCE ON CLEANLINESS, AND FOR THE OUTDOOR RECREATIONAL AREA IT OFFERS CUSTOMERS, EMPLOYEES, AND THE COMMUNITY. TWO SMALL LAKES WITH FOUNTAINS ARE SURROUNDED BY A WALKING PATH DOTTED WITH BENCHES. NEARBY GROUNDS OFFER A CONCRETE BASKETBALL COURT, A PLAYGROUND WITH EQUIPMENT, A COVERED PAVILION WITH PICNIC TABLES, AND A PAR THREE GOLF GREEN (LEFT AND RIGHT).

Most of Karl Chevrolet's large, established customer base is in Iowa, where the dealership is known for customer satisfaction, convenience, dependability, and professionalism. Several of the dealership's sales staff are members of General Motor's Legion of Leaders for high sales volume. The service department was awarded a certificate of achievement from GM in 1997 for meeting all training requirements and standards in every aspect of GM service technology. The general office also has won the Accounting Excellence Team Award from GM every year since the dealership's founding.

Putting the Customer First

Karl Chevrolet operates on the philosophy that taking care of the customer is its first priority. The dealership provides quality products and service, and the highest level of professionalism in every department, in a friendly, no-pressure atmosphere. As a result, Chevrolet consistently lists it among the top 25 of 5,000 Chevrolet dealerships in the nation for customer service. "That's something I'm awfully proud of," Moyer says.

Still, Karl Chevrolet centers its goals around improving service to promote new business and encourage the return of satisfied customers. The dealership is unique in its insistence on cleanliness, and for the outdoor recreational area it offers customers, employees, and the community. Two small lakes

with fountains are surrounded by a walking path dotted with benches. Nearby grounds offer a concrete basketball court, a playground with equipment, a covered pavilion with picnic tables, and a par three golf green. The park-like area has even been the setting for a wedding.

Karl Chevrolet is a major supporter of the local schools, YMCA, and civic organizations. Each year, the company sponsors the annual summertime Air Expo, an exposition and fly-in of antique and vintage aircraft from across the country.

Hot Rod Racing

Carl Moyer, a three-time Pro-Modified Class world champion, has set six national records in the pro-modified division since 1986, when he reentered drag racing competition. Moyer promotes the use of Chevrolet products in his racing, and that exposure has brought his dealership sales

of vehicles and parts to a nationwide clientele.

Karl Chevrolet is the Official Dealership of the International Hot Rod Association and provides a multivehicle package of support trucks for the program. In addition, he has assisted other racers with monetary sponsorships or vehicles and parts at discounted prices. Moyer also owns Eddyville Raceway Park, an NHRA-sanctioned, one-eighth-mile drag strip in Eddyville, Iowa. The dealership's Parts Department Pro Shop offers apparel and memorabilia from the popular GM-sponsored racer Dale Earnhardt, along with Goodwrench vehicle care products.

After more than 20 years in business, Moyer still delights in working with cars and serving his customers well. "There's nothing about this job that's work," he says. "Truthfully, it's somewhat like being on vacation full-time. I love people, and I love what I do."

EARLY MORNING PREPARATIONS ARE UNDER WAY THE DAY OF KARL CHEVROLET'S RE-GRAND OPENING IN 1996. THE EVENT CELEBRATED THE EXPANSION AND DEVELOPMENT OF THE DEALERSHIP (LEFT AND RIGHT).

MOYER (PICTURED IN CENTER) OWNS THE ONE-EIGHTH-MILE EDDYVILLE RACEWAY PARK TRACK IN EDDYVILLE, IOWA, AND PROMOTES MANY OUTINGS FOR GROUPS AND ORGANIZATIONS AT THE RACE TRACK (BOTTOM).

SINCE ITS FOUNDING IN 1982, INVESTORS MANAGEMENT GROUP (IMG) has grown rapidly from a two-person office in Des Moines to one of the Midwest's largest asset managers. IMG's success reflects its emphasis on building a highly talented asset management team in a rewarding professional environment. The firm's portfolio managers are experts in equity and fixed-income portfolio management, and manage individual accounts as well as the firm's own Vintage Funds family. IMG has established a solid investment performance history in managing equity, fixed-income, cash, and balanced accounts over the years.

Investors Management Group is headquartered in Des Moines, creating a natural focus on Iowa client relationships. With additional offices in Rockford and Madison, the firm maintains a strong regional presence across the upper Midwest. Representative clients of the firm include high-net-worth families, endowments and foundations, financial institutions, insurance companies, and public bodies. Examples of the firm's innovative management efforts include the Iowa Schools Joint Investment Trust, the Iowa Public Agency Investment Trust, and the Nebraska Public Agency Investment Trust—three local government investment pools, with roughly 1,000 public entity participants, that serve as models for efforts in other states.

A COMPREHENSIVE APPROACH

Independent research is the foundation upon which IMG anchors its investment process. Consistent attention to an established discipline has enabled the firm to become a well-respected source of investment research and performance. Over the years, the firm has developed proprietary statistical analyses and compiled an extensive database of economic and financial relationships. "Our objective is to provide high-quality asset management services to individuals, corporations, foundations and endowments, and public bodies through independent research and proprietary asset management activities," says Mark A. McClurg, senior managing director.

To avoid distractions to longer-term investment objectives that short-term events can easily cause, IMG's investment discipline focuses on long-term investment performance. Performing well in bull

PERHAPS INVESTORS MANAGEMENT GROUP'S (IMG) MOST VISIBLE CONTRIBUTION TO CENTRAL IOWA IS THE COMPANY'S CORPORATE HEADQUARTERS, THE HISTORIC CRAWFORD MANSION. THE TWO-AND-A-HALF-STORY BRICK HOUSE, DESIGNED IN 1896 BY A PROMINENT LOCAL ARCHITECTURAL FIRM AND ADDED TO THE NATIONAL REGISTER OF HISTORIC PLACES IN 1982, UNDERWENT EXTENSIVE RENOVATION IN 1995.

▲ MULLICA STUDIO

markets and minimizing losses when markets fall is a management philosophy that helps the firm's clients remain committed to long-term investment goals.

EXPANSION BRINGS GROWTH

IMG greatly expanded its operations upon completion of a 1998 merger with AMCORE Financial Inc.'s offices in Madison and Rockford. Following the merger, IMG doubled assets under management to $4 billion, placing it in the top 15 percent of asset management firms in the country. The company now employs more than 60 people in three states.

IMG anticipates continued growth internally from client asset expansion as well as possible additional future acquisitions. "We continually evaluate complementary acquisition and strategic alliance opportunities that might better enable IMG to provide top-quality asset management services to current and future clients into the next century," says David Miles, senior managing director.

The 1998 merger also increased IMG's Vintage Funds family to roughly $1.25 billion, about one-third of the company's total assets under management. The Vintage Funds, a proprietary family of 10 no-load mutual funds, offer investors a series of complementary investment objectives, ranging from aggressive growth to capital preservation. The Vintage Funds are available to investors with very low minimum investment amounts, enabling investors of every size to access the firm's sophisticated asset management skills. Several of the Vintage Funds have received national recognition from Morningstar Inc., a national mutual fund rating service.

Interaction with clients plays a key role in IMG's success. The company's institutional clients are encouraged to speak directly with the portfolio manager making investment decisions on their behalf and to meet with the asset management team at the client's discretion. The company also communicates with clients via special events and the *Economic & Market Survey,* IMG's quarterly journal offering the firm's in-depth economic analysis.

In addition to supporting the asset management needs of clients, IMG actively contributes to the Des Moines community financially and by strongly encouraging employees to participate in civic organizations.

Perhaps IMG's most visible contribution to central Iowa is the company's corporate headquarters, the historic Crawford Mansion. The two-and-a-half-story brick house, designed in 1896 by a prominent local architectural firm and added to the National Register of Historic Places in 1982, underwent extensive renovation in 1995. The carefully restored, ornate exterior and interior of the building reflect the company's commitment to high-quality work products.

Looking forward, Investors Management Group plans to increase its geographic presence beyond the Midwest. Enhanced distribution of the Vintage Funds will be a substantial part of IMG's growth through the end of the 1990s. The company will make its investment products more widely available through strategic alliances and direct presentation of the firm's capabilities to institutional prospects. Armed with strong proprietary research abilities, a proven track record of financial success achieved for clients, and a sound vision for the firm's operating future, IMG is successfully poised to enhance itself and its clients as they enter the new millennium.

MARK McCLURG (LEFT) AND DAVID MILES, IMG'S SENIOR MANAGING DIRECTORS, ARE PICTURED HERE IN FRONT OF THE CRAWFORD MANSION, THE FIRM'S HISTORIC CORPORATE HEADQUARTERS.

MULLICA STUDIO

CONSIDER THIS APPARENT MISMATCH: AN OFFICE ENVIRONMENT that finds metal grain bins within 10 feet of a wood-and-Plexiglas corn crib, and an Internet domain name— outofthebox.com—that describes the creative thinking that the group delivers to its clients. ■ For Meyocks & Priebe

THE AGENCY'S UNIQUE INTERIOR DESIGN REFLECTS THE CREATIVE THINKING IT DELIVERS TO CLIENTS (RIGHT).

THE "CRIB," ONE OF THE AGENCY'S MAJOR CONFERENCE AREAS, IS PHOTO-GRAPHED HERE AS IT RARELY IS—UNOCCU-PIED. AN OPEN, RELAXED ATMOSPHERE FOSTERS COMFORT AND THE FREE EX-CHANGE OF IDEAS FOR BOTH AGENCY CLIENTS AND TEAM MEMBERS (BELOW).

Advertising, Inc., the seeming contrast between its rural-but-contemporary interior architecture and the agency's wacky World Wide Web address is intentional.

"We're a food-chain agency with roots in agriculture," explains Ted Priebe, agency president and chief executive officer. "The global food production systems of the 21st century will be highly focused on meeting specific customer needs, and we recognize that the gaps between the ultimate con-sumer and the food producer are collapsing at a rate difficult for many people to appreciate.

"In this environment, it's our job to help clients use the appro-priate communication tools to create and maintain brands that foster strong relationships, one customer at a time. Because we work with clients who have prod-ucts along all points of the food production continuum, we're in a unique position to deliver on that promise."

STIMULATING CREATIVE MINDS

The approach has paid off for the agency. From its one-person public relations operation in 1984, Meyocks & Priebe has grown to more than 100 people— referred to as team members— working from four cities: the West Des Moines headquarters, as well as offices in Minneapolis, Chicago, and Madison.

The work environment in every location is unique, and each has the goal of stimulating the people inside to raise their creative think-ing standards each day. Another contributor is a decidedly unstruc-tured structure. There are no de-partments, no titles, and only one profit center: the overall bottom line.

The agency's attention to the needs of its team members has attracted strong brand marketers and communicators from across the country. Meyocks & Priebe's team-oriented atmosphere also has had a great deal to do with an amazingly low turnover rate. That has helped the agency grow significantly, tripling in size be-tween 1995 and 1998.

PARTNERING FOR PROFIT

The Meyocks & Priebe plan for the future is to focus more on the food part of the food chain. One example is an agency-created partnership with clients Hy-Vee and Kraft Foods—which

was named a national "case his-tory of the year" by Andersen Consulting for their Successful Selling Solutions program.

The agency constantly encour-ages entrepreneurial innovation among its staff. Two new service groups, Purple Box Design and Purple Box Response, enhance the mix of integrated communi-cation services that the agency can provide to current and poten-tial clients. Purple Box Design moves the agency into the spe-cialized areas of packaging, logo development, and concept design for exhibits and special events. Purple Box Response marries two critical aspects of relation-ship marketing by harnessing the Internet's sophistication and capabilities to the personalization and courtesy necessary for suc-cessful customer service.

The agency is looking to ex-pand in other regions and is build-ing its skills in foreign languages and global communications. Meyocks & Priebe is committed to being the country's largest and most creative food-chain agency, and is well on its way to that goal.

W HEN DAN AND CAROLE KAVANAUGH BEGAN COLLECTING art in the early 1970s, they didn't expect to eventually own a thriving outlet for the creative products of local and world-renowned artists. But since Dan Kavanaugh began his own shop around 1988, the husband-and-wife

team has built one of the finest art galleries in the Midwest.

When the gallery first opened, Kavanaugh planned for it to occupy his time after he retired. He envisioned something fairly small that he could tinker at three or four days each week. Carole joined him as director, and over time, the business blossomed as others began to experience the pleasures of art offered by Kavanaugh Art Gallery. Dan Kavanaugh attributes the growth to an increased appreciation for fine, original artwork in the Midwest, and an appreciation for local and regional artistic work. Indeed, what sets this gallery apart from the rest is the variety of original works. Easy access to some of the best artwork in the world means patrons do not have to travel to New York, Los Angeles, or San Francisco to find a perfect piece for their homes and offices.

Moving Pictures

The Kavanaugh Art Gallery has twice relocated to larger quarters. Currently, its storefront is nestled in the heart of West Des Moines' Valley Junction neighborhood, a center for specialty shops. Hundreds of artists—including the famous Don Hatfield and Henri Plisson—are represented at the gallery, which has shipped artwork all over the United States, as well as to Europe and Japan. The Kavanaugh Art Gallery uses 6,500 square feet of floor space to showcase fine paintings, sculptures, and custom, museum-quality framing. The walls are lined nearly to the ceiling with paintings of everything from gardens and flowers to women sitting in a parlor.

Another draw may be that Kavanaugh Art Gallery offers something in everyone's price range. Posters sell for $40, paintings sell for $40,000, and there's a range of work available for prices anywhere in between.

A Love for Art

The Kavanaugh Art Gallery is a labor of love for its owners. The Kavanaughs have an eagle eye that can spot the types of artwork patrons seek. This skill serves them well not only in finding pieces for their gallery, but also in their consulting work. Carole Kavanaugh can look at the general decor of a room in a home or office and learn the art buyer's likes and dislikes through conversation. Following her assessment, she can recommend specific art pieces within a customer's price range that could put the finishing touch to a room. Traditional furniture may call for a traditional-style painting, while modern furniture may call for a 20th-century piece. And a room with fairly monotone hues may require a splash of color on the wall in the form of a bright painting that draws attention.

Carole, Dan, and their three employees try to pick art for the gallery's clients that offers a style. The couple plans to continue offering high-quality, affordable art to the public. Says Dan Kavanaugh, "There is a customer for every art and style."

WHAT SETS KAVANAUGH ART GALLERY APART FROM THE REST IS THE VARIETY OF ORIGINAL WORKS. EASY ACCESS TO SOME OF THE BEST ARTWORK IN THE WORLD MEANS PATRONS DO NOT HAVE TO TRAVEL TO NEW YORK, LOS ANGELES, OR SAN FRANCISCO TO FIND A PERFECT PIECE FOR THEIR HOMES AND OFFICES.

I N THE MID-1980S, A NEW, HIGH-TECH PIECE OF EQUIPMENT—THE lithotripter—was federally approved, revolutionizing the treatment of urinary stones. Three of Des Moines' hospitals wanted to offer the state-of-the-art medical procedure to its patients, but the high cost for the equipment—a lithotripter originally cost about $1.5

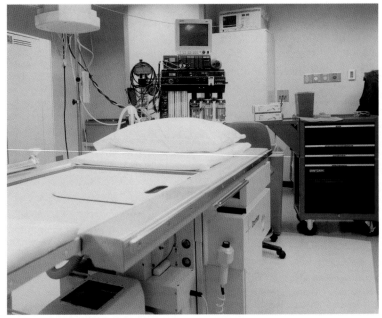

CLOCKWISE FROM TOP:
SINCE THE IOWA KIDNEY STONE CENTER OPENED IN MAY 1986, MORE THAN 9,000 PATIENTS HAVE BEEN TREATED, AND THE NUMBER CONTINUES TO GROW.

THE NONPROFIT IOWA KIDNEY STONE CENTER WAS BORN THROUGH THE PIONEERING EFFORTS OF IOWA LUTHERAN HOSPITAL, IOWA METHODIST MEDICAL CENTER, AND MERCY HOSPITAL MEDICAL CENTER.

A FAMILY ATMOSPHERE HAS EVOLVED AMONG THE SMALL STAFF AT THE IOWA KIDNEY STONE CENTER, WHICH IS COMMITTED TO PROVIDING THE BEST HEALTH CARE POSSIBLE.

million—was too prohibitive for each facility to acquire. In an effort to bring the equipment and procedure to central Iowa, the hospitals joined forces and formed a unique collaborative relationship, sharing the cost of the equipment and the facility where patients would be treated.

Thus, the nonprofit Iowa Kidney Stone Center was born through the pioneering efforts of Iowa Lutheran Hospital, Iowa Methodist Medical Center, and Mercy Hospital Medical Center. A staff of 16 urologists from Ames, Des Moines, Fort Dodge, and Marshalltown travel to the center to perform patient treatments for urinary stones. Anesthesia services are provided by anesthesiologists from Iowa Methodist Medical Center and Mercy Hospital Medical Center in one-week rotations. In combination with the medical staff, the highly trained clinical staff join to provide a caring, supportive environment, working one-on-one with patients and their families. A family atmosphere has evolved among the small staff, which is committed to providing the best health care possible.

THE BEST IN HEALTH CARE

S ince the Iowa Kidney Stone Center opened in May 1986, more than 9,000 patients have been treated, and the number continues to grow. The center now treats more than 1,000 patients annually, some of whom have traveled 50 to 75 miles to Des Moines for the procedure. There is no average person who undergoes a kidney stone procedure—the center has treated a patient as young as three years old and one as mature as 92 years old. About 45 percent of those treated are women, which is consistent with the national trend.

The procedure was revolutionary when it was first introduced. In the past, kidney stones were removed through major surgery that left patients hospitalized for days and recovering for weeks. But lithotripsy helps the body eliminate kidney stones without surgery. During the procedure, a patient rests comfortably on a fluid-filled cushion and an X ray is used to pinpoint the exact location of the stone. Shock waves are focused to break up the stones, which crumble into fine, sandlike particles that pass through the patient's urinary tract. The procedure takes about one hour, and the patient is monitored posttreatment in the center's recovery room.

Active in the American Lithotripsy Society, the staff at the Iowa Kidney Stone Center is committed to offering the latest that technology has to offer. Ancillary equipment and supplies are constantly being updated, and the latest software and hardware are added so patients can benefit from the most up-to-date medical advances. The center has been recognized on a national level within the industry for excellence of care and for being one of the busiest freestanding kidney stone treatment centers in the country.

The Iowa Kidney Stone Center is dedicated to continuing to pursue its mission of offering high-quality patient care, improving its equipment, and providing education to those scheduled for treatment.

SINCE THE LATE 1970S, INCISIONAL REFRACTIVE SURGERY HAS BEEN used to treat myopia, or nearsightedness, allowing persons a freedom from total dependence on glasses or contact lenses. ▓ Recently, refractive surgery, or laser vision correction, experienced a revolution with the FDA approval of the

excimer laser. This technology represents a precise and permanent procedure for treatment of myopia, astigmatism, and farsightedness. More than 25 percent of the population could experience an improved lifestyle with less dependence on corrective lenses with these procedures.

In order to offer these revolutionary procedures to people in central Iowa, three hospitals in Des Moines have capitalized on a cooperative health care effort that started more than a decade earlier. Iowa Lutheran Hospital, Iowa Methodist Medical Center, and Mercy Hospital Medical Center could not individually substantiate purchase of the new and expensive excimer eye laser. They decided to merge resources, as they did when they began the Iowa Kidney Stone Center.

As a result, the three hospitals are now offering another medical breakthrough in health care to central Iowans through the Laser Eye Center of Iowa. The center opened its doors in April 1997, and more than 2,000 people have since been treated. The number of people who are undergoing the surgery—and paying for it themselves, since it is an elective, non-reimbursable procedure according to insurance companies—continues to increase at a phenomenal rate.

STATE-OF-THE-ART TREATMENT
Experienced, certified ophthalmologists from Ames, Des Moines, and Marshalltown provide laser vision correction procedures. The goal is to improve a person's eyesight and lifestyle, and minimize dependence on glasses and contacts.

Physicians on staff at the Laser Eye Center of Iowa use an FDA-approved excimer laser to correct nearsightedness, farsightedness,

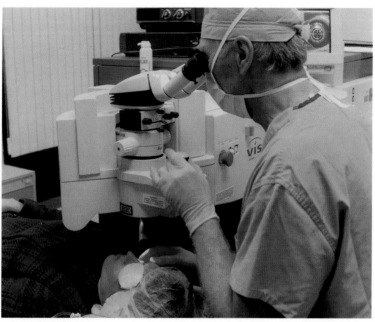

and astigmatism by carefully reshaping the cornea to better refract light. With the accuracy and non-thermal benefits of the laser, this new technology produces more consistent and predictable results than previous laser vision correction procedures.

The Laser Eye Center of Iowa continues to provide the latest software, computer programming, and equipment available to ensure quality results. The most positive consequence of this cooperative health care effort is how pleased

the patients are with the outcomes they experience from these state-of-the-art procedures.

For a patient, finding out about the health of his or her eyes and their refractive error through a complete vision examination and consultation with an eye care professional is the first step toward visual independence. In general, the ideal patient has a healthy cornea and has had a stable prescription for the preceding year. The decision to have laser vision correction is ultimately the patient's.

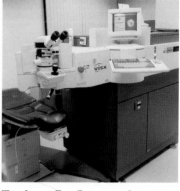

THE LASER EYE CENTER OF IOWA CONTINUES TO PROVIDE THE LATEST SOFTWARE, COMPUTER PROGRAMMING, AND EQUIPMENT AVAILABLE TO ENSURE QUALITY RESULTS.

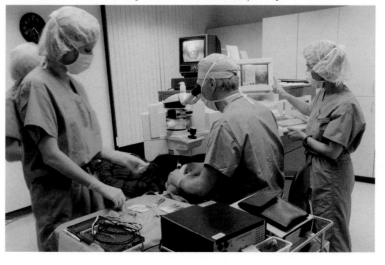

PHYSICIANS ON STAFF AT THE LASER EYE CENTER OF IOWA USE AN FDA-APPROVED EXCIMER LASER TO CORRECT NEARSIGHTEDNESS, FARSIGHTEDNESS, AND ASTIGMATISM BY CAREFULLY RESHAPING THE CORNEA TO BETTER REFRACT LIGHT.

Prairie Meadows Racetrack and Casino is the first entertainment facility in the nation to combine the thrill of live horse racing with the excitement of a 24-hour slot-machine casino. Known as "Your favorite place to play!," Prairie Meadows opened in 1989 as a pari-mutuel horse track and restaurant.

In 1995, Prairie Meadows expanded to include more than 1,100 slot machines covering two floors. There are nearly 600 colorful models available for play, with an average payback of 94.7 percent (August 1998 statistics). Year-round simulcast horse and dog racing and free, nationally recognized entertainment complement the fun.

PRAIRIE MEADOWS IS THE FIRST HORSE TRACK IN THE NATION TO INCLUDE A 24-HOUR CASINO, OFFERING MORE THAN 1,100 FESTIVE SLOT MACHINES WITH NEARLY 600 COLORFUL MODELS AVAILABLE FOR PLAY (RIGHT).

PRAIRIE MEADOWS RACETRACK AND CASINO PROVIDES THE DES MOINES AREA WITH SOPHISTICATED ENTERTAINMENT AND THE THRILL OF LIVE HORSE RACING AND CASINO GAMING, AND IT IS ALSO DEDICATED TO IMPROVING THE COMMUNITY THROUGH ITS PROFITS (BOTTOM).

"Go, Baby, Go!"

When the starting gate opens, the ground rumbles, jockeys shout, and fans cheer as a swarm of thundering hooves rockets past the grandstand. Throughout its live racing season, Prairie Meadows hosts some of the finest racing in the Midwest. Prairie Meadows hosted six graded stakes races in 1998 with purses totaling nearly $600,000 and 52 other stakes totaling more than $2.4 million. Sports Radio KJJC (The Jock) 106.9 FM broadcasts the racing action

every Saturday night, providing complete analysis and live coverage.

Located at I-80 exit 142, next door to Adventureland amusement park and campgrounds, the racetrack is a one-mile, oval dirt track with live racing offered each year

between April and October. Twenty-seven nearby barns stall 1,450 Thoroughbreds, quarter horses, and standardbreds. Viewers can catch the races at their tables complete with monitors in the Clubhouse terraced dining area, or can select a spot in the grandstand. Patrons can also enjoy the beautiful outdoors and get close to the action on the track apron. Prairie Meadows also offers information about racing, promotions, and entertainment on its Web site at www. prairiemeadows.com.

Like other racing facilities in the state, events at Prairie Meadows are conducted under the supervision of the Iowa Racing and Gaming Commission. Unlike any other gaming enterprise in Iowa, Prairie Meadows is directly managed by a locally operated not-for-profit corporation. This arrangement permits all profits to remain in Iowa for reinvestment in the community.

Prairie Meadows— Charitable Giver

Prairie Meadows has solidified its position as an enthusiastic partner in facilitating community programs and services. In 1997, Prairie Meadows donated $3 million to 72 state and local charitable organizations. These grants were made possible exclusively through revenue generated by Prairie Meadows Racetrack and Casino.

Prairie Meadows celebrated its largest funding year ever in 1998, continuing its tradition of providing vital financial assistance to community and social needs, and distinguishing Prairie Meadows Racetrack and Casino as a leader in nonprofit corporate philanthropy. Beneficiaries include Veterans Memorial Auditorium, Polk County Convention Center, Des Moines Art Center, Living History Farms, Iowa Senior Games, Ankeny Substance Abuse Center, Bondurant Medical Clinic, Des Moines Area Religious Council Food Pantry, Homestead Autistic Center, Operation Downtown, Des Moines Symphony, and Polk County Crime Stoppers.

Prairie Meadows' impact has been felt in other ways as well. Since 1995, nearly $193 million has been allocated for county improvements and operations, including $13.8 million for day-to-day county expenses, $10.9 million for school infrastructure, $10.6 million for county construction, $8.3 million for a jail annex, $6.7 million for economic development, and $7.6 million for other community projects. Revenues from Prairie Meadows have also been instrumental in ensuring the 2002 completion of a beltway around the south side of Des Moines to Interstate 35 near West Des Moines.

AN ECONOMIC FORCE IN THE STATE OF IOWA

In 1997, more than 3.4 million visitors entered the doors of Prairie Meadows, nearly 27,000 more visitors than in 1996. Taxable room revenues have increased by a compound average annual growth rate (CAGR) of 12 percent since slot machines were introduced at Prairie Meadows. The CAGR for the prior three-year period was approximately 4.5 percent.

In 1997, Prairie Meadows employed more than 1,400 people. The overall increase in employment in the Des Moines area since the introduction of casino gaming has grown at a higher rate (5.7 percent) than the state average of 4.6 percent.

Taxes paid to the city of Altoona accounted for approximately 15 percent of the city's 1996 tax revenues. The $89 million debt incurred to fund the construction, renovation, and initial operations at Prairie

Meadows through bonds issued by Polk County was repaid in only 20 months.

Prairie Meadows Racetrack and Casino provides the Des Moines area with sophisticated entertainment and the thrill of live horse racing and casino gaming. Prairie Meadows is also dedicated to improving the community through its profits. The continued relationship between Prairie Meadows, Polk County, and the Greater Des Moines area makes everyone a winner.

PRAIRIE MEADOWS PRESENTS LIVE THOROUGHBRED, QUARTER HORSE, AND HARNESS RACING FROM APRIL THROUGH OCTOBER.

I MAGINE CREATING A BREAKTHROUGH IN MARKETING WITH A REVOLUTION in technology. At Relationship Marketing, they do. The agency and its forward-thinking clients have been defining and refining how one revolution, information technology, breathes life into another: one-to-one marketing. ■ After working at some of the top advertising

agencies, Jim Lewis, company founder and president, recognized that there was a better way for companies to communicate with their customers. In 1993, he established Relationship Marketing, an agency that integrates three core competencies in a rare unity—creativity, technology, and unique communication strategies—and named it after the most promising marketing trend of the future.

At Relationship Marketing, customers are individuals, each with unique needs, preferences, and purchase histories. Building powerful relationships with customers is essential to long-term success, and strengthening relationships with customers increases the amount of business customers do with a company over time.

One-to-one communication with customers shows them that

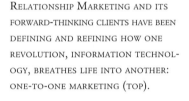

RELATIONSHIP MARKETING AND ITS FORWARD-THINKING CLIENTS HAVE BEEN DEFINING AND REFINING HOW ONE REVOLUTION, INFORMATION TECHNOLOGY, BREATHES LIFE INTO ANOTHER: ONE-TO-ONE MARKETING (TOP).

RELATIONSHIP MARKETING IS A COMPANY THAT OFFERS OPPORTUNITIES AND AN INNOVATIVE ENVIRONMENT THAT EMPLOYEES ARE NOT WILLING TO WALK AWAY FROM (BOTTOM).

a company knows their individual needs better than the competition does. This results in customers who are unwilling to walk away from the relationship. The customers have as much invested in a company as the company has in them.

How It Works

As a full-service agency, Relationship Marketing has all of the resources to make one-to-one communication with customers a reality, beginning with the heart of a winning relationship marketing campaign—a strategic marketing plan. Through a rigorous examination of situations, challenges, and opportunities, Relationship Marketing's experienced account consultants work with clients to create plans intent on gaining share of customer potential.

Once strategic goals have been defined, an award-winning creative team is paired with cutting-edge technology specialists. By combining their skills, customers receive communications tailored to their personal preferences, purchase history, lifestyle, and any other information that can be captured

in the client's database. High-impact print, broadcast, and video communications are not only personalized, but customized. Web sites, multimedia presentations, and direct response communications help customers pick up right where they left off in a progressive interchange of information.

Meanwhile, marketing professionals in Relationship Marketing's Relationship Development Center take client service to another level. They support a company's relationship marketing efforts as a sales force; a research team; and a customized, one-to-one fulfillment operation. They conduct qualitative research, build the database, generate leads, gather customer testimonials, and respond to customer requests.

Creating a Culture

At Relationship Marketing, Lewis's foresight is also driving another revolution. He believes that the battleground of the future will not be for customers, but for top talent. In order to attract and keep top talent, Lewis has developed a culture at Relationship Marketing where innovative, creative employees will thrive.

Structured into client teams, employees with different areas of expertise work together to develop and implement the best strategies for each client. The teams allow more efficient and effective communication and idea generation among coworkers. This structure also provides opportunities for the team members to learn and challenge each other to find better solutions for their clients—even before they ask. In an environment where each individual's ideas matter, the teams proactively search for better marketing tactics, meeting with the clients several times during the year to pitch new ways for them to communicate with their customers.

As team members, employees also play an active role in evaluating their coworkers' performances. To help foster the teams, team-building retreats are held four times per year, and to stay ahead of industry trends, employees are strongly encouraged to attend workshops, seminars, and internal training programs. After three years of meeting goals and exhibiting dedication to the company, employees are invited to become partners at Relationship Marketing.

The culture that attracts hardworking employees also helps them play hard. Once every four months, employees and their guests are invited to get together and cut loose at a Quarterly Disorderly. Past activities have included baseball games, reggae concerts, comedy shows, and holiday dinner parties. During the summer, employees play on the company's coed softball teams and participate in events such as the Des Moines Chamber of Commerce's Golden Circle Games.

Lewis has also started an incentive trip program at Relationship Marketing, dubbed Rejuven8. If the company meets its financial goal, the entire staff and their guests are treated to a five-day vacation of fun and relaxation. Rejuven8 destinations have included Scottsdale and Montego Bay.

THE BATTLEGROUND OF THE FUTURE WILL NOT BE FOR CUSTOMERS, BUT FOR TOP TALENT. IN ORDER TO ATTRACT AND KEEP TOP TALENT, RELATIONSHIP MARKETING FOUNDER AND PRESIDENT JIM LEWIS HAS DEVELOPED A CULTURE AT HIS AGENCY WHERE INNOVATIVE, CREATIVE EMPLOYEES WILL THRIVE.

Relationship Marketing is a company that offers opportunities and an environment that employees are not willing to walk away from.

WINNING RECOGNITION

The agency that specializes in building relationships and its employees is also concerned about building the community. Relationship Marketing partnered with the Animal Rescue League by redesigning the league's communication and marketing plan. The company has also helped Blank Children's Hospital, Children and Families of Iowa, and the Iowa Alliance for Arts Education.

The company has been recognized for its excellence both locally and nationally. Relationship Marketing has received awards for its print, television, radio, Internet, and one-to-one communications. Relationship Marketing has also been featured in magazines, such as *AgriMarketing, Sales and Marketing Management, Desktop Publishing,*

Inside 1 to 1, and *HOW.* Newspapers, such as the *Des Moines Register* and the *Business Record,* have written articles on the agency. Lewis has also been honored for his efforts as a two-time regional finalist for the Ernst & Young Entrepreneur of the Year award.

By continuing to develop the innovative culture and create relationships that customers are unwilling to walk away from, Relationship Marketing is helping define the future of marketing.

THE AGENCY HAS RECEIVED AWARDS FOR ITS PRINT, TELEVISION, RADIO, INTERNET, AND ONE-TO-ONE COMMUNICATIONS. RELATIONSHIP MARKETING HAS ALSO BEEN FEATURED IN MAGAZINES SUCH AS *AGRIMARKETING, SALES AND MARKETING MANAGEMENT, DESKTOP PUBLISHING, INSIDE 1 TO 1,* AND *HOW.*

IN AN EFFORT TO PROVIDE DEPENDABLE AND PRACTICAL WIRELESS communications equipment and service to its customers, United States Cellular Corporation (USCC) has become the nation's eighth-largest cellular provider. Boasting more than just financial success—$853 million in revenues in 1997—the corporation is also proud of how the company has helped to improve people's lives.

USCC's communication products and services routinely help to close business deals, obtain emergency assistance, and even complete such daily tasks as ordering a pizza. Founded in 1983, the Chicago-headquartered company serves more than 140 markets nationwide, representing more than 25 million people.

To help the family of the world's first surviving septuplets, born to Kenneth and Bobbi McCaughey in Des Moines in November 1997, USCC donated two complimentary phones and CarryPhone Home & Away service, which provides a phone with a single number and a single handset that operates as both a cordless and a cellular phone. Within 1,000 feet of the base station, the phone operates on land phone lines. When the handset is beyond the maximum range, it switches to cellular mode. This system will enable the McCaugheys to remain in close contact with family, friends, and community volunteers.

KENNY MCCAUGHEY (CENTER), FATHER OF THE MCCAUGHEY SEPTUPLETS, ACCEPTS A CELLULAR PHONE FROM UNITED STATES CELLULAR CORPORATION (USCC) REPRESENTATIVES NANCY TWINING (LEFT) AND SCOTT HOLLIDAY. USCC GAVE THE IOWA FAMILY FREE CELLULAR SERVICE FOR A YEAR AS WELL AS COMPANY APPAREL.

EVERY YEAR THOUSANDS OF IOWANS VISIT THE USCC BOOTH AT THE IOWA STATE FAIR, ONE OF THE MOST POPULAR BOOTHS IN THE VARIED INDUSTRIES BUILDING.

Sensible Services

USCC entered the Greater Des Moines market in 1992, and now operates retail and service locations in Des Moines, Urbandale, West Des Moines, Ankeny, Altoona, and Ames. The company also has outlets in such retail establishments as Wal-Mart and Kmart, as well as authorized agents trained to sell its products in other venues. Iowa customers enjoy the benefit of statewide, toll-free calling, and because USCC's Midwest service area covers more than 100,000 square miles, callers can reach people in parts of Missouri, Wisconsin, and Illinois.

USCC realizes that customers in rural states like Iowa have unique communications needs. While the company owns or has the right to purchase interests in cellular licenses in 63 metropolitan statistical areas (MSAs), its presence is even stronger outside of cities. In 1989, USCC switched on the continental United States' first cellular rural service area (RSA), operating independently of an MSA. By the end of 1997, some 100 managed RSAs were in operation, and today, USCC owns—or has the right to purchase—more than 115 RSAs nationwide.

To many city dwellers and small-town folk alike, the company's slogan, "United States Cellular—the way people talk around here," is more than just a play on words.

Customer Safety a Priority

In addition to maintaining competitive rates, increasing efficiency and convenience, and providing outstanding customer service, USCC is concerned about keeping its customers safe. It has established an emergency hot line at *55, which operates similarly to the universal 911 emergency number, and travelers can dial #SAFE (7233) to obtain weather conditions across Iowa.

Other programs sponsored by USCC work directly to fight crime. Established by the Cellular Telecommunications Industry Association, Citizens on Phone Patrol partners USCC and local police and sheriff's departments. In the program, USCC provides cellular phones to trained private citizens and uniformed police officers for use in patrolling trouble-prone neighborhoods.

USCC also has initiated and supported programs to help victims of domestic abuse, including Victims of Violence, which donates cellular phones to domestic violence survivors so they can quickly call for help in the event of an emergency. Another program benefiting

from USCC's donations of phones is the Domestic Violence Advocacy Program.

A Caring Company

To handle US CC's rapid success, the company's main office on Hickman Road in Urbandale was remodeled in 1997. Despite the quick growth, USCC is careful not to lose sight of what made it successful: its customers and their communities.

USCC has been involved in an industrywide program called ClassLink, which brings the latest technology to classrooms across the nation. In cooperation with the Cellular Telecommunications Industry Association, USCC has installed state-of-the-art commu-

nication systems in schools, including Roosevelt Middle School in Cedar Rapids. USCC donated airtime and lent support to school personnel to improve learning opportunities through the Internet and strengthen relationships between parents and teachers.

USCC also participates in more than 25 March of Dimes WalkAmerica events annually. Besides sponsorship contributions, the firm provided cellular phone donations, checkpoint stations, and employee walk teams.

USCC has made its resources available during many natural disasters and emergency situations. In the aftermath of the Oklahoma City bombing in 1995, the company responded by orchestrating a major fund drive for victim relief, as well as providing phones for media use. USCC also has supported the American Cancer Society, United Way, Make-A-Wish Foundation, Ronald McDonald House, and Habitat for Humanity.

While USCC looks forward to endless exciting developments in communication—from the arrival of widespread digital networks to increased privacy on cellular calls to extended battery life and up-to-date text messages from Wall Street or sports lines—its primary focus remains the same: to improve the lives of its customers and the community in which it does business.

USCC proudly serves the Des Moines area from its retail outlets in Des Moines, West Des Moines, Urbandale, Ames, Altoona, and Ankeny. The company also has sales kiosks in the Des Moines, West Des Moines, and Ankeny Wal-Marts.

RAGBRAI (the Register's Annual Great Bicycle Ride Across Iowa) is one of Iowa's greatest cultural attractions, drawing riders from every state in the Union as well as around the world. USCC participates in this great event by taking its traveling booth to every overnight stop along the route and providing free phone service to all riders and volunteers.

T HE IOWA CLINIC, P.C. IS AN INDEPENDENT, MULTISPECIALTY clinic based in Des Moines. Founded in 1993, the Iowa Clinic, P.C. was developed by physicians with the desire to keep pace with changes in health care. The Iowa Clinic, P.C. physicians realized the importance of creating a

physician organization that was committed to ensuring the delivery of quality health care to Iowans.

The clinic is comprised of 90 physicians practicing in 16 specialties, making it one of the largest and most comprehensive clinics in the Midwest. "The diversity and number of physicians associated with this clinic are testimony to our commitment to quality and our sensitivity to health care market issues," says Dr. David Boarini, a neurosurgeon and chairman of the clinic's board of directors.

The clinic's creed establishes principles that the physicians and staff apply to their practice of medicine: "The physicians and staff of the Iowa Clinic, P.C. are committed to improving the health of the patients we serve with care and compassion. We believe in this mission and the values that are critical to the profession of medicine. Our people, educational programs, quality of care, level of service, and integrity form the cornerstones of our practice. It is our pledge to uphold the duties of our profession as we

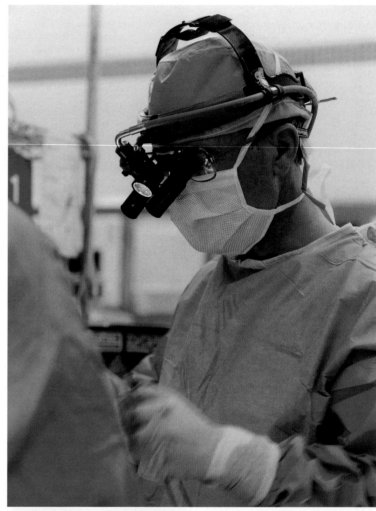

THE IOWA CLINIC, P.C. IS COMPRISED OF 90 PHYSICIANS PRACTICING IN 16 SPECIALTIES, INCLUDING (CLOCKWISE FROM TOP) HOOSHANG SOLTANZADEH, M.D., CARDIOTHORACIC SURGERY; RICHARD GLOOR, M.D., INTERNAL MEDICINE; LOUIS SCHNEIDER, D.O., INTERNAL MEDICINE; AND BERNARD MOUW, M.D., GENERAL SURGERY.

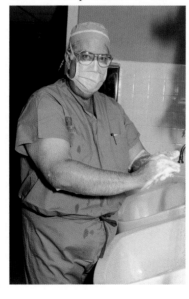

dedicate ourselves to healing those we serve." Through its staff of more than 300 employees, the clinic provides patient care in a friendly and relaxed atmosphere. The clinic's accessibility is also expanded through its more than 20 rural outreach sites across the state. In all, the clinic offers its health care expertise to more than 50,000 patients annually.

EXPERTS IN PROVIDING SPECIALIZED CARE

Patients come to the Iowa Clinic, P.C. for expert care in the areas of gastroenterology; pulmonary disease; cardiology; obstetrics and gynecology; otolaryngology; urology; neurology; neurosurgery; radiation oncology; and vascular, cardiothoracic, general, colorectal, oncological, plastic, and trauma surgery.

All Iowa Clinic, P.C. physicians are either board eligible or board certified in their specialties, which means they have the knowledge, expertise, and compassion to provide the highest-quality medical care. They have trained at the most respected medical centers and universities in the nation, and provide leading-edge medical technology to Iowans. The clinic's partnerships with local and rural hospitals, medical centers, and health care companies help ensure that it can utilize the best and most appropriate means of delivering medical care. Individuals and families who choose the Iowa Clinic, P.C. can have confidence that they will be provided the quality health care and expertise they deserve.

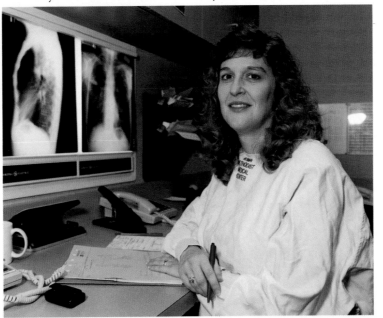

ALL IOWA CLINIC, P.C. PHYSICIANS— INCLUDING STEVEN HERWIG, D.O., OTOLARYNGOLOGY, AND ANGELA COLLINS, M.D., PULMONOLOGY—ARE EITHER BOARD ELIGIBLE OR BOARD CERTIFIED IN THEIR SPECIALTIES (TOP LEFT AND RIGHT).

THROUGH ITS FACILITIES AT IOWA METHODIST HOSPITAL (BOTTOM LEFT AND RIGHT) AND MORE THAN 20 RURAL OUTREACH SITES ACROSS THE STATE, THE CLINIC OFFERS ITS HEALTH CARE EXPERTISE TO MORE THAN 50,000 PATIENTS ANNUALLY.

CREATED IN 1993 BY THE MERGER OF IOWA METHODIST MEDICAL Center, Iowa Lutheran Hospital, and Blank Children's Hospital, Integra Health is the state's largest integrated delivery system. Soon, no Iowan will be more than 30 miles away from an affiliated health care provider or service of Integra Health.

The nonprofit Integra Health unites hospitals and physicians with long traditions of caring, compassion, service, and success. It also involves civic leaders and local volunteers who are open to new approaches and who share a vision of affordable, accessible health care. In addition to its three Des Moines hospitals, Integra Health is the parent company of St. Luke's Hospital in Cedar Rapids, Allen Memorial Hospital in Waterloo, St. Luke's Regional Medical Center in Sioux City, and The Finley Hospital in Dubuque. Integra Health Physicians, a primary care physician group with offices in 30 communities across Iowa, is also an affiliate; other affiliated physicians include Partners In Health, a Des Moines-based primary care practice with more than 40 physicians, and Children's Hospital Physicians, a pediatric multispecialty group providing a wide range of specialty care at Blank Children's Hospital.

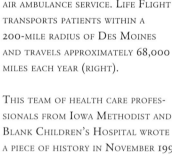

IOWA METHODIST WAS THE FIRST CENTRAL IOWA HOSPITAL TO OFFER AIR AMBULANCE SERVICE. LIFE FLIGHT TRANSPORTS PATIENTS WITHIN A 200-MILE RADIUS OF DES MOINES AND TRAVELS APPROXIMATELY 68,000 MILES EACH YEAR (RIGHT).

THIS TEAM OF HEALTH CARE PROFESSIONALS FROM IOWA METHODIST AND BLANK CHILDREN'S HOSPITAL WROTE A PIECE OF HISTORY IN NOVEMBER 1997 WITH THE SUCCESSFUL DELIVERY AND CARE OF THE WORLD'S FIRST SURVIVING SEPTUPLETS (BOTTOM).

IOWA METHODIST MEDICAL CENTER

Iowa Methodist Medical Center is the state's largest private hospital. Opened in 1901 as a single building with 30 beds, it now occupies a 42-acre campus, offers 710 beds, and employs more than 3,900 people.

In 1979, Iowa Methodist became the first central Iowa hospital to offer an air ambulance service. Today, Iowa Methodist, Iowa Lutheran, and Blank Children's Hospital treat the largest number of emergency patients in central Iowa.

A leader in cancer care, Iowa Methodist established the first radiation therapy department in Des Moines in 1956. In 1991, it opened the John Stoddard Cancer Center, the first central Iowa facility to house all radiation oncology and ancillary services in one location.

The Human Gene Therapy Research Institute at Iowa Methodist, established in 1993, is a nonprofit cancer research institute. In 1996, it became the nation's first community-based clinical facility to receive FDA approval to produce recombinant DNA pharmaceuticals.

Iowa Methodist Medical Center also is a leader in cardiac care. With Iowa Lutheran Hospital and Blank Children's Hospital, the center performs more than 900 open-heart surgeries every year. It also specializes in maternity and women's services, rehabilitation through its Younker Rehabilitation Center, wellness programs, behavioral medicine, surgery, orthopedics, critical care, primary care, geriatric services, and home health care.

IOWA LUTHERAN HOSPITAL

Iowa Lutheran Hospital opened in 1914 in answer to the critical need for a medical center on Des Moines' east side. After seven expansions over the years, it now has 465 beds and operates in conjunction with Iowa Methodist Medical Center.

Built on a site overlooking the Des Moines River, Iowa Lutheran Hospital founded the nation's first polio clinic, the state's first multiple sclerosis center, and the city's first kidney dialysis center.

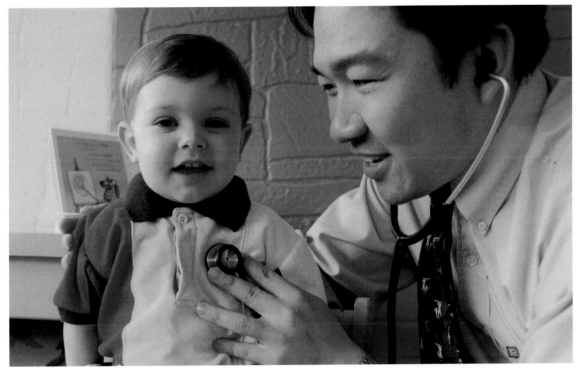

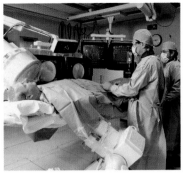

INTEGRA HEALTH HAS DEVELOPED A STATEWIDE, INTEGRATED HEALTH CARE DELIVERY SYSTEM WHERE NO IOWAN WILL BE MORE THAN 30 MILES FROM AN INTEGRA HEALTH PROVIDER OR SERVICE (TOP).

INTEGRA HEALTH PHYSICIANS' 22 CLINICS THROUGHOUT THE DES MOINES METROPOLITAN COMMUNITY OFFER EXTENDED HOURS AND WALK-IN ACCESSIBILITY (LEFT).

In 1969, the hospital achieved another first by allowing fathers in the delivery room. During the next two decades, Iowa Lutheran also brought fathers into the operating room for cesarean deliveries, established birthing rooms, initiated an infant and toddler car-seat loan program, and pioneered single-room maternity care with its Birth Day Suites.

Iowa Lutheran Hospital is home to the state's largest private hospital-based mental health facility. It combines advanced medical care with psychiatric diagnostic and treatment capabilities to address mental illness and emotional or behavioral problems. The hospital includes child and adolescent psychiatry, as well as a dual psychiatric and chemical dependency unit for adolescents.

BLANK CHILDREN'S HOSPITAL

Founded in 1944, Blank Children's Hospital is the only hospital in Iowa just for kids. This 96-bed facility is a leader in pediatric services, including pediatric intensive care, neonatal intensive care, and the only pediatric emergency department in the state. Blank also has the only dedicated children's cancer center in the state that combines inpatient and out-

patient treatment in one unit for continuity of care.

In 1997, Blank Children's Hospital and Iowa Methodist Medical Center became known around the globe for their successful delivery and neonatal care of the seven babies born to Kenneth and Bobbi McCaughey of Carlisle, Iowa—the first recorded case of surviving septuplets in the world.

INTEGRA HEALTH PHYSICIANS

Integra Health Physicians is a 250-member physician medical foundation that serves more than 700,000 patients from 60 locations across central, eastern, and northeastern Iowa. It has a base of primary care physicians in family practice, internal medicine, and pediatrics. In addition, Integra Health Physicians offers services in subspecialty areas, including infectious diseases, endocrinology/diabetes, neurology, obstetrics/gynecology, psychiatry, and rheumatology.

Integra Health Physicians' 22 clinics throughout the Des Moines metropolitan community offer extended hours and walk-in accessibility. The link with Iowa Methodist, Iowa Lutheran, and Blank Children's Hospital allows Integra Health Physicians' patients

access to a full range of exceptional health care services.

A HEALTHY PARTNERSHIP

Integra Health is an opportunity-based partnership built on a mutual understanding that there has never been a better time to translate its shared knowledge and experience into a system that works to deliver health care services of the highest possible quality at the lowest possible cost. By sharing systems, services, and resources, Integra Health affiliates generate meaningful savings in purchasing, administration, information management, human resources, marketing, and planning. Integra Health is successfully working to improve the health of the people and communities of Iowa—one patient at a time.

THE HUMAN GENE THERAPY RESEARCH INSTITUTE AT IOWA METHODIST IS STRIVING TO REVOLUTIONIZE MEDICAL TREATMENT BY DEVELOPING NEW METHODS AND APPLICATIONS OF HUMAN-GENE THERAPY FOR CANCER PREVENTION, TREATMENT, AND CURE.

ROBERTSON LOWSTUTER IS AN ORGANIZATION AND CAREER DEVELopment consulting firm dedicated to helping companies and their executives, managers, and employees. The Des Moines office, established in 1994, successfully serves an ever expanding list of top employers. Locally owned and operated

by Thomas E. Keating, president, and Robert C. Wigger, executive vice president, Robertson Lowstuter specializes in all areas of consulting, counseling, and coaching as they relate to organization, group, and individual effectiveness.

Robertson Lowstuter was originally founded in Chicago in 1981 by Clyde Lowstuter and Dave Robertson, and has assisted thousands of companies and individuals. The firm currently has offices in the upper midwestern states and serves client companies nationally through a network of affiliates. Iowa cities with full-service offices include Des Moines, Sioux City, and the Quad Cities area, in addition to a satellite office in the Waterloo/Cedar Rapids area.

Keating opened the Des Moines office after leaving his position as CEO of an East Coast manufacturing company. Having worked with the Chicago Robertson Lowstuter office through a previous career transition, Keating was

ROBERTSON LOWSTUTER PRINCIPALS THOMAS E. KEATING AND ROBERT C. WIGGER BRING A UNIQUE BLEND OF BUSINESS BACKGROUND AND EXPERIENCE TO THIS ORGANIZATION AND CAREER DEVELOPMENT CONSULTING FIRM. THEIR PERSONAL MANAGEMENT STYLES FIT WELL WITH THE COMPANY'S METHODOLOGY OF COACHING INDIVIDUALS TO CAREER SUCCESS.

asked to establish the first licensed Robertson Lowstuter consulting operation. Keating's broad business acumen made him a prime candidate for launching this groundbreaking office.

Keating and Wigger have both experienced career disruption and transition. In fact, it is a prerequisite at Robertson Lowstuter for all career counselors to have experienced job loss. According to Keating and Wigger, you cannot relate to the emotional, financial, family, and career disruption unless you have been through the situation yourself.

NEGOTIATING A CHANGING MARKETPLACE

Robertson Lowstuter is focused on creating positive, uncommon results that enhance clients' profitability and flexibility, allowing them to react quickly to changes in the marketplace. To that end, the firm offers proven expertise in change management, career

assessment and planning, career enhancement and development, and career transition and outplacement—all designed to help companies and individuals identify and overcome roadblocks to success. Robertson Lowstuter's consulting empowers its clients to make necessary organizational changes with confidence.

Career transition and outplacement are the foundations of the firm's services. In a world characterized by mergers and acquisitions, profit erosion, and international competition, today's corporations turn to Robertson Lowstuter for a full range of individual and group career transition services designed to revitalize the careers of separated employees and to enhance a company's management effectiveness, corporate image, and profit goals. The firm helps exiting employees get back on track as they sort through career options and learn powerful career transition strategies, tactics, and skills.

"We partner with individuals and help them adjust to change, as well as prepare, launch, and manage an effective career search," explains Wigger, who joined the Des Moines team in 1997 and brings with him significant experience in human resource management, employee counseling, and change management through reorganizations and downsizings. Drawing on their own career histories, Keating and Wigger often talk about their personal experiences so those in transition don't feel alone in the process. They also point out that in most cases, an involuntary separation may be due to the nature of circumstances— not performance. Treating individuals with dignity and respect, Robertson Lowstuter helps

transitioning employees work through their emotions so they can concentrate on moving on with their careers. The firm also works with employees who remain within the client company, counseling them as they undergo the emotional roller coaster of seeing associates leave.

In addition to career transition and outplacement, Robertson Lowstuter also offers an array of career assessment and planning services. Robertson Lowstuter consultants focus on helping valued employees within a company examine their own talents, skills, and aspirations so they can take charge of their careers, seek advancement opportunities, and fully achieve their potential, thus improving an organization's effectiveness.

The firm's unique career enhancement and development services are targeted toward employees who have become derailed in their efforts to help their employer meet its corporate mission. Robertson Lowstuter strives to help individuals redirect their performance, behavior, and attitudes, which ensures meaningful contribution to the organization.

The firm also offers significant expertise in the area of change management. For instance, when an office moves from an authoritarian to a participatory leadership style, the corporate culture undergoes a transition that often needs guidance. Similarly, when two companies with diverging cultures merge, Robertson Lowstuter helps the new leadership and the existing employees negotiate and embrace the resulting cultural change. The firm's consultants understand that change can be disruptive and that a company's environment may actually become more difficult before employees see the benefits of the change.

EXCEEDING CLIENT EXPECTATIONS

As Robertson Lowstuter partners with its clients to Create Uncommon Results!®, it

will continue to reach for the goal of exceeding client expectations. The company lives by its mission statement: "Robertson Lowstuter will provide distinctive career counseling and performance enhancement services customized to the unique needs of our client firms and their employees. We are dedicated to delivering unsurpassed excellence in all we do, each and every time, providing greater value and options to our clients. We believe in the greatness of the individual, and that our purpose is to help people optimize their talents, skills, and abilities, while creating breakthrough results in behavior, attitudes, and performance."

Distinguished from its competitors through an uncompromising pledge that its consultants will not disconnect from its clients, Robertson Lowstuter personnel will not rest until an assignment has been completed to the full satisfaction of the customer. The firm expects to continue that pledge as it pursues growth and uncommon results with its clients—all based on the company's mission to help people. Keating says, "We go home every day with a sense that we truly helped someone in their life and their career."

ROBERTSON LOWSTUTER'S CONVENIENTLY LOCATED AURORA AVENUE OFFICES PROVIDE FULL-SERVICE FACILITIES TO THE FIRM'S CLIENTS. THE HIGH-QUALITY OFFICE ENVIRONMENT AND STAFF GIVE EACH INDIVIDUAL PERSONAL AND CUSTOMIZED SUPPORT.

ROBERTSON LOWSTUTER'S TEAM OF CONSULTANTS WORK TOGETHER TO PROVIDE THE BEST POSSIBLE CAREER DEVELOPMENT STRATEGIES THAT BRING CUTTING-EDGE DIFFERENCES TO THEIR CANDIDATES FROM ALL LEVELS WITHIN AN ORGANIZATION.

C OMMERCIAL FEDERAL CORPORATION ENTERED THE IOWA MARKET in 1996, but it was the acquisition of Des Moines-based Liberty Financial Corporation two years later that really put it on the state's banking map. ■ A publicly traded company headquartered in Omaha, Commercial Federal first began its Iowa-

COMMERCIAL FEDERAL CORPORATIONS'S RECENT ACQUISITIONS HAVE ENABLED IT TO BECOME THE FOURTH-LARGEST BANK IN IOWA (BASED ON DEPOSITS) AND THE SECOND-LARGEST IN DES MOINES. RUSSELL G. OLSON, THE COMPANY'S EXECUTIVE VICE PRESIDENT OF COMMERCIAL BANKING, IS SHOWN HERE AT THE DES MOINES SKYWALK BRANCH, ONE OF THE BANK'S 24 LOCATIONS IN GREATER DES MOINES.

COMMERCIAL FEDERAL REMAINS AT THE FOREFRONT OF NEW TECHNOLOGY IN ITS RESPONSE TO CUSTOMERS' NEEDS FOR CONVENIENCE. THE BANK INTRODUCED ITS HOME BANKING SERVICE IN 1996, WHICH ALLOWS CUSTOMERS TO PAY BILLS, TRANSFER FUNDS BETWEEN ACCOUNTS, AND CONDUCT MANY OTHER BANKING TRANSACTIONS ON THEIR PERSONAL COMPUTERS.

based operations in February 1996, when it acquired a single branch bank in Harlan. The company acquired six additional Iowa branches in October 1996, through its purchase of Heritage Financial, Ltd., parent company of Hawkeye Federal Savings Bank.

As Commercial Federal was fueling growth through acquisitions, Liberty Financial Corporation was doing some expanding of its own. In just 13 years, Liberty had climbed from zero assets to nearly $700 million in assets, and had become a significant force in Iowa commercial banking. Commercial Federal acquired Liberty Financial in February 1998, giving the corporation a major boost in the area of commercial banking, while increasing the number of branches in Iowa from seven to 45.

Acquisitions of Perpetual Savings Bank, FSB, of Cedar Rapids in May 1998 and the AmerUs Banks in July 1998 enabled Commercial Federal to become the fourth-largest bank in Iowa (based on deposits) and the second-largest in Des Moines. In the Greater Des Moines area, Commercial Federal's company logo now identifies 24 branches in Des Moines, West Des Moines, Johnston, Urbandale, Waukee, Polk City, Winterset, Boone, Indianola, Ankeny, Marshalltown, Ames, and Clive.

STRENGTH IN COMMERCIAL BANKING

W ith the strength of its Iowa banks behind it, Commercial Federal quickly exported its new strength in commercial banking products throughout its multistate system.

Iowan Russell G. Olson, former president and chief executive officer of Liberty, assumed the role of executive vice president of com-

mercial banking at Commercial Federal. The commercial banking portfolio managed by Olson includes commercial lending, agricultural lending, commercial deposit services, and such nonbanking services as trust, property and casualty insurance, and commercial equipment leasing through a nationwide company.

"Our goal in commercial banking is to project Commercial Federal as an institution that is sensitive to the needs of local citizens in each of our markets," Olson says. "We will conduct our efforts for the purpose of protecting customers' deposits, and stimulating growth and opportunity in each community we serve."

A NEW HOMETOWN BANK

T he Iowa acquisitions enabled Commercial Federal to bring the company's rich, 111-year history of retail customer service to the area. Since its founding as a building and loan association in

1887, Commercial Federal has been devoted to helping families realize their dreams, particularly the dream of home ownership.

Commercial Federal provides a full range of convenient financial services for the retail customer, including checking, savings, trust, insurance, and brokerage transactions. Its service to customers includes account access at Commercial Federal CASHBOX® machines, more than 320,000 ATM locations carrying the Cirrus® logo worldwide, VISA® Check Cards, telephone banking, on-line computer banking, and convenient retail locations throughout the Midwest.

"Above all else," Olson says, "we will deliver extraordinary customer service and operate as a state-of-the-industry commercial bank, but maintain homespun flexibility that identifies us as a caring and approachable hometown bank. This is what community banking is about."

DURING THE PERIOD OF TIME FOLLOWING THE CIVIL WAR, the growth of the banking industry in Des Moines stimulated Polk County's economy and firmly established the capital city as Iowa's financial center. While that strong banking tradition continues into the 21st century,

one of the city's newest financial institutions stands out as unique in its purpose and its services.

The Des Moines office of LaSalle National Bank opened in 1997 in the 801 Grand Avenue building. In Des Moines, the bank's relationships with middle market businesses have generated more than $100 million in credit commitments and $75 million in assets for the Des Moines office in just two years. In Des Moines, LaSalle deals exclusively with commercial clients, and LaSalle offers nontraditional services to meet needs that can't be met by other local banking institutions.

A Commanding Role in Chicago

LaSalle National Bank was established in 1927 as the National Builders Bank of Chicago. The bank grew rapidly through the decades, and adopted its current name in 1940. From the bank's inception in Chicago, it has held an unwavering commitment not only to provide the best service to its customers, but also to make it as easy as possible for customers to access LaSalle's experience, resources, and solutions. This is just as true for local deals as it is for global transactions. In 1979, most of its interests were sold to an Amsterdam-based holding company now known as ABN AMRO Holding N.V.

As a member of the ABN AMRO organization, LaSalle can provide local support to more than 1,900 locations in more than 70 countries. Virtually anywhere a customer's business takes them, LaSalle's international bankers can tap this global network to meet its needs.

LaSalle gives importers and exporters a critical edge in the mar-

ketplace through ABN AMRO's 1,900 locations across the globe. LaSalle's international desk can help open an account in a foreign country or even help arrange multi-source financing for an export transaction.

From the LaSalle National Bank Des Moines office, "we cover the whole state, and will soon expand into Nebraska," says Senior Vice President Aimee Daniels, one of five permanent staff members in Des Moines.

LaSalle assists with the sales, trading, and underwriting of government, corporate, and municipal fixed income securities, as well as U.S. and international institutional equity sales and trading services.

The bank handles merger and acquisition advisory services, and offers a full range of corporate finance and underwriting capabilities and asset management services. LaSalle is a link to access worldwide futures markets for institutions, corporations, and professional investors.

LaSalle offers access to expertise and services that only a well-established, closely connected family of banks can provide. Its experience, resources, and solutions add up to an exceptional advantage. As its customers' needs grow and change, LaSalle can provide the solutions they need, whenever and wherever they need them.

AIMEE DANIELS SERVES AS SENIOR VICE PRESIDENT AT LASALLE NATIONAL BANK'S DES MOINES OFFICE.

A TOP SEED COMPANY AND THE TALL CORN STATE—IN NOVEMBER 1997, a perfect match was made. Asgrow Seed Company LLC moved its headquarters from Kalamazoo to Des Moines, bringing with it superior seed genetics, a wealth of technology, and its new vision to provide "An innovation for every farm."

While employees were still unpacking boxes and settling into their offices, the new corporate vision and values were painted on the headquarter walls. Stenciled words like "innovation," "leadership," and "integrity" decorate the hallways and serve as a constant reminder of the company's focus. "Our vision is to provide innovations to enable every farmer to play a role in delivering higher-quality, innovative crops to meet ever changing world needs and demands," says John Schillinger, co-president of Asgrow/Hartz. "This vision directs our 600 employees, who are scattered around the world."

CLOCKWISE FROM TOP: AT ASGROW'S OPEN HOUSE, THE MANAGEMENT TEAM INTRODUCED THE COMPANY'S NEW VISION, "AN INNOVATION FOR EVERY FARM." PICTURED AT CENTER, ASGROW/HARTZ CO-PRESIDENTS JOHN SCHILLINGER (LEFT) AND DANNY KENNEDY (RIGHT) CUT THE BANNER TO OFFICIALLY OPEN THE COMPANY'S NEW DES MOINES HEADQUARTERS.

TRADITIONAL GENE DISCOVERY PROGRAMS HAVE YIELDED TREMENDOUS BENEFITS FOR FARMERS WORLDWIDE. GENOMICS—ADVANCED GENE DISCOVERY PROGRAMS—ALLOW RESEARCHERS TO IDENTIFY AND CAPTURE BENEFICIAL TRAITS AT A RATE PREVIOUSLY UNIMAGINABLE.

AN INDUSTRY FIRST, ASGROW'S SEED INFORMATION SYSTEM (SIS) ENABLES SALES REPRESENTATIVES EQUIPPED WITH PORTABLE COMPUTERS TO ACCESS HEAD-TO-HEAD PERFORMANCE DATA OF ASGROW AND COMPETITIVE PRODUCTS.

IN 1996, ASGROW INTRODUCED SIX ROUNDUP READY® VARIETIES AND HAD 95 PERCENT OF AVAILABLE UNITS FOR U.S. FARMERS.

Asgrow is wasting no time in working toward its vision. Today, it provides growers with a choice of soybean varieties, corn and sorghum hybrids, as well as new sunflower and alfalfa varieties.

SOYBEAN LEADERSHIP

So many growers have put Asgrow at the top of their list that Asgrow became the number one brand of soybeans in the United States in 1998. Asgrow made headlines in 1996, when it was the dominant seed company to commercially market Roundup Ready® soybeans. *AgriMarketing* magazine took notice of Asgrow's

achievement, and in 1997 honored Asgrow Roundup Ready soybeans with its first Product of the Year award. The product changed the rules with regard to the way growers produce soybeans. "Growers can spray Roundup Ultra™ herbicide over the top of the Roundup Ready soybeans, killing weeds without damaging the crop," says Schillinger. "That's one of the most significant changes ever in soybean production."

Asgrow was also the first to introduce nearly every essential soybean defensive trait, including soybean cyst nematode and Phytophthora root rot resistance. How has all of this been accomplished? Asgrow's vast breeding program is the answer. Asgrow scientists use 13 research stations and four Central and South American winter nurseries to evaluate more than 400,000 lines annually.

In addition to its soybean leadership, Asgrow is committed to building a world-class corn product line. As with soybeans, Asgrow has been aggressive in incorporating insect resistance and disease tolerance into its seed corn. More than 90 percent of the Asgrow

hybrid corn line is proprietary, developed by Asgrow corn breeders from Asgrow germ plasm. The result is consistently high-yielding hybrids across all regions of the Corn Belt. Asgrow's corn breeders make more than a million pollinations annually and test 35,000 new hybrids in 450,000 plots. "Of course, breeding for top yield is a priority, but no Asgrow hybrid reaches the farm without agronomic and defensive traits as well," says Danny Kennedy, co-president of Asgrow/Hartz.

GROWING KNOWLEDGE

Asgrow's innovations don't stop with its seed technologies. The company's *Growing Knowledge™* brand of information services helps growers efficiently manage their crops.

Asgrow's eight Concept Farms, located in key corn and soybean regions, are the most visible of the *Growing Knowledge* services. In Iowa, they are located at Atlantic and Williams. The farms are run by research agronomists intent on discovering the most profitable combination of management practices and products for growers. Working with local growers, research agronomists develop studies that answer specific questions concerning row width, planting dates, and plant populations, as well as herbicide- and insect-tolerant crop management. Research trials involve current and experimental Asgrow and

competitive seed products. The results are made available to more than 70,000 growers through biweekly *Field Report* agronomic newsletters, radio updates, the company's Web site, and year-end yield and crop management reports.

MORE THAN 140 YEARS OF HISTORY

Although Asgrow may be new to Des Moines, the company has a long history as a seed leader. In 1856, Everett B. Clark laid the first cornerstone of the company when he sold cabbage seed for $1.50 per pound. This began his commercial seed venture, and led him to establish Everett B. Clark Seed Co. Clark later merged with

two other seed companies to form Associated Seed Growers, Inc. The cable code name was Asgrow, which later was adopted and registered as the brand name. In the late 1990s, Asgrow's vision for the future remains bright. "Through the company's relationship with Monsanto, Asgrow scientists will continue to lead the industry in the development of new seed technologies," says Kennedy.

Although the smell of fresh paint no longer lingers in the hallways of Asgrow's headquarters, the vision remains fresh in the minds of Asgrow employees. "We want to feed the world. We want to feed it well, feed it safely, and feed it economically," says Schillinger.

CLOCKWISE FROM TOP: ASGROW'S ROUNDUP READY® SOYBEANS WERE HONORED BY *AGRIMARKETING* MAGAZINE AS ITS 1997 PRODUCT OF THE YEAR. ASGROW CUSTOMERS CITE THE PRODUCT FOR ITS EXCELLENT WEED CONTROL, CROP SAFETY, AND GOOD YIELDS.

ASGROW'S STRONG CORN RESEARCH PROGRAM UTILIZES 13 RESEARCH STATIONS. CORN BREEDERS MAKE MORE THAN 1 MILLION POLLINATIONS ANNUALLY.

ASGROW WAS AMONG THE FIRST COMPANIES TO OFFER IMI® CORN, WHICH IS TOLERANT TO IMIDAZOLINONE (IMI) HERBICIDES, AND LIBERTY LINK® CORN, WHICH IS TOLERANT TO LIBERTY® HERBICIDE.

L OCATED JUST SOUTH OF UNIVERSITY AVENUE IN THE RAPIDLY developing business area west of Valley West Mall, Mondo's of West Des Moines is a stylish restaurant, bakery, and bar that has exceeded its customers' grandest expectations since opening in June 1997. With room for 465 customers at a time, the restaurant is finished with rich mahogany, tile, and granite. Warm lighting greets guests of all ages, types, and tastes—from singles to families, from infants to the elderly, from people in designer dresses or dinner jackets to those in sports clothes.

In its first year of business, Mondo's served an average of 1,700 meals each day and quickly became a popular site for business lunches, special-occasion dinners, and afternoon or evening socializing. In March 1998, it was voted Best New Restaurant, Best Place to Entertain Out-of-Town Guests, Best Place for a First Date, and Best Bloody Marys by readers of *Cityview* newspaper.

THE MONDO FAMILY

M ondo's is the culmination of everything we've ever wanted," says President Jim Mondanaro. His management company, Fresh Food Concepts, Inc., currently operates five restaurants in Iowa City—Micky's Irish Pub, Givanni's Italian Cafe, Mondo's Sports Cafe, Mondo's Tomato Pie, and Bread Garden Cafe—as well as Mondo's of West Des Moines and Mondo's of North Palm Beach, Florida.

The West Des Moines Mondo's, which took more than two years to design and build and which cost around $4 million, is the largest of Mondanaro's eateries. The Mondanaros planned it that way: the 15,000-square-foot facility was designed to handle the large-volume business necessary to support a well-paid staff in a beautiful restaurant. Aspiring to attract top-quality, experienced employees, Mondo's provides more than 200 jobs to the Des Moines area, with 75 thoroughly trained employees on duty on a typical shift.

Mondo's 7,500-square-foot, state-of-the-art kitchen is "every chef's dream," says Operations Director Gina Mondanaro, Jim's sister. All cooking equipment is placed on casters for mobility, so the kitchen can be kept immaculate by cleaning with a pressure washer. Cooks have individual

MONDO'S OF WEST DES MOINES IS A STYLISH RESTAURANT, BAKERY, AND BAR THAT HAS EXCEEDED ITS CUSTOMERS' GRANDEST EXPECTATIONS SINCE OPENING IN JUNE 1997.

MONDO'S MENU OFFERS MORE THAN
100 MEAL COMBINATIONS, WITH
ENTRÉES RANGING FROM MEXICAN
FOODS AND ITALIAN CUISINE TO
SEAFOOD, CHICKEN, AND BURGERS.

work areas for their own specialties and communicate with other cooks via radio.

Fresh Foods

In all of his restaurants, Mondanaro takes pride in serving fresh foods, from homemade pasta to mashed potatoes. Mondo's of West Des Moines houses a large bakery section that provides freshly baked bread. Future plans include building an outdoor dining area with additional parking.

Mondo's menu offers more than 100 meal combinations, with entrées ranging from Mexican foods and Italian cuisine to seafood, chicken, and burgers. "The broad menu offers something for everyone," says Gina, "with an emphasis on premium quality, freshness, flavor, and affordability."

All in the Name

Contrary to frequent assumptions, Mondo's is not an abbreviated form of its owner's name. The best explanation of the name, according to Gina, was written by her niece Lani Kastantin: "*Mondo*, the Italian

word for 'world,' epitomizes the business philosophy, market, and purpose embraced by Mondo's. Volume is the means by which Mondo's embodies its name: volume of size, in which the business and its people may comfortably breathe, move, and expand at the steady pace of change; volume of space, which evokes the time and freedom essential to artistic and intellectual expression; and volume of spirit, which stimulates

creativity, passion, and acceptance within and among its individuals.

"While volume empowers Mondo's to attract persons of all ages and horizons, present and future patronage is secured by an unwavering commitment to provide guests and employees alike the finest atmosphere in which to appreciate state-of-the-art products and services. It is an atmosphere of unparalleled warmth and energy that results when passionate people are provided generous working conditions and the most effective tools with which to cultivate their talents. This is the unique commitment of Mondo's: one that ensures prosperity for its concept, for its people, and for the community in which it serves.

"Rich and sound of structure, perennial in design and decor, and eclectic of personality and cuisine, Mondo's is at once traditional and progressive. As the culinary and architectural masterpiece of Fresh Food Concepts, Mondo's is a restaurant for all seasons, one that seeks to nourish and dazzle the universal senses."

ACCORDING TO LANI KASTANTIN,
NIECE OF OPERATIONS DIRECTOR GINA
MONDANARO, "*MONDO*, THE ITALIAN
WORD FOR 'WORLD,' EPITOMIZES THE
BUSINESS PHILOSOPHY, MARKET, AND
PURPOSE EMBRACED BY MONDO'S."

FROM ITS BEGINNINGS AS A SMALL PUBLISHER OF LOCAL NEWSPAPERS in the 1930s, Towery Publishing, Inc. produces a wide range of community-oriented materials, including books (Urban Tapestry Series), business directories, magazines, and Internet sites. Building on its long heritage of excellence, the company is today global in scope, with cities from San Diego to Sydney represented by Towery products. In all its endeavors, this Memphis-based company is synonymous with service, utility, and quality.

A DIVERSITY OF COMMUNITY-BASED PRODUCTS

Over the years, Towery has become the largest—and leading—producer of published materials for North American chambers of commerce. From membership directories that enhance business-to-business communication to visitor and relocation guides tailored to reflect the unique qualities of the communities they cover, the company's chamber-oriented materials offer comprehensive information on dozens of topics, including housing, education, leisure activities, health care, and local government.

In 1998, the company acquired Cincinnati-based Target Marketing, an established provider of detailed city street maps to more than 300 chambers of commerce throughout the United States and Canada. Now a division of Towery, Target offers full-color maps that include local landmarks and points of interest, such as parks, shopping centers, golf courses, schools, industrial parks, city and county limits, subdivision names, public buildings, and even block numbers on most streets.

In 1990, Towery launched the Urban Tapestry Series, an award-winning collection of oversized, hardbound photojournals detailing the people, history, culture, environment, and commerce of various metropolitan areas. These coffee-table books highlight a community through three basic elements: an introductory essay by a noted local individual; an exquisite collection of four-color photographs; and profiles of the companies and organizations that animate the area's business life.

To date, more than 90 Urban Tapestry Series editions have been published in cities around the world, from New York to Vancouver to Sydney. Authors of the books' introductory essays include former President Gerald Ford (Grand Rapids), former Alberta Premier Peter Lougheed (Calgary), CBS anchor Dan Rather (Austin), ABC anchor Hugh Downs (Phoenix), best-selling mystery author Robert B. Parker (Boston), American Movie Classics host Nick Clooney (Cincinnati), Senator Richard Lugar (Indianapolis), and Challenger Center founder June Scobee Rodgers (Chattanooga).

To maintain hands-on quality in all of its periodicals and books, Towery has long used the latest production methods available. The company was the first in the country to combine a desktop workstation environment with advanced graphic systems to provide color separations, image scanning, and finished film delivery under one roof. Today, Towery relies on state-of-the-art digital prepress services to produce more than 8,000 pages each year, containing well over 30,000 high-quality color images.

AN INTERNET PIONEER

By combining its long-standing expertise in community-oriented published materials with advanced production capabilities, a global sales force, and extensive data management expertise, Towery has emerged as a significant Internet provider. In keeping with its overall focus on community-based resources, the company's Internet sites represent a natural step in the evolution of the business. There are two main product lines within the Internet division: introCity™ and the American Community Network.

Towery's introCity sites introduce newcomers, visitors, and longtime residents to every facet of a particular community, while also placing the local chamber of commerce at the forefront of the city's Internet activity. The sites include newcomer information, calendars, photos, citywide business listings with everything from nightlife to shopping to

TOWERY PUBLISHING PRESIDENT AND CEO J. ROBERT TOWERY HAS EXPANDED THE BUSINESS HIS PARENTS STARTED IN THE 1930S TO INCLUDE A GROWING ARRAY OF TRADITIONAL AND ELECTRONIC PUBLISHED MATERIALS, AS WELL AS INTERNET AND MULTIMEDIA SERVICES, THAT ARE MARKETED LOCALLY, NATIONALLY, AND INTERNATIONALLY.

family fun, and on-line maps pinpointing the exact location of businesses, schools, attractions, and much more.

Towery's other Internet product, the American Community Network (ACN), is the only searchable on-line database of statistical information for all of the country's 3,141 counties and 315 metropolitan statistical areas (MSAs). Each community's statistical profile includes vital information on such topics as population, workforce, transportation, education, taxes, and incentives. ACN serves as a national gateway to chambers of commerce, private companies, and other organizations and communities on the Web, making it an ideal resource for finding and comparing data on communities suitable for a plant or office location.

DECADES OF PUBLISHING EXPERTISE

In 1972, current President and CEO J. Robert Towery succeeded his parents in managing the printing and publishing business they had founded nearly four decades earlier. Soon thereafter, he expanded the scope of the company's published materials to include *Memphis* magazine and

other successful regional and national publications. In 1985, after selling its locally focused assets, Towery began the trajectory it continues on today, creating community-oriented materials that are often produced in conjunction with chambers of commerce and other business organizations.

Despite the decades of change, Towery today follows a long-standing family philosophy of unmatched service and unflinching quality. That approach extends throughout the entire organization to include more than 130 employees at the Memphis headquarters, another 60 located in Northern Kentucky outside Cincinnati, and more than 50 sales, marketing, and editorial staff traveling to and working in Towery's growing list of client cities. All of its products, and more information about the company, are featured on the Internet at www.towery.com.

In summing up the company's steady growth, Towery restates the essential formula that has driven the business since its first pages were published: "The creative energies of our staff drive us toward innovation and invention. Our people make the highest possible demands on themselves, so I know that our future is secure if the ingredients for success remain a focus on service and quality."

TOWERY PUBLISHING WAS THE FIRST IN THE COUNTRY TO COMBINE A DIGITAL DESKTOP ENVIRONMENT WITH ADVANCED GRAPHIC SYSTEMS TO PROVIDE COLOR SEPARATIONS, IMAGE SCANNING, AND FINISHED FILM DELIVERY UNDER ONE ROOF. TODAY, THE COMPANY'S STATE-OF-THE-ART NETWORK OF MACINTOSH AND WINDOWS WORKSTATIONS ALLOWS IT TO PRODUCE MORE THAN 8,000 PAGES EACH YEAR, CONTAINING WELL OVER 30,000 HIGH-QUALITY COLOR IMAGES.

THE TOWERY FAMILY'S PUBLISHING ROOTS CAN BE TRACED TO 1935, WHEN R.W. TOWERY BEGAN PRODUCING A SERIES OF COMMUNITY HISTORIES IN TENNESSEE, MISSISSIPPI, AND TEXAS. THROUGHOUT THE COMPANY'S HISTORY, THE FOUNDING FAMILY HAS CONSISTENTLY EXHIBITED A COMMITMENT TO CLARITY, PRECISION, INNOVATION, AND VISION.

◆ © CURTIS STAHR

◆ © JONATHAN POSTAL / TOWERY PUBLISHING, INC.

© BUD LEE / THE ARTISTS AND WRITERS GROUP